James Joyce and the German Novel

JAMES
JOYCE

and the
German Novel
1922-1933

Breon Mitchell

OHIO UNIVERSITY PRESS, Athens, Ohio

Copyright © 1976 by Breon Mitchell
Library of Congress Catalog Number LC75-36980
ISBN 0-8214-0192-0
Printed in the United States of America by Oberlin Printing Company, Inc.

Designed by Hal Stevens 77-2840

FOR JACK AND MAXINE

CONTENTS

PREFACE

In making this study I have used the re-set 1961 Random House text of *Ulysses*. All page references are to this edition. I have designated the episodes by the Homeric titles Joyce originally intended for them:

1. Telemachus	10. Wandering Rocks
2. Nestor	11. Sirens
3. Proteus	12. Cyclops
4. Calypso	13. Nausicaa
5. Lotus-Eaters	14. Oxen of the Sun
6. Hades	15. Circe
7. Aeolus	16. Eumaeus
8. Lestrygonians	17. Ithaca
9. Scylla & Charybdis	18. Penelope

Page references to the first edition of the German *Ulysses* (1927) are preceded by the volume number (I, II, or III). All other references to the German text, unless noted, are based on the 1956 Rhein-Verlag edition.

I have translated all material except literary texts into English. The original text of each translated passage is furnished in the notes. Literary criticism in any language is often difficult to reduce to ordinary English. I have attempted to retain the flavor and sense of the original.

ACKNOWLEDGMENTS

I am indebted to several individuals and institutions for information and assistance in the preparation of this study. I would like to thank in particular Fritz Senn of Zurich for valuable suggestions and material, including permission to quote from several unpublished letters in his possession. Ilse Curtius of Bonn kindly allowed me to quote from unpublished letters to her late husband, and to utilize his library.

Crucial manuscript material was made available to me on many occasions. I am particularly indebted to Signe Trede-Jahnn of Karlslunde for special information, and for permission to quote from her father's unpublished letters, and to Claude Döblin of Nice for permission to quote from the manuscript of his father's novel. Three institutions in particular were extremely helpful over a period of three years: the Deutsches Literaturarchiv of the Schiller-Nationalmuseum, Marbach/Neckar, where I inspected the manuscript of *Berlin Alexanderplatz,* kindly allowed me to reproduce portions of it in this work; the manuscript department of the Staats- und Universitäts-bibliothek Hamburg offered kind personal assistance with the manuscript of *Perrudja* and allowed me to quote from it here; the Beinicke Rare Book Library of Yale University kindly allowed me to inspect the typescripts of *Die Schlafwandler.*

Much of the critical material assembled here could not have been obtained without the kind assistance of individual libraries and archives. I would like to thank: in the United States—the University of Kansas Library (special collections) at Lawrence, University of Texas Library at Austin, University of Southern Illinois Library at Carbondale, Yale University Library at New Haven, and the Northern Illinois University Library at Dekalb; in West Germany—Wissenschaftliche Stadtbibliothek Mannheim, Schul- und Kulturamt der Stadt Neunkirchen (Saar), Stadtbibliothek Mainz, Universitätsbibliothek der freien Universität Berlin (Dahlem), Badische Landesbibliothek Karlsruhe, Stadtbibliothek Stuttgart, Wissenschaftliche Bibliothek der Stadt Essen, Bayerische Stadtsbibliothek München, Universitätsbibliothek Heidelberg, Stadt Dortmund Institut für Zeitungsforschung, Württembergische Landesbibliothek Stuttgart, Stadtarchiv der Stadt Mannheim, Stadtarchiv der Landeshauptstadt Saarbrücken; in East Germany—Sächsische Landesbibliothek Dresden, Deutsche Staatsbibliothek Berlin, Deutsche Bücherei Leipzig, in Switzerland—Zentralbibliothek Zürich, Schweizerische Landesbibliothek Bern; in Austria—Österreichische Nationalbibliothek Wien; and in Czechoslovakia—Státni knihovna Československé socialistické republiky Praha.

In the early stages of the work Frank Budgen provided me with encouragement and information, as did Carola Giedion-Welcker of Zurich. Thanks are also due to the House of El Dieff, Inc. (New York), and Sotheby's of London for information and assistance. I would also like to thank Margaret Jacobs (St. Hugh's) and Gilbert McKay (St. Peter's) in Oxford, and Professor E. L. Stahl, for continuing support and valuable advice.

Grateful acknowledgments are due to *Arcadia, Contemporary Literature*, and the *James Joyce Quarterly*, where portions of this study previously appeared in slightly altered form. I am also grateful to Random House, the Viking Press, The Europäische Verlagsanstalt, the Suhrkamp Verlag, and the Walter-Verlag, for permission to quote from their editions of the works of James Joyce, Hans Henny Jahnn, Alfred Döblin, and Hermann Broch. Finally I would like to thank the Rhodes Scholarship Trust, the Danforth Foundation of St. Louis, and the Alexander von Humboldt-Stiftung of Bad Godesberg, without whose assistance this study would not have been possible.

INTRODUCTION

The temptation to simple speculation is perhaps at its strongest in "influence" studies. The complexity of the problem we face in attempting to trace the impact of a particular novel on the literature of another country seems almost insurmountable. The present study attempts to make as solid a case as the evidence warrants for the direct impact of Joyce's *Ulysses* on three important German novels. It also attempts to set the reception of the novel in the larger context of German culture between the wars. The self-imposed limits are partially intended to keep us as close as possible to the immediate contemporary effect of *Ulysses* on the development of German fiction. But the terminal dates spring naturally to mind: 1922 with the publication of the first edition of *Ulysses*, and 1933 as the political and historical watershed which brought an official end to the availability of Joyce's novel for twelve frightening years.

Our study begins with the story of the genesis of the German translation of *Ulysses*, including the first detailed investigation of that translation, and its effect upon the reception of the novel in German-speaking countries—for the plain fact of the matter is that it was only through this version that the novel came to life for the German reader, including those authors we wish to discuss.

The German critical reception of *Ulysses* is of intrinsic interest, but it also serves as a means of understanding exactly what aspects of the novel seemed original and striking in the twenties. Much of the critical material had to be slowly assembled from libraries scattered throughout several countries. In the light of this fact quotations from many articles which would otherwise be almost inaccessible to the reader are included in this study.[1]

Of the novels written in German within the period under discussion, three have been selected as representative of the direct and profound influence which *Ulysses* seemed to have the power to exercise. This is not to suggest that other novels and novelists did not come under the spell of Joyce's work. Thomas Mann was to praise Joyce highly while working on *Doktor Faustus* (although he denied a first-hand knowledge of *Ulysses*).[2] Franz Werfel met Joyce in Paris in the late thirties, and they drank and sang opera arias together late into the night.[3] Stefan Zweig was interested in Joyce's work as early as 1918, when he offered to translate Joyce's play *Exiles*.[4] Nevertheless the novels selected may be said to constitute the true center of *Ulysses'* impact upon German literature. Once we have examined the respective works of Hans Henny Jahnn, Alfred Döblin, and Hermann Broch in the light of Joyce's novel we will have approached an understanding of the place of *Ulysses* in German fiction.

---

1. Four German articles from this period are mentioned by Marvin Magalaner and Richard Kain in *Joyce: the Man, the Work, the Reputation* (London, 1957), pp. 200-201. Three further items were discussed by Frederick L. Moore in his unpublished M.A. thesis "Blickpunkt: *Ulysses* and the Changing Perspective: a Translation and Evaluation of German Criticism from Three Decades" (Northern Illinois, 1966). Rosemarie Franke discusses the period in question in *James Joyce und der deutsche Sprachbereich: Übersetzung, Verbreitung und Kritik in der Zeit von 1919-1967.* (diss. Berlin, 1970). Due to the scope of her work (which includes a study of the translation and critical reception of all of Joyce's works over the fifty-year period) it is inevitable that the treatment accorded any one aspect is somewhat limited. It is valuable, however, for a general view of Joyce criticism, and includes a helpful bibliography.

2. See *Thomas Mann: Briefe 1937-1947*, ed. Erika Mann (Berlin, 1963), p. 382.

3. See Alma Mahler-Werfel, *Mein Leben* (Berlin, 1960), p. 265.

4. See Richard Ellmann, *James Joyce* (New York, 1959), pp. 457-458.

James Joyce and the German Novel

1

TRANSLATING ULYSSES

The story of the German *Ulysses* begins with an afterthought, in a letter from Joyce to Valery Larbaud of 1924: "I forgot to say last night that the Deutsche Verlag (Stuttgart) wants to do a translation of *Ulysses* under direction of Curtius."[1] This first seed fell on barren ground, but Germany was to have its own version of Joyce's masterpiece in the end. The complicated story behind that translation rivals the tale of the production and publication of the original English edition of *Ulysses* in 1922. The trials and tribulations of finding a publisher and printer courageous enough to produce the first English edition have been portrayed often enough not to need repetition here.[2] In Germany as well, significant legal and financial risks attended the publication of the translation of *Ulysses*. The novel had been banned as pornographic in both England and the United States the moment it appeared, and reaction had ranged from unbounded praise to hostile indignation.

In Germany critics remained silent when confronted with the English version, no doubt due to the linguistic difficulties of the work and the scarcity of copies. Among the first to speak out was Ernst Robert Curtius, who figured in the earliest inquiries about a possible German version. In fact Curtius was not to play even a minor role in the eventual translation, nor did the Deutsche Verlag of Stuttgart finally claim the honor of producing the German *Ulysses*. Joyce's letters give us a hint of the possible reason for the breakdown of negotiations. In 1925 he wrote to his brother Stanislaus: ". . . a Milanese firm wrote asking for Italian rights of *Ulysses*. I never give them till *A Portrait* is first translated. The Spanish and German translations of it appear in November."[3] In all likelihood the German publishers in Stuttgart were not patient enough to invest the time and money involved in the preliminary translation of Joyce's *Portrait*. Although his admiration for *Ulysses* and Joyce never flagged, there is no evidence that Curtius ever began work on a translation.

The rights to *Ulysses* were dependent upon securing the rights to the *Portrait*, and Joyce insisted upon a translator he "knew or trusted."[4] He seemed to have found such a man in Paris: "Goll, whom I knew in Zurich, called. He wants books for a modern anthology and talked of buying German rights of *Portrait* for 7-francs sometime, if possible, perhaps."[5] The likeable Ivan Goll was not only a poet himself, but also the Paris agent for the Rhein-Verlag. That his suit for the rights to the *Portrait* was eventually successful we know from the results. And with them came the rights to *Ulysses*.[6]

Goll did not intend to translate the *Portrait* himself. The Rhein-Verlag selected a former high-school teacher from Witten for the task. The translation of the works of Joyce proved to be the making of Georg Goyert's reputation as a major translator.[7] But it did not automatically follow that the translator of the *Portrait* would also translate *Ulysses*. Instead the Rhein-Verlag held an open competition to choose a translator. Goyert must have felt himself vindicated indeed when he entered the competition and won it. According to the publishing house all further record of the contest has been lost.[8]

Finding a translator solved only one aspect of the Rhein-Verlag's problem. Fear of censorship and the inherent possible legal complications cast a slight pall over the proceedings, particularly since the book was to be largely exported to Germany, where some trouble with the authorities was to be expected. Contemporary German critics immediately recognized the point of the publisher's precautions. As one of them put it: "In order to avoid providing 'material' for the German prosecuting attorneys, the Rhein-Verlag has decided from the beginning in favor of a numbered private edition."[9] The first edition was to appear without the printer's name, and clearly stating that it was based on private subscription and limited to one thousand copies. It was to be produced in a multi-volumed luxury edition bound in half-leather, at a very high price.[10] One hundred special one-volume copies on thin paper were printed for the press.

Having decided upon a translator and format the publishers immediately launched an extensive advertising campaign. A fourteen-page booklet devoted entirely to Joyce was issued through the mail. It was termed a "Report on the Greatest Prose Work of the Twentieth Century," a bold claim typical of the tone of the subsequent publicity. The pamphlet included such sections as "James Joyce and Erotic Literature" and "Attacks of Anglo-Saxon Puritans." The attacks were almost all aimed at the supposed "obscene" nature of the work, while those essays printed in praise of Joyce cited a wide variety of positive strengths in the novel. The total impression given was that only puritanical zealots had raised objections to Ulysses.

The appeal of the novel was apparently increased by two factors: the subscriber's feeling that he belonged to an élite group—not everyone was given the chance to buy the novel after all—and the assumption, based on its having been banned abroad, that Ulysses was indeed pornographic. The latter assumption was implicitly substantiated by at least some of the advertisements and conditions involved in its purchase. One annoyed critic mentioned: "It came under all sorts of rules: the three volume edition would only be sold 'to persons over twenty-five years of age, who could prove a serious literary interest, as well as to doctors of all ages.' "[11] These were the standard conditions imposed upon the purchase of erotic literature in the twenties. There was, of course, little in *Ulysses* to further the science of medicine. Although there were many for whom such advertisements and rules obviously produced only distaste, it does seem that this technique sold copies.[12]

While the advertising campaign was creating an atmosphere of interest and excitement around the German *Ulysses* the translator was hard at work. The publishers were obviously anxious to get the German version out as soon as possible. But Joyce was not interested in rushing out a poor translation. The phrase "checked by the author" in the pre-publication announcements had obviously been one of the conditions under which Joyce sold the rights to the work, and he insisted upon this condition being fulfilled. On 29 August 1926, he wrote to Harriet Weaver:

> I am of a sudden overladen with work. Last week the entire type-script of *Ulysses* in German[13] arrived and on top of it the German translator to revise it with me. We work together all day practically, word for word. They want to bring it out in October!!! . . . I hope the German publisher won't rush the translation—and me.[14]

Evidently Joyce's hopes went unanswered, for on 5 November he wrote:

> I am utterly overworking myself . . . The Germans, having given me four days at Ostende, to revise the translation with the translator (we did 88 pages) are now rushing the translation into print. It is of course full of the absurdest errors and with large gaps. Such is financial literature. If they do not give me a délai, I shall ask Miss Beach to circularize the German press with a disclaimer.[15]

Joyce's threat seems to have had some effect, for in February of the next year (1927) he had the page proofs in his possession and began asking friends to check them over. One of these was Claude Sykes, an English actor with a good knowledge of German, with whom Joyce had once established a theatrical company in Zurich. He wrote to him: "Do you think you could spare any time to look through the German proofs (page) of *Ulysses*. . . . The firm has rather rushed the translation and it would be a pity if it contained bad errors . . ."[16] In a subsequent letter to him Joyce showed that he did not blame Goyert personally for errors in the translation:

> It is not his fault, he is forced to do it on time. The edition will be dear (£10 a copy) very luxurious etc. and [?] not scamped. I cannot control them completely but something I can do. Proofs will be sent to you 100 pp at a time. It is very kind of you to say you will look through them. Any ideas that occur you may jot down in the margin.[17]

In March Joyce was still seeking additional help.[18] He wrote to Miss Weaver: "My desk is loaded with German proofs of *U*. I am trying to get people to read them."[19] Another friend Joyce drew into the task was Eugene Jolas, editor of *transition*. Jolas' wife remembers:

> As regards the German translation. . . . The year, unless I am mistaken, was 1927 (in the summer, for I see my husband lying on the grass in Colombey fuming at having accepted this task for Joyce, comparison as we all know, being almost as much trouble as translating oneself). We were therefore extremely busy . . . and . . . all my husband had agreed to do was to make a number of sondages that would give a general idea of the translation's quality and accuracy. He found a few 'boners,' needless to say, and I recall that we laughed gaily at the rendering of 'in a brown study' with 'in einem braunen Studentenzimmer.'[20]

Meanwhile Joyce was corresponding with Goyert, correcting a sheet the translator had sent to him, losing it and asking for another, and explaining individual phrases:

> . . . Mrs. Purefoy is not a Putzfrau. 'Crab' is a slang word for a pubic parasite (Fr. morpion) "Toby Tostoff' is bogus Russian from the verb 'to toss off' an expression for 'to masturbate.'[21]

In the midst of all this hectic activity Joyce found himself devoting valuable time to a problem with the American periodical *Two Worlds Monthly* (New York). The editor Samuel Roth was printing bowdlerized installments of

Ulysses pirated from the Paris edition.[22] This led in turn to the publication of an international letter of protest signed by one hundred and sixty-seven writers, artists, and scientists.[23] Among the signatories were the following German intellectuals: Rudolf Binding, Ernst Robert Curtius, Albert Einstein, Hugo von Hofmannsthal, Georg Kaiser, Graf Hermann Keyserling, Thomas Mann, and Jakob Wassermann. Although these men had not all necessarily read *Ulysses*, and the petition was primarily against piracy on principle, it is doubtful whether a list of such powerful names could have been assembled had the intellectual climate in Germany not been favorable to Joyce and his novel.

Against this background of controversy the Rhein-Verlag mailed out their last pamphlet inviting subscriptions to the German version. "Germany Awaits Joyce's *Ulysses*" it proclaimed, and the title page termed Joyce "The Homer of Our Time." As late as the middle of September, 1927, the publishers were still waiting for the translation to be completed. At last, on 14 October 1927, the German *Ulysses* appeared, one full year behind schedule.

Two weeks later Joyce received his copy: "I got the German *Ulysses*—a most 'kolossal' and princely edition."[24] Soon thereafter he thanked the director of the Rhein-Verlag personally:

> Sehr geehrter Herr Doktor: Die vier[25] Bände der deutschen Ausgabe meines 'Ulysses' sind mir einige Tagen vor [sic] angekommen. Gestatten Sie dass ich Ihnen meinen besten Dank ausdrücke für Ihre höfliche Gedacht [sic]. Die Ausgabe ist wirklich sehr schön und geschmackvoll und hoffentlich wird sie auch in materiellem sowohl als in literarischem Sinn ein Lohn für alle Ihre Bemühungen.[26]

It is not surprising that Joyce was pleased with the beautiful leather-bound edition. The Rhein-Verlag had cause to be happy as well, for within three weeks the edition was sold out. In spite of the slight friction that had been engendered during the translation, Joyce and the Rhein-Verlag were on good terms. The first complete translation of *Ulysses* had become a reality.

Just two years later, in 1929, things began all over again. The Rhein-Verlag wanted to renew their contract for exclusive rights to *Ulysses*. Once again Joyce slowed them down:

> In addition to all this the German publisher arrived and wanted to rush me into a new contract, but I insisted on Goyert's being brought here [Paris] much to the latter's displeasure in the beginning. He, Gilbert,[27] I and Brody[28] the publisher worked on the German text with the help of Sykes by correspondence . . . He has now gone back and the first half of the book has gone to press . . .[29]

In March of 1930 he reported that the second German edition of *Ulysses* had appeared and that the third was due in June.[30] The second edition was also sold by subscription, and although it was a numbered *Privatdruck* it was printed in a small edition of three thousand copies, in two volumes bound in half-leather. The extent of the revision for this edition went completely unnoticed, and will be discussed in detail below. It differed from the first German version in literally thousands of particulars. A few final changes were incorporated into the third edition, which was also sold by subscription. This finalized the form of the "authorized" edition, which has remained essentially unchanged until this day.[31]

As might be expected, correspondence between Joyce and his translator became less frequent after the German version had been established to their satisfaction. Each had his own new problems to face: Joyce's painful eye condition, and the attendant fear of blindness; Goyert's financial problems and the German political situation. In reply to a request from Goyert in October of 1931 Joyce wrote:

> Dear Mr Goyert: I got both your letters but did not know what to reply.
>   First, I have not seen any of your translation of A.L.P.[32] so can form no judgment.
>   Second, as regards your financial position I do not imagine I could find money for you. The whole world is in crisis . . . The only country that seems to be prospering is this one but no doubt it will go into the maelstrom too.
>   *Ora pro nobis.*[33]

In the coming years the infrequent letters Joyce exchanged with both Goyert and Brody became warmer in tone. By the late thirties Joyce seemed to recall the days they had spent together on the translation with genuine fondness, and mutual good-will.[34]

The difficulty and importance of the service Georg Goyert and the Rhein-Verlag rendered in producing the first German *Ulysses* has received scant appreciation. In spite of the immense biographical literature surrounding James Joyce the story of the German translation is pieced together here for the first time. Joyce himself showed far more interest in the French version: he was constantly available for consultation in Paris, and he was fluent in the language. Stuart Gilbert outlined his own troubles with the French translation:

> It was often not merely a question of finding the *mot juste* but—a far harder task, as all translators know to their cost—*la phrase juste* also. For this one has to be thoroughly familiar with the directive ideas, the ground-plan of each episode, the allusions, Homeric and other, and the cross-correspondences disseminated through the text. One had, indeed, to try to get into the mind of the author, surely one of the most intricate, not to say tortuous minds that have ever existed.[35]

But we must remember that Goyert did not have the advantage of access to the detailed structural plan of *Ulysses* which Joyce revealed privately to Gilbert. If the French team found their task difficult in 1927, how much more so must it have been for Goyert, who had finished his German version before Gilbert even began work on the French. Goyert was faced with a monumental and complex task almost without parallel in modern literature, and he produced a translation which remains an achievement worthy of our respect. In spite of its shortcomings, when viewed in its proper historical setting, it is a major tribute to the man and his ability.[36]

The Rhein-Verlag deserves our respect as well. In spite of the fact that the publishing house was tied to the financial realities of the times, and may have been guilty of rushing things, they took on a responsibility which many would have avoided, in light of the critical and legal battle surrounding the book. To do so required courage as well as business sense. Just as Goyert established his reputation as a major translator with his version of *Ulysses*, so the Rhein-Verlag found in its publication the status of a major publisher. In a sense they grew in stature together with Joyce himself. A feeling of comradeship had developed during the many hours spent working on the German *Ulysses*, and Joyce seems to have regarded with equal good-will both the results of the labor and the men who stood loyally beside him in the years of battle.

1. *Letters of James Joyce*, ed. Richard Ellmann (New York, 1966), III, 109. Ellmann edited vols. II and III of the *Letters*. Volume I was edited by Stuart Gilbert (New York, 1957). All three volumes will hereafter be referred to as *Letters*.

2. For a most readable and complete account see Richard Ellmann, *James Joyce* (New York, 1959), pp. 503 ff.

3. *Letters*, III, 128.

4. *Letters*, II, 455.

5. *Letters*, III, 12. Letter to Ezra Pound of July, 1920.

6. These rights were renewed and retained until 1966, in which year they were sold to the Suhrkamp Verlag, Frankfurt/M.

7. Upon his death in 1966 it was noted: "Erst 1927 als im Rhein-Verlag die damals dreibändige Goyertsche Übersetzung des *Ulysses* . . . erschien, wurde klar, wer und wie modern dieser Studienrat war. . . . Vor allem durch seine Übersetzung der Werke James Joyce gehört er in die nicht zahlreiche Gruppe jener Übersetzer und Editoren, die die Literatur dieses Jahrhunderts in Deutschland wirklich 'sichtbar' machten" (Artur Venn, "Ein Übersetzer: zum Tode von Georg Goyert," *Frankfurter Allgemeine Zeitung*, 14 May 1966).

8. In later years Goyert's election to this monumental task was commonly attributed to prior friendship with Joyce. But Joyce's letters show that he first met Goyert while the translation was already in progress.

9. "Um den deutschen Staatsanwälten nicht erst 'Material' zu liefern, hat sich der Rhein-Verlag von vornherein für einen numerierten Privatdruck entschieden. . ." Gerhart Pohl, "Ulysses," *Die neue Bücherschau*, V (November, 1927), 228. The English edition had been limited for the same reasons.

10. Then, as now, a very expensive edition minimized the chances of prosecution for obscenity, on the grounds that most people couldn't afford the book anyway, and certainly not minors.

11. "Es kam unter allen möglichen Kantelen: die dreibändige Ausgabe wurde nur abgegeben 'an Personen über fünfundzwanzig Jahre, die sich über ernsthaftes literarisches Interesse ausweisen können, sowie an Mediziner jeden Alters'." Paul Fechter, "James Joyce und sein *Ulysses*," *Die schöne Literatur*, XXIX (May, 1928), 239. A prospectus issued in 1930 for the second German edition still held to such conditions; while explaining that *Ulysses* "hat natürlich nichts mit erotischer Literatur zu tun," it was insisted that these

conditions were still necessary to avoid prosecution. The prospectus is reproduced in *Herman Broch/Daniel Brody: Briefwechsel 1930-1951*, ed. Bertold Hack and Marietta Kleiss (Frankfurt/M., 1971), column 99.

12.   A story remained current for many years at the Rhein-Verlag of a sudden rush of orders from Vienna when the book was offered there as plain pornography.

13.   All of this material was lost during the bombing of Goyert's flat in Berlin during World War II, according to his wife.

14.   *Letters*, III, 142.

15.   *Letters*, III, 145.

16.   *Letters*, III, 153.

17.   *Letters*, I, 250.

18.   Joyce may even have thought of advertising for assistance. The Joyce collection at the University of Buffalo includes the following draft (ms X K.4): "Wanted immediately person knowing literary German."

19.   *Letters*, I, 250.

20.   Unpublished letter from Maria Jolas to Fritz Senn, 25 February 1966. Evidently Goyert never realized his mistake, for the 1927 version reads: "des dunklen Arbeitszimmers" (II, 293).

21.   *Letters*, III, 162.

22.   For specific bibliographical details of this piracy see John Slocum and Herbert Cahoon, *A Bibliography of James Joyce: 1882-1941*, The Soho Bibliographies, No. 5 (London, 1953), p. 100.

23.   Published in *transition* (April, 1927), pp. 156-158.

24.   *Letters*, I, 260.

25.   The "four" volumes referred to included the one-volume edition intended for the press. All four were exhibited in 1949 in Paris. They were bound in full leather, and carried a dedication from Walther Lohmeyer, the German publisher. See the catalogue *James Joyce: sa vie, son oeuvre, son rayonnement* (Paris, 1949), items 296-297.

26.   *Letters*, III, 165. NB. This letter was written to Walther Lohmeyer (see preceding note), not to Daniel Brody as given in Ellmann. The confusion probably arose because this letter was in Brody's possession as part of the Rhein-Verlag files. Insufficient credit has been given to Lohmeyer, who directed Rhein-Verlag during the period in which the negotiation for the rights to *Ulysses* took place, as well as during the production of the first edition.

27.   By 1966 Gilbert himself remembered little of this: "About the German I know practically nothing and have always assumed that Joyce 'authorized' it probably by having it or bits of it read to him by some German-speaking friend. I certainly don't think he read every word of it." Unpublished letter from Gilbert to Fritz Senn, 21 March 1966.

28.   Daniel Brody had taken over the direction of the Rhein-Verlag in 1929.

29.   *Letters*, I, 285.

30.   *Letters*, I, 289.

31.   The subsequent correction of several errors in the translation in the fifties was evidently made without the knowledge of the translator, who repeatedly refused to alter the "authorized" version. The changes seem to have been based on a list sent to the Rhein-Verlag by the Danish translator of *Ulysses*, Mogen Boisen.

32.   "Anna Livia Plurabelle," a chapter of *Finnegans Wake*. Goyert's translation has been published by the Suhrkamp Verlag under that title (Frankfurt/M., 1970), along with new translations by Wolfgang Hildesheimer and Hans Wollschläger.

33.   *Letters*, I, 307.

34.   In 1938 Joyce wrote: "Geehrter und lieber Herr Goyert: Es ist eine grosse Freude—für mir [sic]—und welche angenehme Uberraschung!—einen

Brief von Ihnen zu bekommen. Hoffentlich geht es Ihnen immer und ihre werte Familie recht gut. . . . Wann kommen wir wieder zusammen wie damals in Trianons Restaurant?" *Letters*, III, 432. Brody sent his best wishes regularly to Joyce on "Bloomsday," 16 June, and Joyce's cordial reply in 1938 is typical: "Dear Mr Brody: Thanks for your good wishes on this day which you never forget. . . . I am glad to know you are safe and well." *Letters*, III, 424.

35. Stuart Gilbert, "Introduction," *Letters*, I, 28.

36. Renewed German interest in Joyce after the second World War led to a public controversy over the quality of the translation. It was frequently attacked for errors and inadequacies. Goyert, referring to those hours spent with Joyce working over the translation, replied: "Bei diesen Besprechungen wurde der ganze deutsche Text des *Ulysses* von Joyce geprüft und gutgeheissen und somit festgelegt. Weitere oder spätere Korrekturen hat er abgelehnt. . . . Joyce selbst äusserte sich dem Rhein-Verlag gegenüber dahin, dass er die deutsche Übersetzung an vielen Stellen besser fände als das englische Original." Georg Goyert, "Noch einmal: *Ulysses* in Deutschland," *Frankfurter Allgemeine Zeitung*, 6 December 1957. The story that Joyce found the translation better than the original in places arouses one's curiosity. Unfortunately Goyert never became more precise about which passages Joyce considered particularly successful.

2

THE NOVEL NOBODY READ: 1922-1927

> Wenn man in jenen Tagen junge Literaten fragte, in welcher Zeit wir eigentlich lebten, hörte man häufig die Antwort: 'In der James-Joyce-Zeit.'
>
> Max Tau (*Das Land das ich verlassen musste*)

The English text of *Ulysses* was first published in 1922, in an edition of one thousand highly-priced copies. Even English readers found it almost impossible to understand. Nevertheless the critical storm surrounding, and indeed preceding, its appearance, continued unabated both in France and in English-speaking countries. Well-known intellectuals were found on both sides of the fence, as well as several perched on top.

In Germany *Ulysses* became almost a legend. Everyone talked of it, but for five years almost no one read it. The first extended notice of the novel in that country appeared in 1923. W. F. Schirmer referred to *Ulysses* as "a grotesque transcendental joke"[1] and outlined the contents in a brief two-sentence summary. Evidently bare facts such as these formed the basis for extended and heated discussions on the nature of art itself. A critic later recalled:

> Since the [first world] war, approximately, the name James Joyce evoked a mysterious glory, and the shuddering admiration of all literary *Stammtische*. . . . Everyone knew of him by hearsay,

everyone knew what a fabulously daring man he was supposed to be, everyone whispered the rumors of the frightfully shocking passages in his still unpublished *Ulysses*. Almost no one could make a judgment on the basis of first-hand knowledge.[2]

It was left to Ezra Pound to first alert the German reading public to what they were missing: "The whole world should unite in praise of *Ulysses*; those who don't want to go along may satisfy themselves with a place on a lower level of spiritual life."[3] This challenge was clearly intended to shock readers, particularly in view of the fact that they were being asked to praise a book almost none of them had read. Pound's article was important for several reasons. Translated from the English, it was the first full-length essay on *Ulysses* in the German language, and it was published in a widely read periodical *Der Querschnitt*. This literary magazine had been initiated in 1921 and by 1924 had become a quarterly with a circulation of around ten thousand copies.[4] Thus Pound's essay revealed the innovations of the novel to a broad public. He threw down the critical gauntlet ("better than Flaubert and Cervantes") and supported his claim with a discussion of the structure of the novel, its various techniques, and a brief mention of the Homeric parallel. He also alluded to the frankness of Molly's final monologue, with "a tip of the hat to psychoanalysis." Although he maintained that *Ulysses* could not be imitated, he also could not imagine "any future writer" who would remain uninfluenced by Joyce's work. Obviously such remarks stirred up controversy in Germany, and acquainted the German reader, if only superficially, with important details of the work.

The Spring of 1925 marks the appearance of the first real contribution to Joycean criticism in the German language. It came from Bernhard Fehr, then professor of English at the University of Zurich. He reviewed Schirmer's book and noted with thanks "the brief evaluation of the gifted Irishman James Joyce,"[5] suggesting that Joyce's stay in Zurich may have been influential in his development. Fehr's own study appeared in two forms that year: a full-length scholarly article,[6] and a shortened generalized version for a newspaper.[7] The article is note-worthy as a carefully considered, thorough study of *Ulysses*. It is even more remarkable in that it appeared in 1925, at a time when literally no other comparable work was being done. Fehr compared Joyce favorably to D. H. Lawrence, and maintained that even if *Ulysses* had never been published the simple fact of its existence would have been a major event in world literature.[8] But in spite of his praise *Ulysses* remained for him "a Sphinx in the desert." His study provided a valuable introduc-tion to the work, and although it doubtless found few readers at the time, it became one of the standard works on the subject within a few years.

It is interesting to note those innovations in *Ulysses* which particularly struck Fehr: ". . . in the jumble of impressions retained from the book we recognize three general tendencies: a new vision, the clearing away of all conventions to free the view of consciousness in its totality, a selection of new literary styles."[9] Not only did he give a brief account of the whole novel, chapter by chapter, with interspersed comments, but he also gave special attention to the various styles. He pointed out that two-thirds of the entire work consisted of "die *parole interieure*," which he regarded as Joyce's own invention.[10] He was remarkably attuned to the humor of the work at a time when few critics paused to smile. But he also saw a serious philosophical energy informing the whole:

> The entire temporal structure that Joyce has laid over the world of his novel is spatio-mechanical, a construction . . . but *behind* this construction lies the conscious direct experience of absolute reality, constant *creation* of time by the power of intuition. Is that not simply *Bergson*?[11]

In that same year (1925) articles by German critics began to appear in the literary periodicals. The first was that of R. H. Pender in the *Deutsche Rundschau*.[12] He began by suggesting that an article on modern English litera-ture was unlikely to be of interest to the average German reader, since it would consist of a list of little known names whose works were not really examples of great art. The only exception was Joyce: "the mere mention of his name brings up the problem of the modern movement in art: are they artists? Are their works art?"[13] As far as German intellectuals were concerned, Joyce was providing new forms in the novel to replace the old, as well as asserting the right of the artist to depict all aspects of life. In so doing, Pender felt Joyce struck a common chord of sympathy with the contemporary movements in German literature.[14] Although he considered *Ulysses* "one of the greatest creations of English literature" he felt it lacked the formal unity which could have been imposed by a strong personality.[15] (Ironically, Joyce was to be criticized in coming years for imposing his overall formal structure too strictly.)

Pender's article in the long-established and highly respected *Deutsche Rundschau* undoubtedly found many readers, and in several respects his remarks must have echoed the contemporary discussion of *Ulysses* in the coffeehouses. In that same year (1925) Ernst Rowohlt founded *Die literarische Welt* in Berlin. It was to provide a broad international review of important and interesting literary and cultural developments. Contributors to the early numbers included Paul Valéry, Thomas Mann, and Jean Cocteau. But the editor Willy Haas considered his greatest asset to be co-worker E. R. Curtius, who by the second issue had already provided readers with a report on the "new writer" James Joyce.[16] Curtius had obtained a copy of *Ulysses* in 1924. It had a profound effect upon him from the first reading, and he was later to refer to the "shock-effect" of the novel. In 1925 his interest in *Ulysses* was still running ahead of his knowledge of the work. It is clear that he was having great difficulties with the novel, terming it "the most difficult book in modern literature." He was the first to use the phrase "innerer Monolog" (undoubtedly taken over from Valery Larbaud's term "monologue intérieure") to designate Joyce's depiction of the flow of human thought. Curtius characterized it as a process "in which the stream of consciousness of the characters flows past the reader continuously like a film."[17] He felt the general tone of the work to be deadly pessimistic, but closed with the following affirmation:

> No matter what attitude towards Joyce's work might finally be adopted, it will have to be admitted that it rises as one of the very few monumental creations of our time above the vain, flat modernism of contemporary literature. It has that unmistakable greatness which only occurs when untiring artistic endeavor is united with decades of concern for the great traditions of the European spirit.[18]

Although this article could not be considered a substantial contribution to Joycean scholarship it was widely read, and its tone was calculated to arouse an interest in *Ulysses*. Curtius' connection with *Die literarische Welt* was to prove valuable to Joyce in the coming years.

In 1926 Georg Goyert was busily translating *Ulysses*, but there were no further articles on Joyce in the leading German periodicals. Advance announcements of the German *Ulysses* were, however, widely distributed by the Rhein-Verlag. The few pages devoted to Joyce in *Das geistige Europa: Ein Jahrbuch der Kultur* contributed little to the understanding of his work. *Ulysses* was summed up in two sentences which served only to reveal that the author had not really read the novel. Nevertheless he seemed to be impressed: "Joyce knew how to unite all of this in one work which will take a unique place in the literature of our time, regardless of how objectionable it might be from a moral standpoint."[19] Ernst Vowinckel took notice of Joyce in his study of the contemporary English novel. He detected both "impressionistic" and "expressionistic" qualities, and laid special stress upon the stylistic innovations.[20] It is unlikely that either of these discussions was widely read.

The newspapers too were almost totally silent, with the exception of an article by Valeriu Marcu, a Rumanian novelist.[21] It was a rather fuzzy review of the *Portrait* which seemed to hint at a reading of *Ulysses* as well. The essay kept Joyce's name in the papers in the Hamburg and

Berlin area, and has a certain interest as a reflection of a general disappointment on the part of critics in Germany with the *Portrait*, which had appeared in German translation that very year. It was seized upon as the only long prose work by Joyce available in German. But it seemed conventional and rather disappointing on the whole. Marcu noted: "James Joyce is certainly no genius. The rainbow of the phantasy-world which arises from his works and spans his existence, is just as typical and conventional as any other."[22] Although reviewers also had some good words for the *Portrait*[23] the general reaction was to be summed up in a later review of the German *Ulysses*:

> Soon thereafter an earlier book of Joyce's, *A Portrait*, appeared. In the wake of all the talk which was already wide-spread at that time about *Ulysses* and its author the book proved a mild disappointment. It was a piece of autobiography, often interesting but seldom unusual, showing a bright and at times sensitive man, without betraying any qualities which would raise it above the average level of good literature.[24]

Part of this reaction may have been due to Goyert's hasty translation, but the general dissatisfaction seemed to stem from the "traditional" style and content of the work. The interest in German intellectual circles, however, centered upon the possibility of a revolution or renewal of the form of the novel, and an extension of its subject matter into hitherto untouched areas.

In order to savor the experience they were all talking about, German readers were forced to wait until October, 1927, and the appearance of the first edition of the translation of *Ulysses*. That year marked the first great turning point in the reception of the novel in German-speaking countries. In the meantime the last of those articles based on the English original alone appeared in the press.[25]

John Alexander West, writing in a Swiss periodical, characterized *Ulysses* as absolutely nihilistic. Molly's final "yes" was seen as the last flicker of flame from the burnt-out ashfield of the world.[26] While praising *Ulysses*

for its "extraordinary literary qualities" he emphasized
its obscurity:

> Long stretches of the work are difficult to read, not only linguisti-
> cally, but also in terms of the literary content. It is surely acces-
> sible to a smaller number of readers than conversations in the
> literary salons of our major cities would lead us to believe.[27]

His general interpretation of *Ulysses* is of particular interest in light of the emphasis he places upon the city
as a symbol. Stephen is seen as the hero whose desire
for artistic individuality is gradually destroyed by his
contact with Dublin—the symbol of everyday life which
the artist must accept. Leopold Bloom is seen as the
personification of the city itself. Although this interpretation of *Ulysses* as a "sublime parody in revenge against
the superior power of the city"[28] may have little to recommend it today, it did, as we shall see, gain the attention
of Alfred Döblin while he was writing his own novel
Berlin Alexanderplatz. The review takes on special meaning
as we see it through Döblin's eyes, and in relation to his
own review of *Ulysses*.

In June, 1927, the increasingly popular *Literarische Welt*
devoted its entire front page to Joyce. A long leading
article by Ivan Goll, accompanied by a picture of Joyce
and Sylvia Beach, was entitled "The Homer of our Time,"
that phrase which was to be repeated in widely varying
tones by subsequent commentators. The bottom half of
the page, no less importantly, carried "A Chapter from
James Joyce's *Ulysses*. The Burial of Patrick Dignam, attended by the hero of the book, Mr. Bloom." The ex-
tracts from this chapter (in the "only authorized [berech-
tigt] translation, by Georg Goyert") included several
examples of inner monologue. Thus this technique and
the new way in which Joyce used it were made known
to readers five months before the novel actually appeared.

Ivan Goll's article was undoubtedly inspired by a sin-
cere respect for James Joyce and his work. But then
Goll was also the Paris representative of the Rhein-
Verlag, and the man who had originally negotiated the

rights for the German *Ulysses* with Joyce himself. Thus
the article became a page-one advertisement for the edition soon to appear. This was certainly the strongest boost
Joyce received in Germany before the appearance of the
translation. E. R. Curtius must have been instrumental
in convincing his co-workers to devote so much of this
issue to Joyce, in such a prominent fashion.

Goll's article provided no particular new insights into
Ulysses. Its importance was to indicate to a wide audience[29] some of the basic characteristics of the novel in
terms of glowing praise. He described the Homeric parallels briefly, and extolled Joyce's wide-ranging knowledge. Among the innovations of the novel he singled out
"something completely new to most European litera-
tures: inner dialogue [innerer Dialog]." He also pointed
out that Joyce and Lenin had lived near one another in
Zurich during the first world war, linking their names in
print for the first time. He continued: ". . . who knows
but what they will continually stand side by side in later
cultural history. For it is a fact that Joyce has called
forth a revolution in literature every bit as important as
that of Lenin in the political world." Such praise was
later quoted to Joyce's disadvantage in a Germany drifting towards fascism. But regardless of their politics German readers were left waiting impatiently for the appearance of the translation.

At this point we may pause to look back briefly at the
period just considered—1922-1927. *Ulysses* seems to have
been widely discussed, but almost never read. This was
reflected in the relatively scanty criticism in the German
language: only one (admittedly excellent) academic article had been written in five years, and only five articles
had appeared in literary periodicals during the same
period. Undoubtedly the articles in *Der Querschnitt, Die
literarische Welt*, and the *Deutsche Rundschau* provided a
nucleus for discussions in the coffeehouses. Yet the articles themselves offered little insight into the work. In
spite of this most intellectuals were acquainted with

Ulysses on at least a superficial basis. Its great length, obscurity, and revolutionary innovations were almost certainly common knowledge in literary circles. Few could have escaped hearing some form of the term "innerer Monolog," often coupled with references to Freud and the unconscious. And its supposedly scandalous content made it a *cause célèbre* for every person concerned with freedom of artistic expression.

What was still missing was the example on the printed page—the text itself. It was not enough to talk of these innovations. Readers would want to know what they added up to in the novel, and how the various elements of which they had heard could be combined into a work of art. For the answers to these questions German readers were uncommonly dependent upon the translation soon to appear. It is evident from the material already presented that the basic problems posed by *Ulysses* merged in some way with the spirit of the intellectual age in Germany. This is the underlying reason behind the continuing recurrence of Joyce's name at a time when his main work was not available. The scandal of censorship alone would no more have kept it alive than it would a work of simple pornography. *Ulysses* was more —it touched the intellectual heart of the times.

1. "eine Groteske, eine transzendentale Posse" Walter F. Schirmer, *Der englische Roman der neuesten Zeit* (Heidelberg, 1923), p. 76.

2. "Etwa seit dem Kriege ist der Name James Joyce heimlicher Ruhm und schaudernde Bewunderung aller Literatur-stammtische. . . . Jeder hatte nur von ihm gehört, jeder wusste, was für ein unerhört kühner Mann er wäre, jeder munkelte von den furchtbaren Nacktheiten seines immer noch ungedruckten *Ulysses*. Ein Urteil aus eigener Kenntnis hatte fast niemand." Paul Fechter, "James Joyce und sein *Ulysses*," *Die schöne Literatur*, XXIX (May, 1928), 239.

3. Ezra Pound, "James Joyce's *Ulysses*," *Der Querschnitt*, IV (1924), 137. Quoted here from Pound's original article in *The Dial*, LXXII (June, 1922), 623-629.

4. Fritz Schlawe, *Literarische Zeitschriften: 1910-1933*, Sammlung Metzler, No. 24 (Stuttgart, 1962), p. 58.

5. "die kurze Würdigung des geistvollen Iren James Joyce" Bernhard Fehr, "Vom englischen Roman der Gegenwart," *Archiv für das Studium der neueren Sprachen und Literaturen*, LXXX (1925), 49.

6. Bernhard Fehr, "James Joyces *Ulysses*," *Englische Studien*, LX (1925), 180-205.

7. Bernhard Fehr, "Der Roman *Ulysses* von James Joyce," *Basler Nachrichten*, 16 August 1925; reprinted in *Von Englands geistigen Beständen: ausgewählte Aufsätze von Bernhard Fehr*, ed. Max Wildi (Frauenfeld, 1944), pp. 162-167.

8. Fehr, *Englands Beständen* (see note 7, above), pp. 163-164.

9. ". . . in dem Wirrwarr von Eindrücken, die das Werk hinterlässt, lichten sich für uns drei Richtungen. Wir erkennen: ein neues Schauen, ein Wegräumen aller Konventionen, um den Blick frei zu machen für das Bewusstseinsgeschehen in seiner Ganzheit, eine Auswahl neuer Stilarten." Fehr, *Englische Studien*, p. 187.

10. Fehr, *Englands Beständen*, p. 166.

11. "Der ganze Zeitapparat, den Joyce über seine Romanwelt hingelegt hat, ist räumlich-mechanisch, ist Konstruktion. . . . *Hinter* dieser Konstruktion aber liegt innenbewusst das unmittelbare Erleben einer absoluten Wirklichkeit, unaufhörliche Zeit*schöpfung* kraft unserer Intuition. Ist das nicht ganz einfach *Bergson*?". *Ibid.*, p. 165.

12. R. Herman Pender, "Die moderne englische Literatur: ein Überblick," *Deutsche Rundschau*, CCIII (June, 1925), 285-286.

13. "Die blosse Erwähnung dieses Namens wirft das Problem der Modernen auf: sind sie Künstler? Sind ihre Werke Kunst?" Pender, p. 279.

14. Pender, p. 285.

15. Pender, p. 286.

16. Willy Haas, *Die literarische Welt: Erinnerungen* (Munich, 1957), p. 156.

17. "in dem der Bewusstseinsstrom der Personen in ungegliederter Kontinuität filmartig am Leser vorüberzieht" Ernst Robert Curtius, "Das verbotene Buch: *Ulysses*," *Die literarische Welt*, I (October, 1925), 1.

18. "Wie man auch letztlich zu Joyces Werk Stellung nehmen mag, man wird gestehen müssen, dass es als eine der ganz wenigen monumentalen Schöpfungen aus dem flachen und eiteln Modernismus der heutigen Literatur emporragt. Es hat jene unverkennbare Grösse, die nur da entsteht, wo sich eine jahrzentelange Versenkung in die grossen Traditionen des europäischen Geistes mit echter Originalität und nie ermattender künsterlischen Arbeit zusammenfindet." *loc. cit.*

19. "Joyce wusste dies alles in einem Werk zu vereinigen, das so verwerflich es auch vom moralischen Standpunkt aus sein mag, doch etwas Einzigdastehendes in der Romanliteratur unserer Zeit bleiben wird." Ellen Russe, "Englische Literatur," *Das geistige Europa*, ed. Muckermann (Paderborn, 1926), p. 201.

20. Ernst Vowinckel, *Der englische Roman der neuesten Zeit und Gegenwart* (Berlin, 1926), p. 186.

21. It appeared first in the *Berliner Börsen-Courier*, 8 September 1926, and was then reprinted in the *Hamburger Fremdenblatt*, 22 January 1927.

22. "Indes kann James Joyce kein Genie sein. Der Regenbogen der Phantasiewelt, die sich aus seinen Büchern erhebt, über seinem Dasein schwebt, ist so typisch und konventionell wie der anderen." *loc.cit.*

23. See for example Efraim Frisch, *Frankfurter Zeitung*, 12 September 1926.

24. "Wenig später kam in Deutschland ein früheres Buch von Joyce, *Jugendbildnis*, heraus, das infolge des vielen Geredes, das damals bereits über den Autor und seinen *Ulysses* gemacht worden war, eine leichte Enttäuschung wurde. Ein Stück Autobiographie, in vielem interessant, in vielem durchaus nicht aussergewöhnlich, zeigte es einen klugen, da und dort auch ganz feinen Mann, ohne indessen Qualitäten zu verraten, die weit über das Durchschnittsniveau guter Literatur hinausgingen." Paul Fechter, "Der *Ulysses* des James Joyce," *Deutsche Allgemeine Zeitung*, 22 January 1928.

25. A further article, Erich Gottgetreu's "Joyce der Spiesserschreck" (printed in the *Neue Leipziger Zeitung* and the *Neue Wiener Journal*), reprinted in the Rhein-Verlag's pamphlet *Der Homer unserer Zeit: Deutschland in Erwartung des Ulysses von Joyce*, (Basel, 1927), pp. 7-9, contributed to the general enthusiasm over the novel, but did little else.

26. John Alexander West, "Über den *Ulysses*," *Annalen*, I (1927), 516.

27. "Die Lektüre des Werkes ist streckenweise schwierig und nicht nur sprachlich, sondern auch mit Hinsicht auf den dichterischen Gehalt sicher nicht so vielen zugänglich, wie das Gerede hauptstädtischer Literatursalons glauben macht." West, p. 510.

28. West, pp. 511-512.

29. It was also printed in the *Badische Presse Literarische Umschau*, Karlsruhe, No. 42, 1927.

3

THE FIRST GERMAN ULYSSES: 1927

I

The extraordinary length of *Ulysses* (over seven hundred pages in the original edition) became a truly staggering one thousand five hundred and eighty-five pages in the three-volume translation. The "privately printed" edition gave the impression of a dangerous and forbidden work. The translation, although often adequate, was seldom satisfying. A thorough chapter by chapter analysis of the shortcomings of the German *Ulysses* would demonstrate conclusively the need for a complete retranslation.[1] Most of the errors in any translation go unnoticed by the average reader, and this was undoubtedly true of the 1927 *Ulysses*. Nevertheless, three episodes of the novel were *so* inadequately translated that they call for particular attention at this point.

Literary music: the Sirens episode

This chapter is one of the most confusing in the novel for the average reader. The short phrases with which the chapter opens seem meaningless until they begin to reappear in the subsequent text. Joyce intended an analogy to a musical overture, and the recognition of leitmotifs based on former phrases in the text increases the reader's pleasure just as the recognition of musical phrases gives added pleasure to a listener. But the German translation fell so short of the mark as to destroy a great deal of the impact of this experimental technique. Either the translator did not understand the importance of a literal repetition of these phrases in the body of the chapter or he did not take time to look for them carefully. In either case the result was the same—it was certainly impossible for the reader to make a connection when the translator had failed to indicate it clearly in the German version. Of course many of the phrases were handled correctly, or were at least close enough to the opening phrase to give the reader the general idea. But the force of the technique comes from the strictness and thoroughness with which the themes are followed up. The German version lost force and interest through insufficient attention to this convention. In some cases the leitmotifs were not even recognizably approximated.

Even as small a point as the omission of a double space between the opening series of phrases and the body of the chapter could be confusing. This space originally set off the "overture" from the rest of the text and gave a visual hint about the way in which the episode was composed—a hint any reader badly needed. But the German version simply ran the two together.

In the overall structure of Joycean correspondences the "art" of the Sirens episode is music, and the chapter overflows with actual quotations from song, as well as musical metaphors. The 1927 version chose to leave the lines of most songs in the original English. This was disastrous. Several of the opening phrases were, as a result, meaningless in the opening section and meaningless when repeated in the body of the episode (assuming the reader was not fluent in English). The numerous English phrases, combined with the translator's failure to follow up leitmotifs consistently, destroyed much of the effect of this episode. Then too the linguistic musical metaphors were hard to reproduce:

ENGLISH	GERMAN 1927
One rapped on a door, one tapped with a knock, did he knock Paul de Kock, with a loud proud knocker, with a cock carracarracarra cock. Cockcock. (282:35)	Jemand rappelte an einer Tür, jemand bumbste mit einem Nock, machte nock, Paul de Kock, mit stolzem lautem Bumbsen, mit einem Rappelbumbser. Bumbum! (II, 137)

The evident loss of rhythm and musicality in such cases was perhaps unavoidable. The translator was at least trying, and the reader would be aware that a sort of musicality was aimed at. But he was unlikely to be impressed with the result. Both the general aim of the chapter, and the linguistic structure which furthered this purpose, were blurred in translation, and the German reader was deprived of a real acquaintance with the episode.

The problem of historical styles:
the Oxen of the Sun episode

This difficult chapter must have overwhelmed even the most enlightened reader. The basic facts of the narrative were only to emerge slowly after a chaotic beginning which included this monstrous sentence:

> Allgemein wird der Scharfsinn dessen für sehr wenig durch-dringend gehalten, mag er auch noch so viel wissen von dem, was von den mit Klugheit begabten Sterblichen als sehr wissenswert erachtet wird, der nicht weiss, was die Gelehrtesten, die grade wegen dieses hohen Geistesschmuckes alle Verehrung verdienen, immer wieder behaupten und unter allgemeiner Billigung immer wieder versichern, dass, seien auch alle Umstände dieselben, kein äusserer Glanz das Gedeihen einer Nation wirksamer in Erscheinung treten lassen kann, als der Umstand, inwieweit ihre Sorge für den Nachwuchs gegangen ist, der, wenn er fehlt, eine Todsünde, wenn er aber vorhanden ist, ein sicheres Zeichen für das wohltätige Wirken einer unverdorbenen Natur bedeutet. (II, 361)[2]

The reader's discomfort may well be imagined. As in several previous episodes, Joyce was attempting to reflect the subject matter as closely as possible in the form of the chapter. The birth of Mrs. Purefoy's baby was to be paralleled in the text by the historical development of the

English language from a formless state, through the literary highpoints of the centuries, to twentieth-century slang. The chapter was composed of a *pastiche* of literary styles in relatively strict chronological order, including imitations of the styles of Mandeville, Sir Thomas Browne, the Authorized Version of the Bible, Pepys, Swift, Addison, Sterne, Goldsmith, Burke, Gibbon, Lamb, de Quincey, Macaulay, Dickens, Newman, Pater, and Ruskin. Clearly a full appreciation of this *tour de force* demanded a reader with an unusually complete grasp of literary history. It was by its very nature a seemingly insurmountable task for the German translator. The translation limped along as best it could but at most was able to provide the reader with the general impression that something was being attempted, without giving him any real idea what that something was. What was missing in the translation was any real sense of development, of growth, within the chapter. The whole was written in a generally nondescript "translator's German," and many of the most interesting and colorful phrases were simply omitted. The final result was an insipid episode unlikely to arouse anyone's enthusiasm. Any page of the text provided numerous examples of the shortcomings of the translation. Here are three short but typical examples:

> This meanwhile this good sister stood by the door and begged them at the reverence of Jesu our alther liege lord to leave their wassailing for there was above one quick with child a gentle dame, whose time hied fast. (387:35)

> Unterdessen aber stand diese gute Schwester an der Tür und bat sie, um Jesus, unseres Allerhöchsten Herrn willen, abzulassen von ihrem Gelage, denn oben läge eine edle Dame in Kindsnöten, deren Zeit wohl bald gekommen sei. (II, 371)

> 'Tis[3] her ninth chick to live, I hear, and Lady day bit off her last chick's nails that was then a twelvemonth and with other three all breastfed that died written out in a fair hand in the king's bible. Her hub fifty odd and a methodist but takes the Sacrament . . . (397:36)

> Es ist das neunte Kind, höre ich, und am Tag der Verkündigung Mariae biss sie dem Jüngsten, zwölf Monate war es alt, die Nägel ab, und vorher drei andere, alles Brustkinder, und jetzt stehen

ihre Namen in schöner Handschrift in der Bibel. Ihr Mann ist etwa fünfzig, und Methodist ist er, nimmt aber das Abendmahl . . . (II, 394)

> . . . this talkative now applied himself to his dress with animadversions of some heat upon the sudden whimsy of the atmospherics while the company lavished their encomiums upon the project he had advanced. (403:24)

> . . . der Redselige . . . befasste . . . sich mit seinem Anzug und schimpfte über das launische Wetter, während die Gesellschaft seinen Plan weiter lobte.(II, 407)

It is little wonder, if, in 1927, this chapter remained blurred in the mind of the reader; and the reader, once lost, was unlikely to ever find his way again.

Tired metaphors: the Eumaeus episode

With this chapter the reader begins Part III of *Ulysses*, three chapters balancing the opening sections and paralleling the *Nostos* or return in the Homeric original. The techniques of these three episodes are also intended to form complementary halves to the opening three. Thus the first chapter of the book was designated by Joyce as "narrative (young)," to which this chapter corresponds as "narrative (old)." The term "old" as applied to this narrative is more than superficial. It does enter noticeably into the structure and style of the text. Time and again sentences are marked by the drifting and verbose speech of one who is extremely tired. Often the sentences are left unfinished, having drifted away into nothingness:

> —Yes, that's the best, he assured Stephen, to whom for the matter of that Brazen Head or him or anywhere else was all more or less . . . (658:34)

We must expect that the reader in 1927 would realize almost nothing of the interrelation of the techniques of these episodes. The prose here would, unless the translator were extremely careful, seem unintentionally lifeless and flat. The problems presented in this episode are basic ones. The type of phrase with which these sentences

abound are exactly those vague, general, and often meaningless interjections with which normal speech abounds
—and which are often difficult to render in another language. The easiest "solution" is to omit them, and this is
exactly what Goyert did in 1927. No other chapter of
Ulysses had more words omitted per page in translation,
and only the final chapter required more revision for the
1930 edition. But the point of the experiment was, of
course, to leave them in. The more they were omitted,
the more the text changed from an interesting attempt to
portray fatigue in the language itself, into a dead text by a
poor writer. The humor and the interest both disappeared.

Two typical examples will suffice to demonstrate the
damage inflicted by the translation:

> Stephen, who confessed to still feeling poorly and fagged out,
> paused at the, for a moment . . . the door to . . . (660:14)

> Stephan, der bekannte, dass er noch immer matt und müde
> sei, blieb einen Augenblick an der Tür stehen . . . (III, 378)

> Because he more than suspected he had his father's voice to
> bank his hopes on which it was quite on the cards he had so it
> would be just as well, by the way no harm, to trail the conversa-
> tion in the direction of that particular red herring just to . . .
> (659:02)

> Er vermutete ja wohl mit Recht, dass er seines Vaters Stimme
> hätte, was grössere Hoffnung bedeutete, das wäre ganz gut mög-
> lich, und schadete gar nichts, die Unterhaltung auf dieses Ziel zu
> lenken. (III, 375)

These renderings miss the whole stylistic point of the
English original. The German becomes a banal and lifeless statement for the reader. The failure of this episode
to elicit any response from critics in 1927 must rest primarily with the translation.

The delicate task of translating the indelicate

The German version of *Ulysses* was not censored in any
way. It reproduced without flinching all frankness of
language and description. If a criticism is to be made it
tends rather in the opposite direction—the translation in
1927 was often cruder and ruder than the original.

It seems as if the translator, in a sincerely motivated desire to be true to this side of the work, looked a little too closely for indecencies and hidden meanings, and found them at times where they did not in fact exist. The following example bears witness to this observation:

> I know the voice. His fustian shirt, sanguineflowered, trembles its Spanish tassels at his secrets. (43:10)

> Ich kenne die Stimme. Sein Fustianhemd, blutrotgeblümt, die spanischen Quasten baumeln ihm an den Geschlechtsteilen. (I, 90)

This is now more appropriately translated:

> Ich erkenne die Stimme. Sein Fustianhemd, blutrotgeblümt, die spanischen Quasten baumeln, wenn er seine Geheimnisse auskramt. (52)

In spite of its well-publicized frankness, it is interesting to note that *Ulysses* is only occasionally blunt. Often both indefinite ("wind, water, thing, that") and unusual ("lingam, yoni, backgate") words are employed in a vocabulary that is surprisingly inoffensive on the whole. In such cases the German seemed often painfully explicit:

> Coming from the vegetarian. . . . They say it's healthier. Wind and watery though. (155:40)

> Kommen aus dem Vegetarischen. . . . Sie sagen es wäre gesünder. Kann besser furzen und pissen, das stimmt. (I, 344)

> Hauding Sara by the wame. (425:42)

> Packt Sara beim Loch. (II, 459)

> He surprised me in the rere of the premises, your honour . . . (461:09)

> Er überraschte mich auf dem Abort, Euer Gnaden . . . (III, 50)

The last two examples were improved in the 1930 version, but the first has remained unchanged throughout all editions. The unintended overtones the translator sometimes inserted were balanced by those which occasionally escaped his eye:

He said he had seen from the gods my peerless globes as I sat in a box of the *Theatre Royal* . . . (464:25)

Er sagte, er hätte vom Olymp herab meine unvergleichlichen Augen gesehen, während ich . . . in einer Loge des *Theatre Royal* sass. (III, 58)

THE PRISON GATE GIRLS
If you see kay
Tell him he may
See you in tea
Tell him from me. (497:04)

DIE PRISON GATE MÄDCHEN
Wenn du eine Rose siehst
Sag, ich lass sie grüssen![4] (III, 105)

But in general the German translation was less restrained in its handling of indecencies than the English original.

With such a difficult text it is not surprising that *Ulysses* left the reader confused. Some never emerged from this state, but those who seriously attempted to come to terms with the work through re-reading were inevitably handicapped by the inconsistencies and deficiencies of the translation. A general, if oversimplified, notion of the characters and their actions must have remained. The emergence of the unconscious levels of thought through the constant use of inner monologue should also have been clear.

Beyond these general impressions the German version was most likely to be remembered for its rapid variations of style, its length, and its frankness. It is to be expected that those stylistic devices which most noticeably affected the typographic appearance of the text on the page were most likely to be memorable, while those which depended more closely upon the language itself were less likely to succeed. Considered in this light (equivalent to remarking that any translation will tend to be more successful in reproducing general form and structure than in reproducing the detail and finesse of the language) those episodes which captured the eye of the reader typographically would rise above the general level of obscurity:

the Aeolus episode with its newspaper headlines, the Circe episode set in dramatic form, the questions and answers of the Ithaca episode, the uninterrupted final monologue of Molly Bloom. These are the episodes we would expect a reviewer in 1927 to single out for attention—if he has been able to read the work only in translation.

On the other hand those episodes which were not immediately and visually striking were likely to sink into oblivion, especially where the difficulty of the subject matter, or the refinement of the language, made translation a particularly exhausting task. In this light episodes such as Proteus (Stephen's thoughts on the beach), Sirens, Oxen of the Sun, and Eumaeus were likely to be passed over by the reader—in spite of their being, both in terms of content and style, among the most interesting experiments in *Ulysses*.

Thus a reading of the German translation of *Ulysses* in 1927, if our speculations are correct, would have produced both memorable peaks (corresponding for the most part to visual impressions) and patches of total incomprehension. But regardless of how the book was judged as a work of art, the total impact of *Ulysses* was uniquely original.

II

Von dieser Stätte aus ging der Blick zurück, in das Jahr 1927, das Erscheinungsjahr der deutschen Ausgabe des "Ulysses." Die Zeit war von einem überreizten Krisenbewusstsein erfüllt. . . . Es war eine Zeit der fieberhaften Experimente, des gründlichen Missbehagens an den alten Formen und einer versteckten Sehnsucht nach einem neuen, verpflichtenden Sinn.
(Arnim Kesser, *In Memoriam James Joyce*)

The German *Ulysses* appeared on 14 October 1927,[5] followed a scant two weeks later by the first of a flood of reviews. Before the end of the year at least as many lines had been devoted to Joyce in leading newspapers and periodicals as in the five years preceding. The mainstream of the reaction continued well into 1928, in which year more than twenty articles devoted solely to *Ulysses* were to appear.

The six articles which appeared by Christmas of 1927 were evenly divided for and against *Ulysses*. The three unfavorable reactions came from Walter Schmits,[6] Kurt Tucholsky,[7] and Otto Zarek.[8] Favorable reactions came from Gerhart Pohl,[9] Eduard Korrodi,[10] and Ivan Goll[11] (a reply to Tucholsky). Of course the general evaluations were by no means so simple as "for" and "against." As Schmits pointed out "even the bitterest opponents do not deny the power of his talent,"[12] and although his own article was, overall, distinctly unfavorable to *Ulysses*, it included passages praising Joyce's ability to create scenes of great plasticity, as well as his biting wit and fabulous gift of imagination. Indeed the controversy seemed often to center upon whether or not Joyce was truly the equal of Homer. This is the type of question Joyce must have appreciated.

As one would expect, the critical reactions to various aspects of the novel were widely divergent. Thus those points on which all reviewers agreed seem particularly interesting. One such, Joyce's basic talent, has already been mentioned. But the most striking point of general agreement was on the originality of *Ulysses*, that it was something completely new in literature. This originality was seen, almost without exception, to rest in the formal characteristics of the work. And although many of the formal devices of *Ulysses* were discussed, it was the inner monologue which was singled out most often for attention. The following statements are typical:

> . . . in this sense James Joyce's work is of significant importance: as an artistic revolution, and that must always mean a *revolution of form*.[13] (Pohl)

> Stylistically the novel is a coat of many colors. Its own style is a completely new use of the monologue, expressing everything which races through a mind.[14] (Korrodi)

> And here the "inner monologue" begins, which has drawn so much attention . . . and it must be said that it leaves the strongest impression of all. . . . This symphony of thought has nothing to

do with the puny attempts of Arthur Schnitzler and Carl Spitteler. Here everything, but *everything*, is actually said.[15] (Tucholsky)

Such a consensus among those obviously aware of the general literary background of the times is striking, and particularly so when it comes from both favorable and unfavorable reviews. What tended to differentiate these readers into two camps was their evaluation of such new formal innovations. For example Tucholsky reacted as a writer:

Avant-garde professors have a predilection for *Ulysses*, and that's not the only thing that makes me suspicious. I received 1585 pages—but with the exception of two magnificent sections [Circe and Penelope] there is nothing on my plate that I can eat—there is something artificial about the whole, something contrived, and, now let them stone me for all I care, something unimaginative.[16]

Pohl found the revolutionary aspects quite suitable to his Marxist tastes but felt the need for "inner clarity" on the part of Joyce:

If [that clarity] develops quickly and logically he will depict our age effortlessly. For "the rational has always existed, but not always in the most rational form" (Karl Marx). If he does not calm the waves of his cultural disorientation [Bildungschaos] in favor of a more striking and restricted power his great gamble will never succeed. But the indelible accomplishment remains: the creation of an appropriate form for the times, that is, the most rational form.[17]

Schmits's primary objection was a moral one:

Whether or not such fanatical burrowing for truth in malodorous swamps is the task of the artist is a question we may leave to the writers of academic theses.[18]

One was left in little doubt as to Schmits's answer.

Enough has been said to indicate some of the ways in which the reception of *Ulysses* was (predictably) affected by individual *Weltanschauungen*. Although no critic could point to any single important literary antecedent there

was general agreement that the novel gave literary expression to recent developments in psychoanalytic
theory, especially to the ideas of Freud (a notion Joyce
always denied). Such a view was often implied in the use
of the term "Unterbewusstsein" and more often directly
stated: "freudian case-material presented in literary
sketches"[19] (Zarek); "innoculated by his preoccupation
with psychoanalysis"[20] (Pohl). The psychoanalytical background seemed to account for Joyce's exploration of the
subconscious by means of the inner monologue. Bergson
was seen to have contributed to Joyce's particular emphasis on various concepts of time (real, imagined, and
experienced).

Although there was justification for such intellectual
parallels they seemed of little practical help in understanding the novel in 1927. It was clear that most critics
were failing to grasp even the literal meaning of large
sections of the novel. The following examples point up
how helpless most reviewers were when faced with the
text:

> . . . long stretches of the book read like the disconnected, incom-
> prehensible, extremely tedious stammering of a man whose mind
> has gone blank.[21] (Schmits)

> A handful of people from Dublin are out to enjoy sin openly and
> exultantly.[22] (Zarek)

> Impossible to read it straight through. The characters become
> mixed; if there is a plot there I couldn't find it—I don't always
> know what is real, imagined, dreamed or intended.[23] (Tucholsky)

Critics unable to come to grips with the text on the most
literal level expressed their most deeply felt objections to
the work—that it was a bluff, a joke on the reader (particularly frightening to the wary critic), a meaningless chaos
of impressions reflecting the chaos of the times. The
structure provided by the Homeric parallel, and the justification for the varied tone and style of the novel were,
of course, facets of the work which remained unseen by
almost every German critic. Certainly the text itself was
difficult, and it is an easy matter to sympathize with the

task of the reviewer in 1927. On the other hand such complete confusion in respect to so much of the text requires further explanation. Ivan Goll provided the answer in his reply to Tucholsky's attack on *Ulysses*:

> Before arguing with [Tucholsky] one would have to be sure that he was familiar with the commentaries to such a multi-faceted work. He was not familiar with them. Thus the only objection one can confront him with is that he treated this novel, which soars above us all, like any of the throng of "novels" which crowd the Christmas table.[24]

But the "commentaries" to which Goll refers were simply not available to German critics (with the exception of those already mentioned). Goll himself was receiving information about the style and structure of *Ulysses* directly from Joyce, and the detailed plan of the novel was only made widely available in 1930. It was natural that the leading periodicals wanted *Ulysses* reviewed as soon as possible. In order to have something about the novel in print by Christmas, 1927, those involved had to read it within a two or three week period, and then try to write something meaningful. The task was simply beyond even the most intelligent of them. *Ulysses* was not an ordinary novel, and the basic mistake of most critics was to treat it as if it were. In this respect the novel could have been a lesson in practical criticism. At any rate critics in Germany, as elsewhere, had first to learn the lesson before they could approach the text with any real understanding.

The techniques employed in the novel pointed to an increasing lack of concern on the part of the author with the plight of the common reader. *Ulysses* forced the reader to approach it on its own terms. On the structural level this meant imposing an overall plan which had to be reconstructed by the reader himself (thus Joyce decided to drop even the chapter headings, which would have at least identified each episode with its Homeric counterpart for the reader); stylistically it meant dispensing with traditional unity (refusing to allow the reader to settle comfortably into one groove for the whole of the novel); on the linguistic level it meant experimenting freely with grammatical and syntactical structure, the introduction of neologisms and special onomatopoetic effects, and the omission of widely used "guide-words," particularly in representing thought. *Ulysses* thus represented a turning-point in the literary history of the novel, in which the relationship between the reader and the work of art was changed significantly.

Ulysses demanded not only a new type of reader, but also a new approach to translation. The very nature of the work meant that much of its effect was bound to be lost in translation—only an extremely close attention to, and understanding of, the text could produce a truly adequate German image. This was simply not a practical possibility in 1927. Whether or not it was even theoretically possible is questionable. The fact remains that the German translation was riddled with errors, both literal and stylistic. The thought that the translation may have altered the original effect of the text seems never to have occurred to the majority of the critics in the twenties. Several of them dismissed the translation with a few words of easy praise, quite evidently not based on any real investigation: "masterfully translated" (Pohl); "a great achievement on the part of the translator" (Korrodi). Only Tucholsky was careful to draw a line between what he was criticizing (*Ulysses* in German) and the original text, with which he was not familiar. After a few critical remarks on the novel he continued:

> Since we are not dealing with the original text, but rather a translation, we should immediately ask ourselves if this impression may be a result of the way in which the book is translated.[25]

He recognized the difficulty of the English text and said he hesitated to quibble with a translation on which Goyert had perhaps spent years working ("helped, moreover, by the author, who knows German"):

> But I can say one thing after hundreds of random samples during the first reading: It is not yet clear to me what style this book is

written in. But it is certainly not literary German. . . . Either a murder has been committed here, or a corpse has been photographed.[26]

The awareness that something may have been lost in the German rendering of *Ulysses* was rare, and Tucholsky was the first critic to attack the translation.

In spite of everything, almost everyone considered *Ulysses* an important phenomenon in the history of world literature. This feeling, on the part of writers and critics alike, was plainly expressed:

> *Ulysses* will alter the features of civilized prose. For a rigid "art" has here been blasted apart.[27] (Pohl)

> . . . now [the reader] sees how conventional and false the monologues and dialogues in our novels were.[28] (Korrodi)

> *Ulysses* is not comparable to any existing work in world literature: it is unique and completely new. Such prose contains the language and rhythm of the poetry of the future.[29] (Goll)

> James Joyce has opened the door. . . . Joyce has done what could be done. Liebig's meat extract. Inedible. But it will be used to make many a future soup.[30] (Tucholsky)

In 1928 the main body of reviews appeared. More than twenty articles devoted solely to Joyce and *Ulysses* were to be found almost evenly divided among the leading newspapers and periodicals in Germany, Switzerland, and Austria. It is interesting to note to what extent these reviews modify the initial impressions of 1927.

The most striking fact that emerged in 1928 was the overwhelmingly favorable reception of *Ulysses*. Whereas the first articles that appeared immediately after the translation in 1927 were about evenly divided in their evaluations, the following year saw fourteen clearly favorable and only two distinctly negative reviews. Five others managed to avoid making a value judgement, often on the grounds that a meaningful assessment of *Ulysses* would only be possible after a few years had passed. A summary of the critical reception during the entire period 1927-1933 may be seen in Table 1 of this chapter.

TABLE 1

	predominantly favorable	neutral	predominantly unfavorable
1927	Goll Pohl Korrodi		Schmits Tucholsky Zarek
1928	Curtius Döblin Ehrenstein Fechter Fischer Frisch Gaupp Giedion-Welcker Muschg Offenburg Pohl "L. W." Werner Zweig	Binz "L. F." Georg Hennig "Sch."	Franzen Guillemin
1929	Curtius		Thieme
1930	"F.B." Fehr Jahnn		Enkenbach
1931	—		
1932	Blass Giedion-Welcker Goll Jung Lieven Weiss Weltmann	Guillemin Marinoff	Tau
1933	Hentze Kulemeyer Theile		Knapp
total	31	7	9

A second interesting fact to emerge in 1928 was the significant absence of strong attacks against obscenity in *Ulysses*. Whereas in 1927 the immediate reaction was mixed on this point, the vast majority of critics now chose to ignore the subject altogether, or to pass it off with a few words:

> . . . forbidden in England and America because of its erotic flavoring—quite harmless, by the way.[31]

No book could be less pornographic than *Ulysses*—with the sole
exception of the confessional register of sins.[32]

Here anglican Puritanism put the gears of censorship in motion,
blind to the greatness of the work, its wisdom and deep humanity.[33]

At least part of the refusal to attack *Ulysses* as pornographic seemed to be an attempt to avoid alignment with
"English Puritanism." On the other hand a few readers
seemed genuinely disappointed, particularly since they
had paid a high price for what they expected to be a scandalous book. For those who thought it necessary to lend
moral support to *Ulysses* a Swiss critic advanced a standard defense:

Who is at fault, the author or nature, if the bottom layer of the
soul is "slime"? The best thing about *Ulysses* is the courage with
which it breaks down all those barriers which are traditionally
placed in front of the literary image of the human soul.[34]

In general critics continued to agree that *Ulysses* was new
and original. Its technical advances were supposedly
based upon the ideas of Freud and psychoanalysis. The
inner monologue (under various designations) continued
to be viewed as the primary formal contribution. Although Ivan Goll had outlined the bare bones of the
Homeric parallel in his 1927 article, the majority of readers remained ignorant of this aspect. Of the few critics
who did mention it, most were only misleading:

A Dublin night-club is the Underworld. A Dublin home Heaven
and Hell: each according to the hour depicted. A walk through
Dublin's streets is a journey through the universe.[35]

These remarks, confused as they are, bear witness to a
common difficulty, rather than one man's personal inability. Joyce himself commented on an extreme case:

Another American "critic" who wanted to interview me (I de-
clined) told me he had read the book with great interest but that
he could not understand why Bloom came into it. I explained to
him why and he [was] surprised and disappointed for he thought
Stephen was Ulysses.[36]

Some German critics likewise considered Stephen the real hero of the novel, for whom Bloom simply served as a foil: "Bloom seems to exist for no other reason than to make Dedalus visible."[37] Most of them realized that Bloom was Ulysses, but any closer understanding of the Homeric parallel was denied them. As E. R. Curtius pointed out:

> In order to understand *Ulysses* one must understand this double symbolism precisely. But we lack the key to the first layer of symbols: a carefully worked out system of concordances. It exists, but only in the possession of the author and a few friends.[38]

The rapid variations in style within the novel presented a puzzle that few readers could solve. At least one critic thought Joyce himself was simply tired with the effort of writing a particular chapter and switched abruptly to another to spur himself on. Nevertheless the chapters most often referred to remained those which were distinguished by their stylistic innovations. These were the episodes which presented the most striking effect on the printed page—Aeolus, Circe, Ithaca, and Penelope. The Scylla and Charybdis chapter was also singled out for attention at times, undoubtedly because the long and involved discussion of Shakespeare appealed to German readers. A statistical summary of the frequency with which the various episodes were specifically mentioned (for the entire period 1922-1933) is given in Table 2.

TABLE 2

Episode	*times specifically mentioned*				
1. Telemachus					0
2. Nestor					0
3. Proteus				1	1
4. Calypso					0
5. Lotus					0
6. Hades		1		1	2
7. Aeolus	3	5	1	1	10
8. Lestrygon				1	1

	1923-7	1927	1928	1929	1930	1931-3	Total
9. Scylla			4		1		5
10. Rocks	1		2				3
11. Sirens			2	1		2	5
12. Cyclops			2	1		2	5
13. Nausicaa			2			1	3
14. Oxen-Sun	3		1		1	1	6
15. Circe	3	4	8	1	2	4	22
16. Eumaeus			2			1	3
17. Ithaca	2	4	9	1	1	2	19
18. Penelope	3	3	13	1	1	8	29

Many critics attempted to relate *Ulysses* to the intellectual and cultural climate of the twenties. Some saw it as an expression of the age:

[*Ulysses*] is unthinkable outside of the spiritual climate of the last twenty years, and that period, one could say, is hard to conceive of now without this book.[39]

. . . thus one arrives at the realization that this is a standard work, which, by the very fact that it sums up a whole epoch, already points into the future.[40]

Others felt that *Ulysses* was definitely ahead of its time[41] and there was at least one critic who saw it as coming ten years too late.[42]

It was of course true that the German *Ulysses* was only available five years after the novel had first appeared. Much had happened in those five years, and many readers saw in *Ulysses* an implicit critique of the age that spared neither the reader nor the world:

This book sums up the age with a radicalism never before experienced and unlikely ever to be exceeded. . . . The x-ray picture makes things so transparent that we see naked chaos grinning behind it.[43]

You can't find ten pages of sincere kindness, devotion, goodness, or friendliness among the fifteen hundred. . . . Joyce's genius is based on hate and finds its only release in irony.[44]

It was perhaps partly as a result of the general unrest of the times that so many readers reacted almost physically to the revolutionary aspects of *Ulysses*. One critic after another emphasized the disturbing ability the novel had to displace the reader from the literary rut of the day. E. R. Curtius spoke of the "shock-like effect"[45] it produced, and Manfred Georg's reaction was not completely atypical:

> I must be completely honest: the first two times I jumped up suddenly after a short while, because I felt a strange pressure in my brain. The feeling of nervous dizzyness that overtakes one all at once on a fast merry-go-round, or when a plane makes a sudden dip in an air-pocket.[46]

The existence of *Ulysses* had to be assimilated by those who were seriously interested in the problem of artistic expression. The necessity to come to terms with the novel may have been experienced by only a small group of readers—but these readers represented individuals profoundly and personally involved with the struggle for adequate expression in German literature. Korrodi had already suggested the year before that "in order to understand Joyce, the world-critic, completely, one must be a poet."[47] And in 1928 novelists and poets continued to be both attracted and daunted by the possibilities of *Ulysses*:

> Even though it has been accessible to only a limited circle up to now, this book must weigh upon the whole of our literature like an incubus. For—no matter how one feels about the novel—one has to admit in all honesty that we will progress no further without having come to terms with it.[48]

Alfred Döblin, whose own struggles with the "crisis" of the novel had already won him a limited but enthusiastic circle of readers, stressed the same idea:

> . . . it is . . . of the greatest importance, for authors and public alike, that someone has taken the path he has chosen with such determination and confidence. This book has opened many people's eyes; they can now see what kind of trade they ply in their dim garrets. . . . The first thing on the list of every serious writer should be to involve himself with this book.[49]

Döblin stressed the "scientific" qualities of the novel. This feature of *Ulysses* was to take on special importance for German writers. Insofar as the novel was scientific and exact it seemed to reflect both the most recent developments of the age, and the particular stylistic tendencies of "neue Sachlichkeit." Joyce was characterized as the first author (in any language) to follow these tendencies to their logical conclusion. E. R. Curtius emphasized this towards the end of 1928:

> The shock-like effect of *Ulysses* comes, in large part, from the fact that in this book all repressions are released. And what makes it new is that it has been done methodically . . . never has this whole realm been illuminated with such cool scientific thoroughness.[50]

The new literary techniques introduced in *Ulysses* brought forth an enthusiastic response from most writers. As Döblin put it, "now new literature can be 'created' left and right." Reviewers repeatedly stressed the fact that these techniques went far beyond anything that had been seen thus far in German literature. Albert Ehrenstein, also a novelist, wrote:

> I remember twenty years ago making use of a certain whispering of the soul in some story. . . . Ernst Weiss and Richard Hülsenbeck did too, in their own ways. But none of us—including Döblin—has written such a thick text-book of psychology as that produced by James Joyce.[51]

German novelists, taken as a separate group, were almost unanimously enthusiastic over *Ulysses* (although by 1928 only a few had expressed themselves in print). One of the few exceptions was Kurt Tucholsky, and even he had attacked the novel very cautiously. His remarks had been directed primarily at the translation, and when *Ulysses* was defended by Ivan Goll there is evidence that Tucholsky may have had a change of heart. In any case he soon could write (in a review of a novel by Arnolt Bronnen):

> In order to depict erotic situations in almost medical detail one must possess the power of someone like James Joyce; what Bronnen has produced is plain pornography.[52]

A second major body of opinion was formed by those reviewers who felt that *Ulysses*, for all its greatness, was almost certainly sterile. Stefan Zweig expressed this view most clearly:

> Actually no analogy one might make to this unique experiment will hold—the inner isolation of James Joyce admits of no connection with the past, it refuses to embrace another, and as a result will probably produce no descendents. Today in any case we say: show respect for this stubborn, vehement and seductive effort, and respect, respect for James Joyce![53]

The bulk of reviews of *Ulysses* had appeared in the first few months of 1928. Joyce's name had appeared in almost every leading periodical and newspaper in the German-speaking countries of Europe. The geographical extent of this coverage was equally broad, and by the end of 1928, although only a few hundred people may have read *Ulysses*, the basic facts about the novel and about Joyce himself were made available to thousands. The literary centers of Berlin and Zurich continued to dominate the discussion, but voices were also heard in Frankfurt, Bern, Prague, Vienna, Salzburg, Leipzig, and many other cities. Among many leading periodicals reviewing *Ulysses* were included: *Die deutsche Rundschau, Die neue Rundschau, Die Literatur, Die schöne Literatur, Die Weltbühne, Die neue Bücherschau,* and *Die neue Schweizer Rundschau.*

Looking back over 1928 there was little evidence that *Ulysses* was really understood by those who wrote about it, whether favorably or unfavorably. Although many saw in it a great work of art, with an important message for the future of literature, almost no critic escaped from the mistaken impression that *Ulysses* was chaotic and unformed. Thus it was that at one and the same time they could praise it for its technical innovations and unparalleled realism, and yet see in it simply a mirror held up to the face of a meaningless and chaotic world. Gert Pohl, in that same year 1928, attacked his fellow literary critics with a vengeance:

James Joyce's great work, unconventional and new in every respect, was a proficiency test for German literary critics. Unfortunately the majority of the candidates failed brilliantly. . . . *Being
a critic means serving as a herald and pacemaker for literature. Today we have
no literary criticism.*[54]

It remained for E. R. Curtius, writing in November of
1928 (and with the advantage of inside knowledge about
the structure of *Ulysses*), to make the important statement:

But whoever becomes seriously involved with *Ulysses* will find himself enriched by a fantastic intellectual experience. It is possible to
understand *Ulysses,* or at least to learn to understand it. For unlike
certain products of Dada or Surrealism which are the result of a
willed orgy of the irrational, an explosion of meaningless auto-
matic writing, this work is a complicated construction which is
thoroughly rational and conscious, and therefore accessible to
intellectual analysis.[55]

The flow of articles which had already begun to lessen
by the end of 1928 was reduced to a trickle during the
next year. This was largely a simple matter of satura-
tion—almost every leading literary periodical had published something on *Ulysses* and, in the absence of new
material or insights, there seemed little more to say for
the moment. In January of 1929 the *Neue Schweizer Rundschau* published what was to become the standard work of
German Joycean criticism, "Technik und Thematik von
James Joyce," by E. R. Curtius. Its importance rested
primarily in the way in which it followed up with concrete examples the suggestion:

. . . only those will do justice to the art of Joyce who analyze the
complexity of the almost incalculable number of motifs in this
work.[56]

Curtius proceeded to demonstrate the way in which association, to which he attributed the primary role in
Joyce's method, functioned in several specific passages of
Ulysses. He also stressed the difference between the
thoughts of Stephen and Bloom, thus showing the man-

ner in which the inner monologue could transcend more traditional methods of recording individual thoughts. Certain basic themes in the novel, such as the father-son problem, were also analyzed. Curtius thus provided, in a very practical sense, a guide for the way in which the novel should be approached. The result of his approach was to bring order into what was at first sight chaos.[57]

His discussion of the Sirens episode represented the first real attempt by a German critic to come to grips with this chapter. Curtius suggested that verbal phrases, unlike those in music, were not immediately aesthetically satisfying:

> The word-motive, however, remains a meaningless fragment, and assumes its meaning only in the objective context. I am unable to do anything with "Horrid! And gold flushed more." Joyce has intentionally ignored this profound difference in substance of sound and word. For that reason his experiment remains questionable.[58]

Such criticism (within the very favorably-toned article) was a welcome change from unreasoned arguments, and Joyce showed his appreciation by requesting that a translation of the article be reprinted in transition:

> Ihre Exegese ist sicher die beste, die ich bisher in irgend einer Sprache über Ulysses gesehen habe. Herr Joyce selbst interessiert sich dafür, dass der Aufsatz in transition erscheint.[59]

The article was of further interest in that it denied any profound relationship between Joyce's methods and psychoanalysis. By 1929 Freud's name was so commonly coupled with Joyce's that Curtius felt it necessary to dwell upon this point:

> Ulysses unmasks, exposes, demolishes, degrades humanity with a sharpness and completeness which has no counterpart in modern thinking. It is wrong to mistake this for psycho-analysis . . . Joyce stands on a higher plane. He knows that the ultimate intellectual decisions are metaphysical and religious.[60]

In spite of what Curtius termed "metaphysical nihilism" in Joyce's work he made it quite clear that this was not the last word—the final function of *Ulysses* was cathartic, and the novel itself was not metaphorical Hell, but Purgatory.

Later in the year Karl Thieme, writing in the *Christliche Welt*, had little charity to spare for a renegade Catholic:

> The whole of Joyce in a nutshell: self-tormenting universal disgust and the empty lyricism of an erudite Alexandrian clearly unaware of the fact that he is incapable of emotion—[the sum total amounting to] boundless filth . . .[61]

This vitriolic attack included a rather one-sided view of Leopold Bloom as a "most dull and dirty Irish jew." But by 1929 such a reaction to *Ulysses* appeared an isolated case against the background of criticism which had already been published. In the meantime fragments of Joyce's new novel, referred to for the time being only as "Work in Progress," were beginning to appear in *transition*. Carola Giedion-Welcker wrote the first article in German to appear on the subject. One can imagine the consternation of those for whom long stretches of *Ulysses* had been almost incomprehensible when they were told:

> Joyce's latest work makes considerably greater demands on the reader's mental alertness and cooperation than *Ulysses* did in 1922.[62]

In 1930 the task of German critics (at least those with some knowledge of English) was made considerably easier by the publication of Stuart Gilbert's "detailed and revealing study,"[63] *James Joyce's Ulysses* (London, 1930). Gilbert outlined in great detail the "secret" structure of the novel, thus opening the eyes of many readers for the first time to the overall plan of the work. Prior to this point critics had been only vaguely aware that each chapter had its own technique, color, symbol, hour, and parallel to the *Odyssey*. Now these were set forth clearly and with the weight of authority (Joyce had read and approved of the whole of the study, according to Gilbert, as well as furnishing him with many of the details). This information, accompanied by a lengthy commentary, furnished the groundwork from which that intellectual analysis referred to by Curtius could proceed. Even those who, like Curtius, had been privy to the outline of the parallels had lacked up to this time anything like the thorough exegesis provided by Gilbert's study. Thus the publication of this book opened the way for serious academic consideration of the merits of *Ulysses*. And of course it was of particular importance as a guide to the non-English reader.

Meanwhile enough time had passed for some critics to feel called upon to review the situation historically. Although little had been written specifically about Joyce in 1929, two German novels had appeared with which his name was often linked: *Berlin Alexanderplatz* by Alfred Döblin, and *Perrudja* by Hans Henny Jahnn. The first of these had been a literary sensation and brought Döblin to the forefront of literary discussion. It was his first and last popular success. *Perrudja*, appearing in a limited edition, had excited less attention, but reviewers had been quick to point out its similarities to certain features of *Ulysses*. Walter Enkenbach, writing in *Der Scheinwerfer* (Essen), took the occasion to attack Joyce and the whole development of the modern German novel. He began by giving an interesting account of his difficulties in obtaining a copy:

> Only a few copies of this book were in circulation. Yet every writer heard of it. It was hard to get hold of; one was constantly being asked: Have you read Joyce?—but the supposed owner of a copy was always saying: Pity, I've just loaned it out. The book became legendary.[64]

According to Enkenbach the German novel had become "burned out" between 1927 and 1930. Then the novelists "discovered" science and accepted James Joyce as their leader. Foremost among Joyce's disciples, in his view, was Alfred Döblin, who had turned to *Ulysses* for inspiration:

> Alfred Döblin used it as a writing pad in 1930, while working on *Berlin Alexanderplatz*. Of course there's nothing wrong with writing

pads—as long as the person using them knows whether they are
any good, and how they should be employed.[65]

Enkenbach saw Joyce and the misguided German writers
who followed him as tardy schoolboys who hadn't
learned their lessons, and who pretended to be giving
something new to the public in serving up a catalogue of
old knowledge. *Ulysses* was as unscientific as possible,
vague and inexact. Joyce was a bohemian, and therefore
did not deserve to be taken seriously. Enkenbach's article
had one unique feature: it claimed that there was absolutely nothing new in *Ulysses*.

The year 1930 marked another dividing point in the
critical reception of *Ulysses* in German-speaking
countries: Not only critics, but also the publishers of the
novel, were beginning to review its history. All in all the
first edition had been tremendously successful. Not only
had it been well received, but much praise had also been
showered upon the Rhein-Verlag for publishing it. The
dangers of prosecution on the grounds of obscenity had
apparently been avoided and nothing stood in the way of
bringing out a second edition, which could be expected
to sell out almost immediately. Just to be on the safe
side the second edition was also to be subscribed.

As we have seen, the 1927 version of *Ulysses* left much
to be desired as a translation—and Joyce knew it. He
insisted on the right to revise it thoroughly. The story of
the German *Ulysses* after 1930 must take into account the
importance of that revised edition, and its implications
for this study.

---

1. After obtaining the rights to *Ulysses* in 1966, the Suhrkamp Verlag
commissioned a new translation of *Ulysses*, the first for over forty years. It has at
last appeared (Spring, 1976) as this book goes to press.
2. The English original is completely unpunctuated, and the second German version (1930) correctly omitted the commas present in 1927.
3. Misprinted " 'This" in the Random House edition.
4. The last two lines of Heine's "Leise zieht durch mein Gemüt" are: "Wenn
du eine Rose schaust,/ Sag, ich lass' sie grüssen."
5. Announced on that date in the *Börsenblatt für den deutschen Buchhandel*,
XCIV (1927), 9352.
6. Walter Schmits, "James Joyce," *Die Kölnische Zeitung*, 3 November 1927.

7. Kurt Tucholsky, "*Ulysses,*" *Die Weltbühne,* XXIII (November, 1927), 788-793.

8. Otto Zarek, "Der *Ulysses* des James Joyce," *Das Tagebuch,* VIII (December, 1927), 1963-1966.

9. Gerhart Pohl, "*Ulysses,*" *Die neue Bücherschau,* V (November, 1927), 224-228.

10. E[duard] K[orrodi], "Kritizimus im europäischen Roman," *Neue Zürcher Zeitung,* 11 November 1927.

11. Ivan Goll, "*Ulysses: Sub specie aeternitatis,*" *Die Weltbühne,* XXIII (December, 1927), 960-963.

12. "auch die grimmigsten Gegner bestreiten nicht sein starkes Talent". Schmits, *loc.cit.*

13. "in diesem Sinne ist James Joyces Werk von eminenter Bedeutung: als Kunst-Revolution und das muss immer heissen *Form-Revolution.*" Pohl, p. 226.

14. "Der Roman reitet alle Stilsättel. Sein eigener ist eine völlig neue Verwendung des Monologs, der alles ausspricht, was durch ein Hirn rast." Korrodi, *loc.cit.*

15. "Und hier setzt nun der 'innere Monolog' ein, der so viel Aufsehen gemacht hat . . . und es muss gesagt werden, dass dies der stärkste Eindruck von allem ist. . . . Mit den winzigen Versuchen Arthur Schnitzlers und Carl Spittelers hat diese Orgelsymphonie der Gedanken nichts zu tun. Hier ist tatsächlich alles, aber auch alles, gesagt." Tucholsky, p. 792.

16. "Fortschrittliche Professoren haben für den *Ulysses* eine Vorliebe gefasst, und es ist nicht nur das, was mich mistrauisch macht. Ich habe 1585 Seiten bekommen—aber mit Ausnahme jener zwei grandiosen Stücke ist da nichts auf meinem Teller, bis jetzt kann ich das nicht essen—es ist irgend etwas Künstliches an der Sache, etwas Konstruiertes, und, nun will ich mich getrost steinigen lassen; etwas Phantasieloses." Tucholsky, p. 790.

17. "Schreitet sie schnell und konsequent genug fort, wird er unsere Zeit mühelos gestalten. Denn 'Vernunft hat immer existiert, nur nicht immer in der vernünftigsten Form' (Karl Marx). Glätten sich die Wellen des Bildungschaos nicht zugunsten einer schlagkräftigen Beschränkung, wird ihm der grosse Wurf nie gelingen. Unverwischbar aber bleibt die Tat: Schöpfung der zeitgemässen, also der vernünftigsten Form." Pohl, p. 228.

18. "Ob ein solches wahrheitsfanatisches Durchwühlen stinkenden Schlammes Aufgabe des Künstlers sein kann, ist eine schwierige Doktorfrage." Schmits, *loc.cit.*

19. "freudianische Tatbestände zeichnerisch festgehalten". Zarek, p. 1964.

20. "Viele Beschäftigung mit der Psychoanalyse impfte ihm ein." Pohl, p. 227.

21. "muten lange Strecken des Buches wie zusammenhangloses, unverständliches, sehr langweiliges Gestammel eines Menschen an, der an Ideenflucht leidet". Schmits, *loc.cit.*

22. "Menschen, zwei oder drei Menschen aus Dublin, wollen jauchzend die 'Sünde' geniessen." Zarek, p. 1963.

23. "Unmöglich, alles hintereinander zu lesen. Die Personen verwirren sich; wenn eine Handlung darin ist, habe ich sie nicht verstanden—ich weiss nicht immer, was real, gedacht, geträumt oder beabsichtigt ist." Tucholsky, p. 788.

24. "Bevor man mit [Tucholsky] . . . streitet, müsste man sicher sein, dass ihm die Kommentare zu einem so verzweigten Werk bekannt waren. Sie waren ihm nicht bekannt. Also kann man ihm nichts andres vorwerfen, als dass er dies Epos, das weit über uns alle hinausragt, wie irgendeinen der vielen 'Romane' behandelt hat, die den Weihnachtstisch belagerten." Goll, p. 962.

25. "hier ist nun, da wir es nicht mit einem Originaltext, sondern mit einer Übersetzung zu tun haben, sogleich zu untersuchen, ob dieser Eindruck an der Übersetzung liegen kann." Tucholsky, p. 789.

26. "Wohl aber kann ich nach Hunderten von Stichproben bei der ersten Lektüre eines sagen: In welchem Stil dieses Buch abgefasst ist, steht dahin. Dichterisches Deutsch ist es bestimmt nicht. . . . Hier ist entweder ein Mord geschehen oder eine Leiche photographiert." *Ibid.*

27. "*Ulysses* wird das Gesicht der zivilisierten Prosa ändern. Denn hier wurde die starre 'Kunst' gesprengt." Pohl, p. 224.

28. "nun sieht [der Leser] wie konventionell und verlogen unsere Romanmonologe und Dialoge waren". Korrodi, *loc.cit.*

29. "Der *Ulysses* ist mit keinem existierenden Buch der Weltliteratur vergleichbar: es ist einzig und ganz neu. Solche Prosa ist die Sprache und der Rhythmus der kommenden Dichtung." Goll, p. 962.

30. "James Joyce hat eine Tür aufgestossen. . . . Was gemacht werden konnte, hat Joyce gemacht. Liebigs Fleischextrakt. Mann kann es nicht essen. Aber es werden noch viele Suppen damit zubereitet werden." Tucholsky, p. 793.

31. "verboten in England und Amerika seines übrigs harmlosen erotischen Einschlags wegen". Bernard Guillemin, "Die Irrfahrt des James Joyce in seinem Roman *Ulysses*," *Berliner Börsen-Courier*, 7 March 1928.

32. "Es gibt kein Buch, das weniger pornographisch wäre als der *Ulysses*— mit einziger Ausnahme des Beichtspiegels." Erich Franzen, "Zum *Ulysses* von Joyce," *Die literarische Welt*, IV (April, 1928), 5.

33. "Hier setzte der anglikanische Puritanismus die Hebel der Zensur in Bewegung, blind für die Grösse des Kunstwerkes, für seine Weisheit und tiefe Menschlichkeit . . ." A. J. Fischer, "James Joyce in Salzburg," *Salzburger Volksblatt*, 25 August 1928.

34. "Wer ist schuld, Autor oder Natur, wenn der Seelenboden 'Schlamm' ist? Der Hauptvorzug des *Ulysses* ist der Mut, mit dem alle Schranken zerschlagen werden, die sich vor dem literarischen Abbild der Menschenseele immer wieder errichten wollen." H[elmut?] Sch[lien?], "*Ulysses* von James Joyce," *Der Bund*, Beilage: *Der kleine Bund*, Bern, 7 January 1928, p. 13.

35. "Ein Dubliner Nachtlokal ist die Unterwelt. Ein Dubliner Bürgerhaus Himmel und Hölle: je nach der Stunde, die geschildert wird. Ein Gang durch Dublins Strassen eine Wanderung durch das Weltall." "L. W.," "*Ulysses*," *Deutsche Zeitung Bohemia*, Prague, 24 February 1928.

36. *Letters*, I, 184.

37. "Bloom scheint nur da, um Dädalus sichtbar zu machen." Efraim Frisch, "*Ulysses*: zu dem Werk von James Joyce," *Frankfurter Zeitung*, 11 January 1928.

38. "Um *Ulysses* ganz zu verstehen, müsste man die Durchführung dieses doppelten Symbolismus genau erfassen. Aber zum ersten Symbolismus fehlt uns der Schlüssel: ein genau ausgearbeitetes System von Konkordanzen. Es existiert, aber im Besitz des Autors und weniger eingeweihten Freunde." Ernst Robert Curtius, "James Joyce," *Die Literatur*, XXXI (November, 1928), 126.

39. "[*Ulysses*] ist undenkbar ohne das Seelenklima unserer letzten zwanzig Jahre, und dieses ist, so möchte man schon meinen, schwer denkbar ohne dieses Buch." "H. Sch.," *loc.cit.* (see note 34, above).

40. ". . . so kommt man doch zur Erkenntnis, hier ein Standardwerk vor sich zu haben, das eben durch die Tatsache, dass es einen Bilanzstrich unter eine ganze Epoche setzt, bereits wieder in die Zukunft deutet." Bruno E. Werner, "Der *Ulysses* des James Joyce," *Deutsche Rundschau*, LIV (June, 1928), 270.

41. Frisch, *loc.cit.*

42. Fritz Gaupp, "Kritisches zum *Ulysses* von James Joyce," *Badische Presse*, Karlsruhe, 4 April 1928.

43. "Dieses Buch zieht die Bilanz eines Zeitalters mit einem Radikalismus, wie dies bisher nicht geschehen ist und wohl auch nicht übertroffen werden wird. . . . Das Röntgenbild wird so transparent, dass dahinter das nackte Nichts grinst." Werner, *loc.cit.*

44. "Keine zehn Seiten Herzlichkeit, Hingebung, Güte, Freundlichkeit findet man unter den fünfzehnhundert. . . . Das eigentliche Genie von Joyce sitzt im Hass und erlöst sich einzig in Ironie." Stefan Zwieg, "Anmerkung zum *Ulysses*," *Die neue Rundschau*, XXXIX (Oktober, 1928), 477-478.

45. "schock-artige Wirkung" Curtius, p. 124.

46. "Ich muss ganz ehrlich sein: die ersten beiden Male sprang ich nach einer gewissen Zeit rasch ab, weil sich in meinem Gehirn ein merkwürdiger Druck einstellte. Jenes nervöse Schwindelgefühl, das man urplötzlich bei einem zu geschwinden Karussell oder beim Absacken eines Flugzeuges in ein Luftloch empfindet." Manfred Georg, "Der *Ulysses* des James Joyce," *Badische Presse*, Karlsruhe, 4 January 1928.

47. "dass der Leser, um den Welt-Kritiker Joyce ganz zu verstehen, ein Dichter sein müsste". Korrodi, *loc.cit.*

48. "Dieses Buch, wenn auch nur einem begrenzten Kreis bisher zugänglich, müsste wie ein Alp auf unserem gesamten Schrifttum liegen. Denn—man mag zu ihm stehen wie man will—man sollte ehrlich erkennen, dass man nicht weiter kommt, ohne sich mit ihm auseinandergesetz zu haben." Gaupp, *loc.cit.*

49. ". . . es ist gut und von grösster Wichtigkeit für Autoren und Publikum, dass von einem einzelnen der Weg, den er begeht, so entschlossen und sicher begangen wird. Mit diesem Buch wird vielen der Star gestochen; sie können nun sehen, was für ein Handwerk sie in ihren trüben Stuben betreiben. . . . Zunächst hat jeder ernste Schriftsteller sich mit diesem Buch zu befassen." Alfred Döblin, "*Ulysses* von Joyce," *Döblin: Aufsätze zur Literatur*, ed. Walter Muschg (Olten, 1963), pp. 288 and 290; article reprinted from *Das deutsche Buch*, VIII (1928), 84-85.

50. "Die schock-artige Wirkung von *Ulysses* kommt nicht zuletzt daher, dass in diesem Buch alle Verdrängungen durchbrochen werden. Und zwar—dies ist das Neue—mit Methode . . . nie ist mit so kühler wissenschaftlicher Gründlichkeit der ganze Bereich alles dessen abgeleuchtet worden." Curtius, *loc.cit.*

51. "Ich entsinne mich, vor zwanzig Jahren erzählerisch von einem gewissen Raunen der Seele Gebrauch gemacht zu haben. . . . Ernst Weiss und Richard Hülsenbeck taten auf ihre Weise desgleichen. Aber keiner von uns—auch Döblin nicht—hat ein so dickes Lehrbuch der Psychologie verfasst, wie James Joyce." Albert Ehrenstein, "James Joyce," *Albert Ehrenstein: Ausgewählte Aufsätze*, ed. M. Y. Bengavriel (Darmstadt, 1961), p. 75; reprinted from the *Berliner Tageblatt*, 5 April 1928.

52. "Um eine erotische Situation bis in die medizinischen Einzelheiten zu gestalten, muss man die Stärke etwa von James Joyce besitzen, was aber Bronnen gemacht hat, ist blanke Pornographie." Kurt Tucholsky, "Ein besserer Herr," *Gesammelte Werke 1929-1932*, ed. Mary Gerold-Tucholsky (Reinbeck bei Hamburg, 1961), p. 110; reprinted from *Die Weltbühne*, XXV (June, 1929), 935 ff.

53. "In Wirklichkeit geht jeder Vergleich für dieses einmalige Experiment glatt daneben—die innere Isolation von James Joyce duldet keine Bindung an Gewesenes, sie paart nicht und wird darum wohl auch keine Nachfahren zeugen. . . . Jedenfalls schon heute: Respekt vor dieser eigenwillig vehementen und versucherischen Leistung, Respekt, Respekt vor James Joyce!" Zwieg, p. 479.

54. "James Joyces grosses Werk, in jeder Hinsicht traditionslos und neu, war ein Befähigungsnachweis für die deutsche Literatur-Kritik. Leider ist der Kandidaten Mehrzahl glänzend durchgefallen. . . . *Kritiker zu sein bedeutet als Schrittmacher und Wegweiser der Dichtung zu dienen. Wir haben heute keine Literatur-Kritik.*" Gerhart Pohl, "*Ulysses* und die deutsche Literatur-Kritik," *Die neue Bücherschau,* VI (1928), 89.

55. "Aber wer sich ernstlich um *Ulysses* bemüht, wird sich um eine phantastische geistige Erfahrung bereichert finden. Man kann *Ulysses* verstehen oder wenigstens verstehen lernen. Dann dies Werk ist nicht wie gewisse Produkte des Dadaismus oder des Überrealismus eine gewollte Orgie des Irrationalen, eine Explosion von sinnlosen Automatismen, sondern eine komplizierte Konstruktion von äusserster Bewusstheit, und darum der intellektuellen Analyse zugänglich." Curtius, p. 121.

56. ". . . nur der wird der Kunst von Joyce ganz gerecht werden, der die fast unübersehbare motivische Verschlungenheit des Werkes analysiert." Ernst Robert Curtius, "Technik und Thematik von James Joyce," *Neue Schweizer Rundschau,* XXII (January, 1929), 54. Translation taken from *transition,* No. 16-17 (June, 1929), p. 315.

57. Professor Curtius' own copy of *Ulysses* (Paris, 1924) bears witness to the thoroughness with which he followed themes and variations. His marginal notations include detailed cross-references with page numbers—a system which allowed him to gain a much greater appreciation of the intricacies of the work than almost any of his fellow critics.

58. "Diesen tiefen Wesenunterschied von Klang und Wort hat Joyce absichtlich ignoriert. Darum bleibt sein Experiment fragwürdig." Curtius, p. 64. Translation, p. 322 (see note 56, above).

59. Letter from Eugene Jolas to Ernst Robert Curtius, 25 April 1929, unpublished.

60. "*Ulysses* entlarvt, exponiert, demoliert und degradiert das Menschentum mit einer Schärfe und Vollständigkeit, die im modernen Denken kein Gegenstück hat. Man verwechsle das nicht mit der Psychoanalyse. . . . Joyce steht auf einer höheren Ebene. Er weiss, dass die letzten geistigen Entscheidungen metaphysisch-religiöser Art sind." Curtius, p. 68. Translation, p. 325 (see note 56, above).

61. "*In nuce* der ganze Joyce: Selbstquälerischer Weltekel und leere Lyrik eines wohlunterrichteten Alexandriners bei offen unbekannter Unfähigkeit zur Passion—also grenzenloser Schmutz . . ." Karl Thieme, "Der Unsägliche und die Sprache," *Christliche Welt,* XLIII (1929), 291.

62. "Der neueste Joyce . . . stellt an die geistige Bereitschaft und Mitarbeit des Lesers erheblich grössere Anforderungen, als es 1922 der *Ulysses* tat." Carola Giedion-Welcker, "Work in Progress: Ein sprachliches Experiment von James Joyce," *Neue Schweizer Rundschau,* XXII (September, 1929), 660.

63. "eingehende und erstaunliche Studie" Bernhard Fehr, *Die englische Literatur der Gegenwart* (Leipzig, 1930), p. 65. Fehr was the first critic to make use of Gilbert, in a chapter of the work cited here.

64. "Nur eine geringe Zahl von Exemplaren dieses Buches kam in Umlauf. Aber alle Schriftsteller hörten davon. Es war schwer zu fassen; immer wurde gefragt: Haben Sie Joyce gelesen?—und immer sagte der angebliche Besitzer eines Exemplars: Schade, ich habe es gerade ausgeliehen. Das Buch wurde legendär." Walter Enkenbach, "Die Odyssee der verspäteten Schüler," *Der Scheinwerfer,* No. 14 (April, 1930), p. 7.

65. "1930 benutzte es Alfred Döblin . . . bei der Niederschrift seines *Berlin Alexanderplatz* als Schreibunterlage. Bitte, kein Wort gegen Schreibunterlagen; nur müsste, wer sie benutzt, wissen, ob sie tauglich sind, und wie sie zu verwenden sind." *Ibid.* Enkenbach does not explain how Döblin could still be working on his novel in 1930, when it had been published the year before.

4

THE SECOND GERMAN ULYSSES: 1930

I

Almost no one realized the extent to which the second version of *Ulysses* varied from the first. Both versions were published with the notice "vom Verfasser geprüft," without any suggestion that extensive revision had taken place. The translator and publisher remained unchanged. Yet a close comparison of the two versions reveals that literally thousands of changes were made—changes which had an important effect upon the quality of the translation, and made possible a greater appreciation of the novel in German-speaking countries.

Dissatisfied with the 1927 version, Joyce had insisted upon the chance to rework the translation. He had enlisted the aid of several friends for this purpose, and the second edition incorporated their suggestions as well as his own. It is of course impossible to accurately determine whether any particular change was made with Joyce's approval, or at his command. Nevertheless, in light of the changes made, the first edition becomes a sort of working manuscript of the translation, from which we might expect to learn something of interest about the novel itself. Joyce's knowledge of German, although far from perfect, was reasonably thorough, and his linguistical genius was such that he could make creative suggestions in another language.

A comparison of the two versions is also revealing in historical terms. Those people most interested in *Ulysses*, if unable to read it in the original, were not likely to pass up the earliest opportunity to read it in their native language. It was unlikely that they would wait three years for the second edition. As a result, the critical reception of *Ulysses* in German-speaking countries centered largely upon the 1927 edition. We shall want to know then in what way the first version differed significantly from the second, and what we may learn from the variations involved. The answer to these questions calls for a close look at the text of the two editions.

The 1930 edition of the German *Ulysses* incorporated 6,306 changes from the first edition—excluding changes of spelling and punctuation.[1] Of these, 4,463 were changes of style in which the meaning of the phrase or sentence was not substantially affected. But 1,203 changes resulted in phrases or sentences whose meaning was altered significantly from that of the first edition. There were 492 words or phrases omitted in 1927 but translated and included in 1930, and 328 cases in which a word or phrase left in English in the first version was translated into German for the second. A chapter by chapter breakdown of the alterations shows that every episode of *Ulysses* was substantially reworked (see Table 3).

TABLE 3

Chapter		change style	change meaning	word(s) omitted	Eng.- Ger.	total changes
Telemachus	1	116	22	3	1	142
Nestor	2	40	21	1	2	64
Proteus	3	103	19	4	1	127
Calypso	4	79	11	4	0	94
Lotus	5	77	18	7	1	103
Hades	6	104	19	1	9	133
Aeolus	7	140	28	11	5	184
Lestrygonians	8	193	31	3	18	245
Scylla	9	116	41	2	13	172
Rocks	10	124	34	7	18	183

Sirens	11	232	63	10	67	372
Cyclops	12	329	67	18	38	452
Nausicaa	13	181	67	9	20	277
Oxen-Sun	14	258	74	43	10	385
Circe	15	867	223	94	39	1223
Eumaeus	16	482	78	91	24	675
Ithaca	17	591	83	110	35	819
Penelope	18	431	124	74	27	656
		4463	1023	492	328	6306

These general figures demonstrate that the revision of the German translation was thorough and relatively complete. Such changes were not concentrated in a few of the more difficult chapters. Each episode was substantially affected. On the average page there were between seven and eight changes, of which one or more involved a significant change of meaning. The figures also give empirical weight to the evidence pieced together previously from letters and statements alone. For example it was Joyce's contention that he and the translator were rushed while working on the first edition. If time were short it would be natural for the last chapters to receive the least attention. And in fact this was true. The number of alterations required (adjusted to a per page average) for each episode shows this quite clearly. A case in point is the number of words or phrases omitted in 1927. This number is negligible (less than one word every three or four pages) until the final three chapters, in which the average was one or two words or phrases omitted *on every page*. A similar upswing, if not so extreme, is seen in changes involving meaning and style. A closer look at each of the categories listed will aid in understanding the extent to which the two versions differ and how this might have affected the German reader.

"theres real beauty and poetry for you":
4,463 changes of style.

There is an important sense in which every change of style involves a change of meaning, and more importantly a change in the response of the reader. Such changes are more subtle and pervasive than the obvious correction of simple errors. Included in this category is any change which did not alter the basic meaning of the phrase involved, regardless of how great an effect such a change might have produced. Many such revisions were aimed at simply making the language flow more easily, and making leitmotifs consistent throughout the work. Yet even on this level, in which basic meanings remain unaffected from one version to the other, the importance of such revisions can scarcely be overstressed, affecting as they do the reader's most profound reaction to the work. A few examples of the types of changes involved will elucidate this point (variations italicized for comparison):

	ENGLISH	GERMAN-1927	GERMAN-1930
1.	His hand took his hat from the peg . . . (56:36)	*Er* nahm den Hut vom Haken . . . (I, 115)	*Seine Hand* nahm den Hut vom Haken . . . (I, 90)
2.	Her ear too is a shell, the peeping lobe there. (281:21)	Auch ihr Ohr ist eine Muschel, Ohrmuschel *ist sichtbar.* (II, 134)	Auch ihr Ohr ist eine Muschel, Ohrmuschel *lugt hervor.* (I, 458)
3.	Oaths of a man roar, mutter, cease. (430:11)	*Ein Mann brüllt, flucht, knurrt, dann Stille.* (III, 3)	*Männerflüche brüllen, knurren, verstummen.* (II, 83)
4.	I feel a strong weakness. (134:24)	*"Mir wird ganz schwach."* (I, 281)	*"Ich fühle eine starke Schwäche."* (I, 218)
5.	Show us the entrance out. (335:22)	*". . . wo geht's denn raus?"* (II, 252)	*". . . zeig mir mal den Eingang nach draussen."* (I, 550)
6.	a morbid upwards and outwards philo-pro-genative erection (305:07)	*eine krankhafte Erection mit Samen-entleerung* (II, 184)	*morbide und philoprogenerative vertikalhorizontale Erektion* (I, 498)
7.	the discharge of fluid from the thunderhead (395:13)	Entladung *einer Gewitterwolke* (II, 388)	Entladung *des Fluidums eines Donnerzentrums* (II, 22)
8.	The final bout of fireworks was a gruelling for both champions. (318:32)	*Im letzten Gang ging es ganz be-sonders scharf her.* (II, 215)	*Die Endrunde mit ihrem Feuerwerk von Hieben war für beiden Champions gleich ver-hängnisvoll.* (I, 521)

9.	He expresses himself with much marked refinement of phraseology. (590:07)	Er drückt sich *sehr gewählt* aus. (III, 242)	Er drückt sich *mit sehr ausgesprochenem Raffinement der Phraseologie* aus. (II, 274)
10.	before transferring his rapt attention to the floor. (622:13)	bevor er *wieder vor sich niedersah.* (III, 293)	bevor er *seine volle Aufmerksamkeit wieder dem Fussboden zu-wandte.* (II, 315)

These few examples are chosen as a sample of some, but by no means all, of the variations of style employed in *Ulysses*. They include characteristic Joycean grammatical twists (1, 3, 10), the flavor of Dublin wit (4, 5), the voice of the scientist (6, 7), the sports announcer (8), and the pedant (9). These clear variations of tone and style simply disappeared in the first German version, and there remained little trace of an author worthy of our attention. There is no reason to believe that one and the same person might not have said or written every phrase in the 1927 column. The 1930 version goes a long way toward rectifying this impression by sharpening the stylistic variations.

The changes introduced went beyond phrases to individual words, hundreds of which were replaced by more descriptive and striking synonyms in an attempt to capture more fully the flavor of the original text:

	became	
nimmt		grapscht
fallen		sausen
bedeckt		festoniert
gefahren		geschaukelt
öffnete		riss . . . auf
etc.		etc.

The realization that almost 4,500 changes of this and similar nature were incorporated into the second German version gives some impression of the inadequacy of the first and improvement of the second.

"as if any fool wouldnt know what that meant":
1,023 changes of meaning.

Those revisions which resulted in an actual change of meaning in the text were occasioned almost without exception by simple mistranslations. That the number of such changes is so high attests both to the difficulty of the task of translating *Ulysses* and the high rate of speed at which the translator was forced to work. Thus most of the mistakes fell into two categories—mistranslations of difficult passages (difficult because they involved local slang, specialized knowledge, archaic or obscure words, etc.) and mistranslations due simply to carelessness. No doubt careless mistakes—

red	"translated"	gelb
number nine		Nummer 10
Joe		Alf
finely		schliesslich
1		ich
etc.		etc.

often passed unnoticed by the reader. But there were many which must have puzzled him. On more than thirty occasions the translator gave the exact opposite of the true meaning. Here is a sample:

	ENGLISH	GERMAN-1927
1.	The father *is rotto*[2] *with money.* (22:17)	Der Vater *hat alles Geld verloren.* (I, 45)
2.	*In ferial tone* he addressed . . . (141:26)	*Feierlich* redete er . . . an. (I, 294)
3.	—Are you a strict t.t? says Joe. —*Not taking anything between drinks,* says I. (293:17)	"Bist du strenger Teesäufer?" sagt Joe. "*Nehme nichts anderes, wenn ich am Saufen bin,*" sagt ich. (II, 159)
4.	the fighting navy . . . *that keeps our foes at bay?* (328:36)	Kriegsmarine . . . *die unsere Feinde in der Bai liegen haben.* (II, 238)

5. STEPHEN. *Pas seul!* (He   STEPHAN. *Pas seul!* (Er . . .
    . . . *takes the floor* . . .)   *bleibt stehen* . . .)
    (578:14)   (III, 225)

In these and similar cases the author's point was not only missed but directly contravened, which could result, as above, in a false reading of: (1) the motives involved, (2) the tone of the conversation, (3) the character's habits, (4) the situation, or (5) the action. Such passages are usually inconsistent with the text immediately preceding or following—an inconsistency the reader might be likely to see as a weakness on the part of the author.

As is the case with most errors in translation there was no way for the reader to know when he was a victim without recourse to the original, and in most cases simply finding the corresponding passage in the English text would have been a large task in itself. Inconsistencies in the text, characters who suddenly acted out of character, and meaningless sentences were no doubt attributed to Joyce. There was no way that the German reader could have appreciated the internal consistency of images and ideas in the novel.

Such mistakes as were discovered in the 1927 version were unacceptable to Joyce, even if they might have passed completely unnoticed by the same reader who objected to the stylistic shortcomings of the translation. Although in any particular case they might not have upset the flow of ideas or narrative the cumulative effect of more than a thousand such errors could only be detrimental to the author's purpose.

"asking me had I frequent omissions":
492 words or phrases left out.

It is taken for granted that a translation at least *attempts* to be complete. Even when the version offered is somewhat unsatisfactory something is considered better than nothing. The omission of words and phrases harms the work in direct proportion to the importance of those words or phrases within the framework of the whole.

Joyce spent long hours searching for the right word in the right place, and it is not an exaggeration to say that he considered every word and every phrase in *Ulysses* to have its own *raison d'être*.[3] He was very upset by gaps in the translation and attempted to ensure that they would be filled. Many were not, and in the final five chapters (and particularly the last three) the number of omissions was high by any standard. This must be attributed in part to the rush in which the translation was completed. Some idea of the effect of such omissions may be seen in the following examples (phrases italicized were omitted in the German version):

ENGLISH	GERMAN-1927
1. . . . the cogitation of which *by sejunct females* is to tumescence conducive or eases issue *in the high sunbright wellbuilt fair home of mothers when, ostensibly far gone and reproductitive, it is come by her thereto to lie in, her term up.* (384:40)	. . . deren Betrachtung ja die Entwicklung der Leibesfrucht fördert und die Geburt erleichtert. (II, 365)
2. . . . by a questioning poise of the head . . . *to which was united an equivalent but contrary balance of the head* asked . . . (404:16)	. . . fragt den Erzähler mit fragender Gebärde . . . (II, 409)
3. making shelter for their straws with *a clout or* kerchief (397:03)	schützten den Strohhut mit dem Taschentuch (II, 392)
4. was prone to disparage, and even . . . deprecate him, *or whatever you like to call it,* which in Blooms humble opinion (664:42)	dazu neigte ihn . . . zu verunglimpfen und zwar gewissermassen . . . ihn heruntermachte, was, nach Blooms bescheidener Meinung (III, 388)
5. winding, *coiling, simply swirling,* writhing in the skies (414:38)	er windet, dreht sich am Himmel (II, 433)
6. narrated to his son Leopold Bloom (aged 6) *a retrospective arrangement* of migrations and settlements (724:23)	erzählte seinem sechsjährigen Sohne Leopold Bloom von Wanderungen und Niederlassung (III, 522)

7.	he *accommodatingly* dragged his shirt more open (631:20)	öffnete er das Hemd noch mehr (III, 313)
8.	*I hate those buggers.* (631:18)	[omitted] (III, 313)
9.	*Do you?* (633:31)	[omitted] (III, 318)

The first two examples are from the Oxen of the Sun episode, and the complex language is basic to Joyce's purpose—a reflection of the history of the development of the English language. Admittedly this is an impossible task for the translator, yet leaving out sections of the text seems far from satisfactory. Such a practice results in a simplicity and modernity of language which runs directly counter to the intention of the original text. In the third example we may suspect that the translator felt the word "clout" to be an unnecessary repetition (it means "a piece of cloth"). But it was just the type of word Joyce needed for the archaic flavor of the passage. The fourth example is likewise necessary in a way the translator never realized. Joyce was attempting to portray Bloom's mental fatigue by a rambling prose which tends toward repetition and cliché. Leaving such "unnecessary" phrases out destroys the whole stylistic intention. Examples five and six show the omission of important leitmotifs which are structural elements of the novel ("your head it simply swirls"—Blazes Boylan's song of the seaside girls, and "in a kind of retrospective arrangement"—a favorite phrase of Tom Kernan's which keeps passing through Bloom's mind during the day). The translator sometimes omitted entire sentences. But most often the gaps consisted of single words, as in the following italicized examples:

limbo *gloom*
to *plausibly* suggest
hydraulic millwheels
hirsute comets
preexisting acquaintance
surviving male heir
etc.

All of the above were corrected in the 1930 version. Of the 492 such omissions in the 1927 version, 412 occurred in the last five chapters. In practical terms this means that the first version was not significantly affected by omissions in the initial thirteen chapters. In the last five episodes, however, we must reckon with the fact that, as with the other categories, the cumulative effect upon the work must have been detrimental.

In fairness both to Joyce and the German reading public it was necessary that the translation be truly complete, and as far as was possible within the bounds of the language, that every phrase be given its equivalent in the German version. With a few exceptions the 1930 edition corrected these shortcomings and gave to the reader, for the first time, a truly complete text of *Ulysses* in German.

"leave us as wise as we were before":
328 words and phrases left in English.

The preceding categories pointed up clear shortcomings in the translation. The present category of changes differs in that it results from a more or less legitimate decision to leave a word or phrase in English, in the first version. Proper names of persons and places were retained, with at most slight changes to make them more familiar to the German reader (thus "Stephen" became "Stephan"). But in other cases retaining the English could be highly confusing.

The decision in 1927 was to leave almost all poetry, songs, book-titles, and quotations (when so indicated) in the original language. Although the translator followed common practice in this respect, the results were far from satisfactory. As Hodgart and Worthington aptly pointed out concerning musical quotations the "potentiality that song has of emptying itself of and refilling itself with meaning is what interested Joyce. He took the songs that he heard about him, as he did the clichés of everyday talk, presented them in the flattest form, with every significance drained away, then invested

them with the greatest possible symbolical weight relevant to his narrative."[4] Musical quotations become structural elements which help hold the whole work together,
and they appear again and again, both recited aloud
and in the minds of the characters. Since most readers
turn to a translation precisely because they lack an intimate knowledge of the original language in question we
must expect that every such line left in English represented a stumbling-block for the reader. In 1930 the decision was made to translate almost all such passages
into German, and as a result the later version became
much clearer and more meaningful. The following are
a few examples of the way in which leaving such phrases
in English could be harmful to the work:

ENGLISH	GERMAN-1927
1. Dignam's potted meat. Cannibals would with lemon and rice. White missionary too salty. . . . Expect the chief consumes the parts of honour. Ought to be tough from exercise. His wives in a row to watch the effect. *There was a right royal old nigger. Who ate or something the somethings of the reverend Mr MacTrigger.* (171:34)	Dignams Fleischkonserve. Kannibalen würden mit Zitronen und Reis. Weisser Missionar zu salzig. . . . Vermutlich bekommt der Häuptling die Ehrenstücke. Sind sicher zäh vom vielen Gebrauch. Seine Weiber in einer Reihe beobachten die Wirkung. *There was a right royal old nigger who ate something or the somethings of the reverend Mr Mac Trigger.* (I, 357)
2. *—When first I saw that form endearing.* . . . Braintipped, cheek touched with flame, they listened feeling that flow endearing glow over skin limbs human heart soul spine. . . . *—Sorrow from me seemed to depart.* . . . Good, good to hear: sorrow from them each seemed to from both depart when first they heard. When first they saw. . . (273:30)	*When first I saw that form endearing.* . . . Ergriffen, mit flammenberührter Wange, hörten sie zu, fühlten jene lockende Flut über Haut Glieder menschliches Herz Seele Rückgrat fluten. . . . *Sorrow from me seemed to depart.* Herrlich, herrlich zu hören: Sorge schien von jedem, von beiden, abzufallen, als sie zum erstenmal hörten. Als sie zum erstenmal sahen . . . (II, 117)

3. . . . cheap reprints of the World's Twelve Worst Books: *Froggy and Fritz* (politic), *Care of the Baby* (infantilic), *50 Meals for 7/6* (culinic), *Was Jesus a Sun Myth?* (historic), *Expel that Pain* (medic) . . . (485:29)	. . . billige Nachdrucke der zwölf schlechtesten Bücher der Welt: *Froggy and Fritz* (politisch), *Care of the Baby* (kindlich), *50 Meals for 7/6* (kulinarisch), *Was Jesus a Sun Myth?* (historisch), *Expel that Pain* (medizinisch) . . . (III, 88)

The point of the entire passage must have been lost upon the reader to whom such English phrases were unintelligible. The first example concerns a limerick that Bloom is trying to recall. In the next few moments he succeeds in remembering: *"His five hundred wives. Had the time of their lives. . . . It grew bigger and bigger and bigger."* Not only are the phrases important as links in the associative chain, they also concern a central theme of the work —that of sexual power and impotence. It is no accident that the conversation about Molly Bloom's new singing tour with her "organizer," Blazes Boylan, seems to help Bloom remember. "Who's getting it up?" asks Flynn. *"Their lives. I have it. It grew bigger and bigger and bigger. —Getting it up? he said. Well . . ."* The German reader missing all this was perhaps, at best, aware that he was being left out of something interesting.

The second example is from the Sirens episode, where the failure to translate lines from the songs was disastrous. Both of the phrases in question are quite obviously linked stylistically and thematically with the corresponding passages. The connection is lost, however, in translation, and it is particularly unfortunate for the German reader since the phrase recurs in Bloom's mind later on. Having left the hotel he sees a prostitute approaching, with whom he once made an "appointment." She looks "a fright in the day" and his mind jumps back immediately to "when first he saw that form endearing." Not only was the irony of this remark lost in the German version (translated this time, it appears simply out of place) but also its origin, since the German reader could not know that Bloom had just heard it sung in the hotel.

The final example demonstrates the way in which the author's intention could be obstructed by failing to translate titles. The humor rests almost entirely upon the titles chosen in each category. In the German version the reader would be most likely to find the whole passage boring, since the major part of it would be unintelligible.

There were many phrases left in English which even common practice could not excuse. They seem to be the result of the translator's carelessness or capitulation in the face of a difficult passage. But if a phrase is troublesome it may be suggested that it is the translator's job to do the work of figuring it out, and not the reader's. A phrase the translator had trouble understanding is unlikely to mean anything to a reader unfamiliar with English. Thus when words like

> acid
> concert rooms
> rapparee
> sandwichmen
> at peak of tide[5]
> backtothelander

were left in English it could only have resulted in confusion.

Puns are another, and especially difficult, problem for the translator. They may be left in English, but the result is far from satisfactory for the reader:

> . . . er hatte eine köstliche herrliche Stimme Phoebe dearest goodbye sweetheart so sang er es immer nicht wie Bartell D'Arcy sweet tart goodbye . . . (III, 641)

Here is the way this example was handled in the 1930 version:

> . . . er hatte eine köstliche herrliche Stimme Phoebe Teure lebe wohl Geliebte so sang er es immer nicht wie Bartell D'Arcy Gelippte lebe wohl . . .

Almost fifty examples have been selected in the preceding pages to typify the vast difference between the first and second German editions of *Ulysses*. On the whole the second edition was a tremendous improvement over the first: hundreds of drab phrases were replaced by more colorful and descriptive ones, the prose became more colloquial and flowed more easily. The changes of style from chapter to chapter were sharpened and improved. Leitmotifs were drawn more clearly and consistently. The remaining gaps were filled, and previously untranslated phrases were attended to. That thousands of such improvements were necessary at all indicates the inadequacy of the first edition. And we must remember that for the most part it was upon this version that attention centered.

The further significance of these revisions is closely bound up with the question of the status of the authorized edition. The answer to this question is important for three reasons: (1) many critics assumed that the German *Ulysses* was carefully checked and authorized by Joyce himself, and judged it accordingly, (2) if it was authorized in this sense the changes introduced will be of special interest, and (3) attempts to improve and correct the translation have been hampered by the feeling that Joyce wanted it left the way it was.[6]

One is immediately struck by the fact that the *first* German version was published with the imprint "checked by the author." Yet we know Joyce was unhappy with it, and rightly so. The thousands of changes required to get it in acceptable form ridicule the supposition that the notice meant every phrase could be taken as approved by Joyce himself. But the changes for the second edition present a greater problem. It is quite possible that Joyce himself suggested many of them, and barely possible (though obviously unlikely) that he approved of all of them. Perhaps he did say he wanted it left as it was in 1930, with no further corrections or changes, as Goyert claimed. If so, much might be learned by investigating the changes more closely. But such an investigation leads immediately to several problems, all of which shed light ultimately on the general question of what authorization meant in the case of *Ulysses*. A few examples will suffice to point this up.

Since two forms of personal address exist in German, the translator is faced with an immediate problem in how to translate the English "you." This involves determining the relationship of the characters. Is, for example, Buck Mulligan a close enough friend to use the familiar form of address with Stephen Dedalus? Should Bloom and Stephen ever use the familiar form? The fact is that in the 1927 version Stephen used the familiar form "du" with Mulligan, Haines, and Bloom (among others). In the 1930 version this was changed in the case of Haines and Bloom to the polite. The pervasive change resulting for the German reader is of great importance. Stephen's distance from and irritation with Haines is now clear (he could reasonably use the familiar form with him under the circumstances—but he doesn't). But it is particularly in the case of Bloom that the change is vital. It is a linguistic sign that the spiritual son and spiritual father are never really united. Had their conversation been left in the familiar the effect would have been the opposite.

Presumably Joyce requested these changes in order to portray the relationship of these characters correctly. Mulligan and Stephen are on intimate terms—Bloom and Stephen, who are, after all, barely acquainted with one another, remain more formal. Surely here if anywhere we could assume Joyce's approval, considering the importance of such changes to the German reader. But there is a difficulty. The French version, also authorized, faces the same problem in the first case (Mulligan and Stephen) but handles it differently. In the French version the two are on "polite" terms. Since Joyce worked on both versions, and since this problem occurs on the very first page of *Ulysses* we can only conclude that the real degree of intimacy between the two cannot be determined by reference to an "authorized" translation.[7]

There is also the problem of changes in the 1930 version where the improvement is at best doubtful. It is difficult to believe that Joyce would have approved of several of these alterations. In some cases the 1927 version seems clearly superior.[8] To take only one example—the 1930 version seems to tone down its language in one interesting area. It may be true that the local Dubliner has a greater variety of expressions at his command, but the following seems unduly narrowing:

bloody	translated	verdammt
ah curse you		Oh, verdammt
by God		verdammt
for God's sake		verdammt noch mal
by Jaspers		verdammt
blast you		verdammt noch mal
by Jesus		verdammt
begob		verdammt
by the holy farmer		verdammt
maledicity		verdammt
Gad's bud		verdammt noch mal
demme		verdammt noch mal
fucking		verdammt

Several of these phrases were much more colorfully expressed in 1927. Of course not every curse in the novel was translated by verdammt in every occurrence, but the 1930 version seems inferior in variety and liveliness when it comes to swearing.

Finally it must be said that the German version still contained many, many errors, even after 1930. That it was a great improvement over that of 1927 is unquestionable. That it still left a great deal to be desired can be shown in hundreds of instances. Clear mistranslations were still present in unacceptably high number, and stylistic deficiencies abounded. A sufficient number of the shortcomings of the 1930 version will be presented to convince us that Joyce would never have "authorized" their canonization as a final text.

"You must have repetition. That's the whole secret."

To begin with a matter of style—the opening phrases in the Sirens episode are to be repeated in the body of the chapter in a prose analogy to the statement and development of musical themes. But at least three of them were still translated so differently in the body of the chapter that the most attentive German reader would never have realized that they were to be a repetition of the opening phrases. The total loss of effect as far as the German version goes is obvious. Here is one example:

ENGLISH	GERMAN-1930
Peep! Who's in the . . . (256:10)	Sieh! Wer ist in dem . . .
Peep! Who's in the corner? (262:13)	Guckguck! Wer sitzt da in der Ecke?

and another:

ENGLISH	GERMAN-1930
Warbling. Ah . . . Alluring. (256:28)	Trillern. Ah . . . Anlocken.
. . . throat warbling. . . . Ah, alluring. (275:25)	. . . singende Kehle. . . . Ach, anlockend.

Yet another example is the phrase "Jingle jingle jaunted jingling" in the opening overture. It is the leitmotif of jaunty Blazes Boylan and his jingling mode of transportation—as well as, significantly, the jingling of the loose brass quoits of the Bloom bedstead. The German translation had two basic faults—it did not follow the motif consistently through the novel and it gave Blazes' "jingle" to several other persons and things not included in the motif. Thus when Joyce indicated the loose quoits, in the first chapter devoted to Bloom, the translation got off immediately on the wrong foot (motif italicized):

ENGLISH	GERMAN
. . . she turned over and the loose brass quoits of the bedstead *jingled*. (56:27)	. . . als sie sich auf die andere Seite legte und die lockeren Messingscheiben an der Bettstelle *klirrten*.

Since "jingle" is translated "klingen" in general, the linguistic connection between the bed and Boylan is lost completely. Boylan's other characteristic description ("jaunty") has no single equivalent in the German version. Following this motif in the Sirens episode we find:

ENGLISH	GERMAN
Jingle jingle *jaunted* jingling. (256:15)	Klingen, klingen, *rüttelte* klingen.
Jingle *jaunty* jingle. (262:17)	Klingeln *munteres* Klingeln.
. . . waited for Boylan . . . for jingle *jaunty* blazes boy. (263:25)	. . . wartete . . . auf Boylan . . . auf den klingenden *kecken* boy.
Jingle *jaunted* by the curb and stopped. (264:29)	Klingen eines Wagens *ertönte* am Bordstein und hörte auf.
Jingle a tinkle *jaunted*. (267:42)	*Lustig klang* klingendes Klingen.

"Jaunty" is simply non-existent as a motif in the German version. But "klingen" seems to be used fairly consistently. Unfortunately there are too many noises of this kind in the Sirens episode. Joyce is careful to distinguish the following (italicized) sounds in the chapter:

Hoofirons, steely*ringing* (256:01)	Hufeisen, stahl*klingend*
And a *call* . . . Longindying *call*. (256:12)	Und ein *Klang* . . . Langsamersterbender *Klang*.
Coin *rang*. (256:16)	Münze *klang*.
Deep*sounding*. (256:42)	Tief*klingend*.
Will lift your *tschink* with *tschunk*. (257:18)	Heben ihr Glas. *Kling Klang*.
Acoustics that is. *Tinkling*. (282:29)	Das is Akustik. *Klingeln*.

Ringing, sounding tinkling, tschinking, tschunking, calling—all "klingen" throughout this chapter (the first five are themselves introductory phrases repeated at least once in the course of the chapter, and often more). Thus Blazes' leitmotif blurs and blends with many other sounds and as a consequence is greatly weakened. This is only one example of several leitmotifs which are inadequately handled in the authorized edition.

Although we praised the 1930 edition for stylistic improvements, we must add that far too many lackluster phrases remained:

ENGLISH	was still translated	GERMAN
laconic epistolary compositions (686:27)		einen kurzen Brief
circumjacent to a cicatrice (710:37)		um eine Narbe
An exquisite dulcet epithalame of most mollificative suadency (393:07)		Ein ausgezeichnetes, melodisches, beruhigendes Epithalam
this chaffering allincluding most farraginous chronicle (423:26)		dieser vermischten, allumfassenden, sehr gemischten Chronik
A truce to threnes and trentals and jeremies and all such congenital defunctive music (424:03)		zum Teufel mit den Klagen und all dem Kram, den Jeremiaden und all dieser angeborenen Totenmusik

In these cases the stylistic shortcomings are obvious —Joyce's purpose, whether it be to parody scientific and pedantic language, or to give a passage an archaic flavor, or simply to take pleasure in the words themselves— all was lost in translation.

Scores of individual words remained neutral and colorless in the 1930 version:

	was still translated	
incuneated		gesteckt
inclined		gestellt
ubicity		das "Wo"
benignant		leicht
cessile		weich
dexter optic		rechtes Auge
inverecund		schamlos
eructation		Rülpsen

These translations were not incorrect, they simply transformed a group of unusual, carefully chosen words into the language of a child.

Beyond its stylistic shortcomings the authorized edition still contains many mistranslations involving the meaning of the sentence or passage. Here are a few examples of the many errors (italicized) still remaining:

ENGLISH

GERMAN—1930

1. Now who is he I'd like to know? *Now, I'd give a trifle to know who he is.* (109:30)

1. Möchte doch zu gerne wissen wer er ist. *Na, ist ja auch ganz pipe.*

2. Underfed she looks too. Potatoes and marge, marge and potatoes. It's after they feel it. *Proof of the pudding.* Undermines the constitution. (152:08)

2. Sieht auch unterernährt aus. Kartoffeln und Marga, Marga und Kartoffeln. Merken sie erst später. *Genau wie mit Pudding.* Untergräbt die Gesundheit.

3. POST NO BILLS. POST 110 PILLS. *Some chap with a dose burning him.* (153:37)

3. NICHT ANKLEBEN, 110 PILLEN NEHMEN. *Einer hat mal zu viel genommen.*

4. *—The rain kept off.* (181:11)

4. *"Hat aufgehört zu regnen."*

5. I shall call rebutting evidence to prove up to the hilt that the hidden hand is again at its old game. *When in doubt persecute Bloom.* (464:10)

5. Ich werde ein gegenteiliges Zeugnis beibringen und klipp und klar beweisen, dass die geheimnisvolle Hand hier wieder ihr Spiel treibt. *Gelingt mir das nicht, dann verfolgen Sie Bloom.*

6. (*Old* Sleepy Hollow calls over the *wold*) (542:05)

6. (Schlaftal ruft über die *Welt*)

7. . . . I wished I could have picked every morsel of that chicken out of my fingers . . . *only for I didn't want to eat everything on my plate* . . . (750:08)

7. . . . hätte am liebsten das Hünnchen in die Finger genommen und abgenagt . . . *das andere schmeckte gar nicht so gut* . . .

In these examples the translation is at times exactly opposite to what is intended (1, 4). Others involve a failure to recognize a familiar saying (2, "the proof of the pudding is in the eating") or slang phrase (3, "a dose of the clap"). The remaining examples are more or less clearly a case of misreading (5-7). Surely Joyce did not knowingly agree to these and similar mistranslations. Nothing we know of Joyce indicates that he would willingly allow the more than thirty examples chosen above to remain unchanged. Since we cannot believe or accept that Joyce "approved" mistranslations and inconsistencies we must assume that he was not really aware of them—that the sheer volume involved in checking the translation word for word was too much for a man already overburdened with work. Finally it must also be remembered that Joyce's knowledge of German was less thorough than is commonly believed.

In all fairness to the translator it should be pointed out that Joyce did spend more hours working with the translation of *Ulysses* than any normal author would probably have done. And on the whole the second German edition is, as we have seen, a vast improvement over the first. It would be unfair to fail to lay stress on the tremendous difficulty of the task faced, or to fail to give credit to the translator for the many problems he successfully solved.

Joyce helped to the best of his time and ability in making the German translation of *Ulysses* accurate and stylistically acceptable. But he did not approve of every change, nor was he necessarily aware of each one. The reader must realize that the value of the translation as an academic tool for exegesis of the novel is limited. Any given phrase under consideration may never have been checked or approved by Joyce himself, and any given change may have been introduced by any of at least four people other than Joyce. The reader is thus thrown back on his own knowledge and understanding of the work. He must judge each instance in the traditional terms of internal consistency and fitness in context.

Publishers and translators have now realized that they are not offending against Joyce's wishes in continuing to rework, in whole or in part, the authorized translation. To allow mistakes and inadequate translations to stand in any version, authorized or otherwise, is unfair to both the author and the reading public.

To return to our historical perspective, the possible effect of a mistaken notion of the term "checked by the author," as well as the existence of two widely varying versions, must be recognized in assessing the critical reception of *Ulysses* and its impact on the German novel.

II

The 1930 version of *Ulysses* consisted of three thousand copies and was almost immediately sold out. As a result a third edition, containing a relatively small number of further revisions, appeared in the same year. Because almost every leading periodical and newspaper had already given space to the first German edition, the actual number of new reviews was almost negligible. For those literary periodicals which had failed, for one reason or another, to take account of *Ulysses* in the late twenties, the appearance of the new revised edition provided an excuse to make good this omission. Hans Henny Jahnn reviewed *Ulysses* with an enthusiasm particularly interesting in light of the appearance, a short time previously, of his own first novel *Perrudja*. Reviewers had already commented upon certain similarities between the two works. Some idea of the importance of *Ulysses'* still powerful impression may be seen in Jahnn's closing words:

> In short, *Ulysses* should be in every book-case, even the most modest. Any collection of modern literature, however large, remains incomplete when this novel is missing, and the most unassuming group of half a dozen books seems almost inexhaustible when this Irish author is present. Buy the book, read it again and again. And whoever is shocked by it had better ask himself if his own existence is not founded upon deafness, blindness, and lies.[9]

According to Franz Blei, the effect upon other novelists was no less earth-shaking:

> Insofar as they are serious about their work they will, of course, have to forego their yearly novel. For studying *Ulysses* will destroy their courage. They will have to use the time for learning.[10]

These two reviews testified to the continuing power of *Ulysses* to seize the imagination of those directly concerned with the act of artistic creation.

Throughout 1931 Joyce's name appeared sporadically in newspapers and journals. Although it was one of the quietest years of Joycean criticism there were a few interesting developments. For the first time the radio made itself felt in the controversy, with a program devoted solely to *Ulysses*. Under the title "The Radio Comes Alive" a reporter wrote:

> . . . this arrangement of *Ulysses* demonstrated that intellectual propaganda may be practiced within the framework of a radio program. An author's work, available as a book to only a small circle of literary people, was presented for the first time to a large

public by several readers; and for one hour this work, only in excerpts of course, affected the listener so intensely that intellectual propaganda indeed became poetry.[11]

Among those arranging this program was Ivan Goll, while Helene Weigel was numbered among the readers. The program took place in Berlin, and by chance a copy of the text of the presentation has been preserved.[12] From it we see that this special introduction to *Ulysses* was accompanied by detailed commentary concerning the Homeric parallels and several of the primary motifs of the work. The actual reading of the selections, interspersed with commentary linking the various episodes, was followed by a discussion concerning the general merits of *Ulysses*. This was by no means one-sided. Kurt Hirschfeld brought up the standard objections: "We have reached the end, Herr Goll. Is this chaotic confusion supposed to be a great work of art? . . . is it art at all?" Goll answered this query with the arguments he had been practising since the middle of the twenties, laying stress on the strict formal structure of *Ulysses*. The program closed with a recording of James Joyce himself reading aloud from the novel, thus allowing German listeners a rare opportunity to hear the voice of this controversial man. Goll's presence on the program is further evidence of the combination of sincere enthusiasm and sound business sense that characterized the publicity surrounding *Ulysses*. Ivan Goll was still an official agent for the Rhein-Verlag and was undoubtedly instrumental in arranging the affair.

Berlin remained the principal center of Joycean discussion in Germany, but as E. R. Curtius points out some of the most important work on the novel was being done in Switzerland, a fact which he found an interesting commentary upon German cultural life.[13] The developments in the political arena of central Europe during these years were inevitably beginning to creep into the area of literary criticism, and Curtius found it necessary to attack an approach to *Ulysses* which attempted to evaluate Joyce in political terms: "They are in for a profound disappointment. Joyce is a difficult character, that's even one of his most striking characteristics: he is equally difficult to handle in terms of the doctrines of politics and modernity."[14] In spite of such warnings *Ulysses* was to be caught up in the political currents of the times.

The year 1932 marks the second high-water mark of Joycean criticism in the German language. This may be explained by the concurrence at that time of two important events: Joyce's fiftieth birthday, and the publication of Stuart Gilbert's key to the mysteries of *Ulysses*, in German translation.

Ten years had passed since the original appearance of *Ulysses*, and five since the first German edition. It seemed an obvious moment at which to stop and take stock. The basic nature of articles about *Ulysses* altered noticeably. They ceased analyzing the work itself and were content with a retrospective evaluation of its place in the history of literature. The immediate reaction to *Ulysses* had been, on the whole, very favorable, and by 1932 this attitude seemed to have crystallized into an almost total acceptance. Of nine major articles devoted to Joyce in 1932, only one was distinctly unfavorable.

Max Tau described the difficulties he encountered trying to publish his negative appraisal of *Ulysses*. He maintained that literary periodicals were so tied to the mood of the times, which seemed to favor Joyce, that they shied away from an objective analysis of the work.[15] His article, when finally published,[16] was an attempt to demonstrate Joyce's failure as a true artist, as Tau defined that concept. But such a negative evaluation remained the exception until *Ulysses* was officially banned in Germany.

Stuart Gilbert's investigation of the themes and structure of *Ulysses* was not without faults, in spite of the fact that it bore the stamp of approval of Joyce himself. Nevertheless this work was of tremendous importance in so far as it silenced once and for all those critics who saw the novel as formless and chaotic. If anything, the novel was too closely structured, too form-conscious, too cerebral for some readers. But the revelations of Gilbert's work contributed noticeably to the decline of completely wrong-headed notions about *Ulysses*. In making clear the inherent structure of the novel, Gilbert made an invaluable contribution to Joycean criticism in all countries.

The German articles written in 1932 reflected this perfectly. Most of them mentioned Gilbert's work specifically, and several more demonstrated an acquaintance with it indirectly. Almost all references to "chaos" and the Dada movement disappeared. It is in this negative sense that the effect of Gilbert's work was most noticeable—rather than in the appearance of any sudden increase in appreciation and awareness of the novel on a more profound level. Most critics contented themselves with simply repeating facts garnered from Gilbert. As may be expected, some critics rebelled at the idea of a work so difficult that it needed this type of explication. Hugo Lieven spoke for many: "a contemporary work which needs a volume of commentary is several shades more exacting in its demands than seems necessary."[17]

The major German-language article on Joyce which appeared in 1932 had a long story behind it. Almost from the day of its initial appearance, *Ulysses* had been linked with psychoanalysis and the work of Sigmund Freud. Joyce's portrayal of the subconscious levels of thought, and his use of the inner monologue and association technique, seemed to reflect the latest developments in the field. It was not surprising then, that the Rhein-Verlag requested an introductory essay to the 1930 edition of *Ulysses* from one of the leading psychoanalysts of the time—Carl Jung. But if they hoped for an enthusiastic burst of praise they were sorely disappointed. Jung had begun reading the book (in English) in 1929 and had laid it aside, both annoyed and bored. Nevertheless he agreed to write the essay. When the publishers showed the finished typescript to Ivan Goll and other friends, they advised against printing it. Joyce too was disappointed, but wired the firm to proceed with publication, indicating that he felt the essay would do greater damage to Jung's reputation than to his own. Joyce wrote to a friend: "He [Jung] seems to have read *Ulysses* from first to last without one smile. The only thing to do in such a case is to change one's drink!"[18] The result of the whole affair was that the essay was not printed. But in the meantime Jung had returned to reading *Ulysses*, in a pleasanter disposition. Still "bored to tears" from time to time, he nevertheless began to see in the work certain valuable features. He found it most helpful to approach the novel as a significant expression of the cultural and aesthetic developments of the time:

> Joyce has had a considerable influence upon his contemporaries. And that is the fact that interested me most about *Ulysses* at first. If this book had disappeared soundlessly into the depths I would probably never have fished it back out.[19]

His article, rewritten in a mellower tone, finally appeared in 1932. It is clear that one important factor behind his changed opinion of *Ulysses* was his reading of Stuart Gilbert's book. The boredom he had originally experienced now seemed transfigured into a powerful force of nature:

> Everything is new and at the same time that which has always existed. . . . What riches and what—boredom! Joyce bores me to tears, but it is an evil, dangerous boredom. . . . It is the boredom of nature, the desolate roar of the wind upon the rock cliffs of the Hebrides, the sunrise and sunset of the Sahara, the roar of the sea. . .[20]

Hostile critics had suggested as early as 1927 that Joyce was suffering from mental disorder. Jung was in a position to comment on this suggestion, and his conclusion must have been disheartening for those who viewed *Ulysses* as the sick product of a sick mind:

> It would never occur to me to explain *Ulysses* as the product of a schizophrenic. . . . *Ulysses* is as healthy as the whole of modern art. . . . Therefore we may ascribe positive creative value not only to *Ulysses* but also to that art which is spiritually related to it.[21]

According to Jung, the value of Joyce's work consisted in the way in which it destroyed outmoded criteria of beauty and meaning. *Ulysses* was a pessimistic but necessary book which attempted to speak to modern man, to awaken him to his own reality and thus free him:

> For this reason such negative prophets as Joyce (or Freud) are necessary . . . As strange as it might sound, it is nevertheless true, that the world of *Ulysses* is a better one than the world of those who are hopelessly bound to the gloom of their spiritual birth-place.[22]

It was in a personal letter to Joyce that Jung expressed himself most enthusiastically about *Ulysses*. This testimony undoubtedly served to salve any wounded feelings Jung's initial reaction to the novel may have engendered:

> I also don't know whether you will enjoy what I have written about *Ulysses* because I couldn't help telling the world how much I was bored, how I grumbled, how I cursed and how I admired. The 40 pages of non-stop run in the end is a string of veritable psychological peaches. I suppose the devil's grandmother knows so much about the real psychology of a woman. I didn't.[23]

The events of the year 1933 in Germany marked a turning point in world history which overshadowed art and literature. The burning of the works of unwanted authors was but a symbol of the more far-reaching and terrible destruction to come. Two features of *Ulysses* seemed open to political interpretation: its revolutionary style, and the race of its hero. Ivan Goll had been the first critic to couple the name of James Joyce with that of Lenin, and to draw the parallel between them in terms of revolution. By 1932 such comparisons were already fairly commonplace,[24] but in the midst of the political tension of the times they were sometimes viewed with suspicion. In 1933 one critic expressed his feelings in these terms: "It is characteristic that the name of the author is placed beside that of Lenin with pleasure, and with a tacit implication. One recognizes by this what kind of people would like to make him their prophet."[25] *Ulysses* also upset those prone

to fascist racial theories. Most readers had no idea why
Leopold Bloom was portrayed as a Jew, and given the
climate of the time, many must have wondered. Included
among those most mystified and most interested were
Jewish readers in Germany. Lutz Weltmann, writing in
the *Bayerische Israelitische Gemeindezeitung*, addressed himself to this problem:

> James Joyce's Ulysses is a Jew . . . No external feature of
> Leopold Bloom seems Jewish: . . . what are his spiritual charac-
> teristics? A strong interest in material details—that is certainly
> Jewish, but not specifically so. Bloom's actions are not determined
> by his Jewishness but rather by his parallel to the hero of the
> Odyssey.[26]

Weltmann's suggestion was that Joyce had made Bloom
a Jew for other reasons:

> Joyce, who owes so much to psychoanalysis, wished, perhaps
> unknowingly, to create a monument to Sigmund Freud, the Jewish
> founder of psychoanalysis, and the author Arthur Schnitzler, who
> first travelled this path, and intuitively foreshadowed Joyce's
> narrative technique.[27]

Ulysses was officially banned and burned in 1934,[28] but
for many (including those who had never read the novel)
it had always represented the worst of the "moderns."
A certain aura of danger surrounded it—the feeling of
danger inspired by ignorance. The novel seemed to lack
any clear-cut set of moral values, it seemed to attack
all conventions, to be negative and nihilistic. And it was
said to be pornographic. Many of the writers who had
greeted the novel so enthusiastically were themselves
"unwanted," and many of the critics who had reacted
favorably to it were soon to be leaving Germany, or had
never been there.

In the midst of such political turmoil it is not surprising
that literary discussions of *Ulysses*, at least in print,
dropped off sharply, and particularly after the formation
of the new "chambers of culture" under the direction of
Goebbels. Only two relevant articles appeared in the
periodicals in 1933. Harald Theile, writing in February of

that year, made it clear that the novel still seemed both revolutionary and relevant:

> Compared with *Ulysses* any previous literary "revolution" is a perhaps noisy but ultimately harmless affair. . . . Joyce was a chemist who intended nothing less than to discover and express the formula by which Europe exploded and disintegrated.[29]

No other article appeared until September of that year. Otto Knapp attacked those who wished to make a prophet of the author of *Ulysses*, pointing out the suspect political views of critics who had coupled the names Joyce and Lenin. *Ulysses*, under the newly reigning point of view, had nothing to do with true literature (which consisted of "noble simplicity and quiet grandeur"). Another sign of the times was to be seen in the fact that Knapp was the first critic in years to attack *Ulysses* on the grounds of its frankness: "The extraordinarily free and detailed representation of the lower reaches of human life is also beyond the bounds of art and poetry. . . . To go on at length about such things is not to portray nature but to pervert it."[30] In spite of this regression in critical appreciation it was still impossible by 1933 to attack *Ulysses* as "formless" or "chaotic." The primary objection centered instead upon moral considerations.

Paradoxically 1933 marked the beginning of academic work on Joyce by a new generation in Germany. Two Ph.D. theses were presented in that year dealing primarily with *Ulysses*. This pointed to a new and more profound interest in the structure and style of the novel, and in the later thirties it was only in the relatively obscure regions of graduate academic research that Joyce's name was kept alive in Germany.

The first Joycean thesis in the German language was Rudolf Hentze's "Die proteische Wandlung im 'Ulysses' von James Joyce." Young German scholars were able to undertake such studies with the aid of the German translation and Stuart Gilbert's analysis. As a frontispiece to his thesis Hentze reproduced Gilbert's table of the individual episodes of *Ulysses* arranged according to time, place, technique, etc. The entire thesis is concerned with a close examination of the text of the novel, demonstrating Joyce's various themes and techniques, and the way in which they constantly change: "Its [*Ulysses*] particular quality lies precisely in the way in which the fleeting impression of the changing moment is captured, thus indicating the denial of everything fixed and static."[31] The study is commendable in several respects, and in particular for the way in which it elucidates the form and structure of the novel. The previous work of E. R. Curtius was carefully noted and utilized in the thesis. Hentze also made several valid criticisms of the German translation. The very fact that *Ulysses* was considered a fitting subject for a thesis indicates the degree of its acceptance in academic circles by 1933. Hentze's admiration for the novel was not without reserve, for he felt it lacked human sympathy. Nevertheless he saw in it humane values: "This gigantic work of the spirit leads man to the recognition of his limitations, and in this sense *Ulysses* may function as a purgatorium."[32]

Günther Kulemeyer, in November of 1933, presented his inaugural dissertation at the Ernst-Moritz-Arndt University in Greifswald. It was entitled "Studien zur Psychologie im neuen englischen Roman (Dorothy Richardson und James Joyce)." It was an attempt to determine the effectiveness of the portrayal of the psychic processes through the stream-of-consciousness technique. The study was not as thorough as that of Hentze, but within its more limited scope it was respectable enough. The basic structure of *Ulysses* was explicated with the help of Gilbert, and several passages of text were analyzed. "Because of the difficulty of the English text" Kulemeyer quoted constantly from Goyert's 1930 version. The final evaluation of Joyce's success with the inner monologue was distinctly positive:

> We . . . must grant him the successful representation of the vitality and mobility of the psychical processes. . . . It is impossible to represent the reality of consciousness with complete

faithfulness . . . But insofar as it is possible to approach the living truth of things by dint of differentiation, nuance, and dynamics, Joyce has achieved this approximation.[33]

Nevertheless he reserved final judgment, leaving the ultimate value of such a work a question for future generations. By 1933 it becomes hard to distinguish between the normal academic reluctance to take a stand on matters of value in contemporary literature and a reluctance engendered by the increasingly threatening political atmosphere—an atmosphere in which university intellectuals were considered particularly suspect.

Glancing back we may see that between the years 1922 and 1933 Joycean criticism in the German language went through three major stages: 1) a practically dormant period from 1922 to 1927, when *Ulysses* was the object of heated discussions but almost no one had read the book; 2) a period of abundant and enthusiastic reaction from 1927 to 1930, based upon the publication of the first German translation, but demonstrating little grasp of what the novel was all about; and 3) a new surge of favorable criticism from 1930 to 1933, more accurate and perceptive in its detail, brought about by the concurrence of the improved second version of *Ulysses* and Gilbert's key to its mysteries. When the year 1933 placed a political limit on the impact of *Ulysses* in Germany, the novel went underground, harbored within a few academic communities, to re-emerge only after the war.

Joyce himself was keenly interested in the critical reception of his work in Germany. It is unfortunate that he was never aware of the broad range of approval that *Ulysses* had gained in Germany before 1933. In 1929 he wrote to Valery Larbaud: "First the small news, the French press on *Ulysses* was much better than the German. . . ."[34] Georg Goyert did his best to send him articles which had appeared in German, and Joyce was always grateful for them. But in the coming years Joyce was to suffer both pain and hardship. He was working as steadily as his failing eyes would allow him upon what was to be *Finnegans Wake*, yet he realized that the political situation was highly unfavorable to the success of his novel. Under such stress he tended to look back on the twenties and the translation of *Ulysses* with a certain nostalgia, reinforced by a sad awareness of the fate which might befall his work. Thus, in a letter to Goyert of 11 October 1938, he closed with these words:

Wann kommen wir wieder zusammen wie damals in Trianons Restaurant? Der Himmel weiss was für ein Schicksal die Kritik für meinem [sic] Buch reservirt. Das ist mir aber schlussegal—um etwas unverblümtes nicht zu sagen—aber vielleicht habe ich noch eine Zukunft als Strassensänger—hinter mich [sic].[35]

1.   The figures quoted in the analysis are the result of a word-for-word comparison of the first and second German editions, during which every variation between the two texts was recorded, with the exception of changes of punctuation and spelling (unless obviously important). The changes were broken down into four categories: 1) changes of style; 2) changes of meaning; 3) words or phrases first omitted, but now translated; and 4) words or phrases first left in English, but now translated.

The last two categories (3 and 4) presented no special problems in decision making. In categorizing the remaining variations the benefit of the doubt was always given to the translator (in borderline cases the change was treated as an improvement of style—for the purpose of tabulation—rather than as the correction of an error). Each variation was tabulated only once (even if the change resulted in more than one actual alteration, e.g.—a change from the polite to the familiar form of address which resulted in several actual alterations was tabulated only once). No alteration was placed in more than one category.

2.   A misprint in the first English edition (Paris, 1922), giving "rotten," was probably responsible for this particular mistranslation. By the 1926 printing of the English edition this misprint had been corrected.

3.   "I have the words already. What I am seeking is the perfect order of the words in the sentence. There is an order in every way appropriate. I think I have it." Quoted in Frank Budgen, *James Joyce and the Making of Ulysses* (London, 1934), p. 20.

4.   Matthew Hodgart and Mabel Worthington, *Song in the Works of James Joyce* (New York, 1959), p. 3.

5.   To add to the confusion of the German reader, this phrase was misprinted as "at peak of side."

6.   See note 36 to chapter 1.

7.   It may be that the problem in the French version could be resolved by reference to social convention in forms of address in the France of 1904. But French Joycean scholars with whom I have spoken say they too are puzzled in this case.

8.   Fritz Senn has pointed out to me that Goyert turned to the French translation for ideas on difficult points. Mr. Senn has conducted research into this facet of the German translation, and he has been kind enough to allow

me to view his results. Most strikingly, Goyert seemed to make as many new errors by this process as he corrected old ones.

9.   "Kurz, der *Ulysses* gehört in jedes, auch in das bescheidenste Büchergestell. Eine noch so grosse Sammlung moderner Literatur ist unvollständig, wenn dieser Roman fehlt, und das bescheidenste Paket von einem halben Dutzend Büchern wirkt beinahe unausschöpflich, wenn sich dieser Ire darin findet. Kauft das Buch, lest es und lest es immer wieder. Und wer darüber erschrickt, prüfe sich ob er seine Existenz nicht auf Blindheit, Taubheit, und Lügen aufgebaut hat." Hans Henny Jahnn, "*Ulysses*," *Der Kreis*, VII (July-August, 1930), 473.

10.   "Soweit sie es mit ihrer Arbeit ehrlich treiben, werden sie allerdings darauf verzichten müssen, den jährlich fälligen Roman zu liefern. Denn das Studium des *Ulysses* wird ihnen die Courage dazu nehmen. Sie werden die Zeit zum Lernen nützen müssen." F[ranz] B[lei], "James Joyce: *Ulysses*," *Neue Revue* (1930), p. 139.

11.   ". . . so hat uns diese . . . Einrichtung des *Ulysses* gezeigt, das man auch im Rahmen einer Funk-Veranstaltung geistige Propaganda treiben kann. Man hat das Werk eines Dichters, das in Buchform nur einer kleinen Gemeinde von literarisch Interessierten zugängig war, durch eine Anzahl Sprecher . . . zum ersten Male vor ein grosses Publikum gebracht; und man hat dieses Werk, natürlich nur in Bruchstücken, eine Stunde lang so intensiv auf den Hörer wirkenlassen, dass hier in der Tat die Propaganda für den Geist eine Dichtung wurde." "H. S.," "Der Rundfunk regt sich," *Das Tagebuch*, XII (April, 1931), 633.

12.   In the possession of Fritz Senn.

13.   Ernst Robert Curtius, "Philologie oder Literaturkritik," *Die literarische Welt*, VII (April, 1931), 7.

14.   "Es dürften ihnen schwere Entäuschungen vorbehalten sein. Joyce ist unbequem, das ist sogar eine seiner auffallendsten Eigenschaften: er ist gleich unbequem für die Doktrinäre der Politik und der Modernität." Curtius, *loc.cit.* Annette Kolb found Joyce "unbequem" for women too. She mentions in passing: "Doch auch der Bolschewismus, nachdem er alles kurz und klein schlug, spricht nur von Aufbau. Auch Joyce kann auf seinen subversiven Wegen nicht weiter . . . Aber zugegeben: über den "Ulysses" auszusagen, steht mir nicht zu. Ich bin nicht befugt. Es ist ein Männerbuch. Mögen sie es nur behalten." ("Randglossen zur heutigen englischen Literatur," *Die neue Rundschau*, XLII [1931], p. 115).

15.   Max Tau, *Das Land das ich verlassen musste* (Hamburg, 1961), p. 203.

16.   Max Tau, "James Joyce," *Die neueren Sprachen*, XL (August, 1932), 352.

17.   "ein zeitgenössisches Werk, das eines Kommentars bedarf, ist um einige Nuancen anspruchsvoller aufgemacht, als dies nötig wäre." Hugo Lieven, "Das Rätsel *Ulysses*," *Dresdener Neueste Nachrichten*, No. 84, 1932.

18.   *Letters*, III, 262.

19.   "Joyce hat eine ganz erhebliche Wirkung auf seine Zeitgenossen. Und das ist die Tatsache, die mich am *Ulysses* zunächst am meisten interessierte. Wäre dieses Buch sang- und klanglos in der Tiefe der Vergessenheit verschwunden, so hätte ich es wohl nicht mehr zurückgeholt." Carl Jung, "*Ulysses*: Ein Monolog," *Europäische Revue*, VIII (September, 1932), 552.

20.   "Alles ist neu und stets das von Anfang an Vorhandene. . . . Welcher Reichtum und welche—Langeweile! Joyce langweilt mich zu Tränen, aber es ist eine böse gefährliche Langeweile. . . . Es ist die Langeweile der Natur, das öde Sausen des Windes um die Felsklippen der Hebriden, das Sonnenauf- und Untergehen der Sahara, das Rauschen des Meeres . . ." Jung, p. 551.

21.   "Es würde mir nie einfallen, den *Ulysses* für ein schizophrenes Produkt zu erklären. . . . Der *Ulysses* ist ebensowenig ein krankhaftes Produkt wie die ganze moderne Kunst. . . . Deshalb dürfen wir nicht nur dem *Ulysses* sondern

auch der ihm geistesverwandten Kunst überhaupt positiven schöpferischen Wert und Sinn beimessen." Jung, p. 554.

22. "Darum bedarf es solcher Negative-Propheten wie Joyce (oder Freud) . . . So seltsam dies klingen mag, so ist es doch wahr, dass die Welt des *Ulysses* eine bessere ist als derer, welche hoffnungslos an das Düster ihrer geistigen Geburtsörtlichkeit gebunden sind." Jung, p. 558.

23. *Letters*, III, 253.

24. See the articles by Weltmann, Goll, and Giedion-Welcker.

25. "Es ist bezeichnend, dass der Name des Verfassers mit stummer Deutung und stiller Freude neben den Lenins gestellt wird. Man erkennt daran, welche Leute ihn zu ihrem Propheten machen möchten." Otto Knapp, "Das Bild des Menschen im neuen englischen Roman," *Das Hochland*, XXX (September, 1933), 542.

26. "Der Ulysses von James Joyce ist ein Jude . . . Kein äusseres Merkmal Leopold Blooms verrät den Juden: . . . wie ist die geistige Charakterisierung? Starkes Interesse für materielle Einzelheiten—das ist wohl jüdisch, aber nicht spezifisch jüdisch. . . . Blooms Verhalten wird nicht von dem Jüdischen in ihm bestimmt, vielmehr den seiner Analogie zum Helden der Odyssee." Lutz Weltmann, "Momentaufnahme: James Joyce," *Bayerische Israelitische Gemeindezeitung*, VIII (February, 1932), 37.

27. "Joyce, welcher der Psychoanalyse so viel verdankt, hat vielleicht unbewusst . . . dem jüdischen Entdecker der Psychoanalyse, Sigmund Freud, und dem Dichter, der vor dieser Entdeckung als erster ihre Wege ging und ahnungsvoll zu Joycens Romantechnik vorstiess, Arthur Schnitzler, ein Denkmal setzen wollen." Weltmann, *loc.cit.*

28. According to Georg Goyert, "James Joyce," *Prisma*, Munich, No. 17 (1948), p. 17.

29. "Mit dem *Ulysses* verglichen ist jede bisherige 'Revolution' der Dichtung eine vielleicht lärmvolle, aber harmlose Sache. . . . So war Joyce ein Chemiker, dem an nichts mehr gelegen war, als im kleinen Experiment und Abbild die Formel zu finden und darzustellen, nach der Europa explodierte und zersetzt wurde." Harald Theile, "Credo der Ausgestossenheit: zu James Joyces *Ulysses*," *Eckart*, IX (February, 1933), 72, 78.

30. "Auch die unerhört freie und breite Darstellung des niedrig Natürlichen hat mit Kunst und Dichtung nichts mehr zu tun. . . . Sich über solche Dinge weitläufig auslassen, ist nicht Natur, sondern Unnatur." Knapp, p. 540.

31. "Seine Eigenart liegt gerade im Auffangen des flüchtigen Eindrucks wechselnder Momente und bedeutet so die Verneinung alles Festen." Rudolf Hentze, *Die proteische Wandlung im Ulysses von James Joyce und ihre Spiegelung im Stil*, (diss. Marburg, 1933) published as *Die neuren Sprachen, Beiheft* 27 (1933), p. 23.

32. "So führt gerade dieses Riesenwerk des Geistes den Menschen zur Erkenntnis seiner Bedingtheit, und in diesem Sinne kann der *Ulysses* zu einem Purgatorium werden." Hentze, p. 120.

33. "Wir . . . müssen ihm zugestehen, dass ihm die Darstellung der Lebendigkeit und Bewegtheit des psychischen Geschehens gelungen ist. . . . Es ist unmöglich, das wirkliche Bewusstsein vollständig und getreu darzustellen . . . So weit aber durch Differenzierung, Nüanzierung und Dynamik eine Annäherung an die lebendige Wahrheit der Dinge überhaupt möglich ist, soweit ist diese Annäherung bei Joyce gegeben." Günther Kulemeyer, *Studien zur Psychologie im neuen englischen Roman: Dorothy Richardson und James Joyce* (diss. Greifswald, 1933), p. 35.

34. *Letters*, I, 282.

35. *Letters*, III, 433.

5

JOYCE AND THE LITERARY TRENDS
OF THE TWENTIES

In spite of the fact that *Ulysses* attracted relatively few readers in the first ten years after its publication, it quickly established itself as one of the most important works of the century. In Germany the disparity between the actual size of the novel's audience and its profound literary impact was particularly apparent. This impact was transmitted primarily through the works of three major German authors: Hans Henny Jahnn, Alfred Döblin, and Hermann Broch. All three were working on novels when they first read *Ulysses* in German translation, and in each case this reading left clearly discernible marks upon both the original manuscripts and the final published versions of their works. But before examining these novels in detail it will be worthwhile to discuss some of Joyce's major innovations in the light of German literary history.

The seeds of several of the most striking and original aspects of *Ulysses* may be found in German literature prior to 1922. Whether they would have borne fruit without its example is questionable. Joyce's novel served both as a literary case-book and as a spiritual inspiration. Authors not only learned from Joyce, they also gained courage from his example.

It is often said that James Joyce introduced the "stream of consciousness" into the modern novel. In the most meaningful sense this is true. Yet Joyce never denied that he took this technique from Edouard Dujardin's *Les lauriers sont coupés* (1887).[1] The resolution of this apparent paradox lies in a careful scrutiny of just what inner monologue consists of. A great deal of time and energy has been devoted to the task of defining the concept involved.[2] The conclusion we reach is not too surprising. Joyce borrowed from Dujardin the simple idea, he made of it an important and viable literary technique. The inner monologue as developed, enlarged, and enlivened by Joyce is a far cry from the pages of *Les lauriers sont coupés*. And when we say that Joyce added a new technique to the arsenal of the creative writer we mean precisely in so far as that technique differs from, and enlarges upon, Dujardin's first experiment. It is necessary to examine the chronological history of the inner monologue in German literature in order to determine what it was about this technique in *Ulysses* that made it seem so new and different in 1927.

German literature has almost always been involved with the exploration of human thought, and at least since Novalis with that area of the mind today referred to as the unconscious. But it was not until around 1900 that an Austrian writer made use of the inner monologue, representing the thoughts of the characters directly, and without any intervention on the part of the author. This writer was Arthur Schnitzler.[3] In 1900 Schnitzler published "Leutnant Gustl," a short story which consists almost entirely of the thoughts of the main character placed directly on the page. From the first line of the story we are in the mind of the "hero":

> Wie lange wird denn das noch dauern? Ich muss auf die Uhr schauen . . . schickt sich wahrscheinlich nicht in einem so ernsten Konzert. Aber wer sieht's denn? Wenn's einer sieht, so passt er gerade so wenig auf, wie ich, und vor dem brauch' ich mich nicht zu genieren . . . Erst viertel auf zehn? . . . Mir kommt vor, ich sitz' schon drei Stunden in dem Konzert.[4]

Here we can see the external defining characteristics of
inner monologue—the thoughts are expressed in the first
person and the tense remains the natural one for the
situation. Moreover the passage exhibits other attributes
of actual thought. The language is non-literary, and
marked by habits of normal speech, including the use of
such forms as "brauch' " and "sitz'," which are usually
restricted to reports of actual speech. The interconnec-
tion of the thoughts is also loosely associative rather than
literary. The existence of "Leutnant Gustl" alone is sufficient proof that the inner monologue existed in German
literature at least twenty years before Joyce wrote *Ulysses*.
And it is interesting to note in passing that Schnitzler's
source of inspiration for this technique was also—
Edouard Dujardin.[5]

Experiments of this nature did not cease with
Schnitzler's first efforts. Alfred Döblin's early novel, *Der
schwarze Vorhang* (written 1902/3, published 1919), although
now almost forgotten, was an interesting if tentative attempt to portray the states of his characters' souls
through passages of inner monologue alternating with
more traditional narrative techniques. Albert Ehrenstein,
Richard Hülsenbeck, and Ernst Weiss had also experi-
mented with related techniques well before the German
Ulysses appeared. Other cases were to be recalled by later
critics and writers. Bertolt Brecht, discussing Joyce around
1938, remarked: "Rein formal hatten wir einen 'inneren
Monolog,' den gerade wir sehr schätzten, ich denke an
Tucholskys Stücke."[6] And indeed Tucholsky had utilized,
and even expanded, the possibilities of the inner
monologue, in several short pieces written during the
twenties. Most of them appeared in *Die Schaubühne*
(later *Die Weltbühne*), a periodical for which he labored under
five different pseudonyms, and for a time served as
editor. Two typical examples will show his bent for experimentation in this direction. In 1926 a two-page
sketch appeared entitled "Herr Wendriner kann nicht
einschlafen." Herr Wendriner's thoughts are given in one
long inner monologue, including this typical passage:

Nicht möglich, zu schlafen. Ich weiss nicht, was das ist. Das Glas Bier abends kanns nicht sein, geraucht hab ich heute auch nicht—ich muss mal mit Friedmann drüber sprechen. Sport! sagt er immer—treiben Sie Sport! Wir können ja Fussball auf dem Kurfürstendamm zusammen spielen . . . lächerlich![7]

This is clearly recognizable as inner monologue, and it bears obvious affinities to Molly Bloom's night thoughts at the end of *Ulysses*. In fact the suspicion that *Ulysses'* influence may lie behind this sketch cannot be automatically dismissed, since this idea was among the most widely known about *Ulysses* at the time. Tucholsky was obviously in the middle of the current of discussion which surrounded the novel prior to 1927, as may be gathered from his review of *Ulysses* in that year (one of the first to appear). Nevertheless it is also clear that Tucholsky did not actually read *Ulysses* until 1927, and the most he might have gained from it was an interesting idea dropped in conversation.

A further example from the year 1926 is Tucholsky's "Konversation":

Magda spricht. Arthurchen hört zu.

Magda (presto):
"Gott, Sie verstehen doch was vom Theater—endlich mal einer, der was vom Theater versteht. Ich werde Ihnen das also ganz genau erzählen. Die Leute hatten zunächst die Straub engagiert, die sollte den Dragonerrittmeister spielen . . ."

Arthurchen (denkt):
Das kann man wohl sagen, dass ich was vom Theater verstehe—das hat sie ganz hübsch gesagt. Natürlich versteh' ich was vom Theater. Nu leg mal los. Sie ist ja doch pikant, die hat was. Nette Beine. Ob sie einen Büstenhalter trägt? . . .[8]

This non-conversation continues for two pages. It is an interesting and humorous attempt to represent on the page the way in which many conversations are actually conducted—and technically it represents a step, in one direction, beyond the experiments of Arthur Schnitzler.

What has been said so far has established the fact that

a rudimentary form of inner monologue existed in German literature from around 1900 and continued to crop up during the opening decades of the twentieth century, prior to the publication of the first German translation of *Ulysses*. At the same time many German novels continued to express thoughts in the traditional manner, prefacing them with "he thought" and enclosing them in quotation marks.[9] In such cases the presence of the intervening author is (even visually) evident. The importance of the omission of such "signals" must not be underestimated, for it is precisely their omission which grants the inner monologue its all-important directness, in addition to the stylistic differences soon to be discussed. Many German novels also utilized that form of narrated monologue we term "erlebte Rede," in which the characters' thoughts appear to us through the filter, as it were, of the narrator. And of course mixtures of these techniques were fairly common. The question remains: granted the existence not only of traditional forms related to inner monologue, but also of German prose works which unquestionably *were* written in inner monologue, how are we to explain the amazing effect of *Ulysses* on the German-speaking world in 1927? Nowhere is the answer to this question more obvious than in Kurt Tucholsky's own writings. In May, 1927, he had discussed the inner monologue in a short article in the *Vossische Zeitung*. He opened with a direct reference to *Ulysses*:

> . . . since the appearance of this strange book there has been a constant literary discussion in France about an affair which has been christened the "inner monologue." . . . The literary form is nothing new to us. Schnitzler . . . already had given us something similar in "Leutnant Gustl" . . .[10]

Exactly what this inner monologue consisted of was, according to Tucholsky, simple to explain—it was the literary portrayal of the thoughts of an individual talking to himself or meditating "for instance during a sleepless night." These remarks recall immediately the short sketch we have already quoted. Tucholsky went on to outline the difficulties of this technique, particularly its inability to accurately reproduce thought in a form truly corresponding to psychological reality.

Tucholsky's attitude towards the inner monologue, and in particular to what he had heard about *Ulysses*, obviously did not prepare him for what he experienced in reading the novel, for his first reaction was to underline the fact that Joyce's technique *was* new. And in so doing he repudiated exactly those views he had expressed in May:

> And here the "inner monologue" begins, which has drawn so much attention . . . and it must be said that it leaves the strongest impression of all. . . . This symphony of thought has nothing to do with the puny attempts of Arthur Schnitzler and Carl Spitteler. Here everything, but *everything*, is actually said.[11]

Clearly Tucholsky had not expected anything like the manner in which Joyce developed the inner monologue. His admiration for Joyce's achievement ("an admirable production based on ability, artistic courage, and a knowledge of the soul") included his recognition of "the profound authenticity" of the thinking process as portrayed by Joyce—the very thing he had declared theoretically impossible in May of the same year. Tucholsky's reaction is a classic case, and points up the gap that separated those who had only heard about the novel from those who had actually read it.

All in all, in spite of those earlier manifestations of inner monologue in German literature, German critics believed that Joyce gave something new and startling to the world of art. It is this belief that influenced their own actions and words. Thus Bertolt Brecht could speak of Tucholsky's use of the inner monologue on a "purely formal" level and still maintain, as he did,[12] that it was James Joyce who introduced the technique into literature.

Tucholsky had applied the word "puny" ("winzig") to previous attempts at the use of inner monologue. This term hints at one of the distinguishing features of all earlier efforts in this direction. From Schnitzler onwards, and up until the appearance of *Ulysses*, inner monologue was simply an interesting game with form. It seemed by its very nature to be restricted to very short prose works. To be inside the character's mind was interesting, but as soon as the novelty wore off the technique threatened to become simply boring. What Joyce did in *Ulysses* was to employ, for the first time, full-scale inner monologue in a work of epic proportions. In so doing he opened the door to the use of this technique in the novel. At the same time he demonstrated how this could be done without becoming boring.[13] His answer was two-fold: first to use inner monologue in conjunction with more traditional techniques, and secondly to amplify, extend, and vary the inner monologue itself.

As an example of Joyce's special blend of narrative techniques we may examine the first clear instance of inner monologue in the first chapter of *Ulysses*:

> —Look at yourself, he said, you dreadful bard. Stephen bent forward and peered at the mirror held out to him, cleft by a crooked crack on end. As he and others see me. Who chose this face for me? This dogsbody to rid of vermin. It asks me too.
> —I pinched it out of the skivvy's room, Buck Mulligan said. (6:26)

After four pages of text written in a more or less traditional third person narrative, suddenly, and without warning, in the middle of a paragraph, the reader is put in direct contact with Stephen's mind. From this point onwards there is a relatively constant oscillation between the two points of view. Gone are obvious attempts to smooth the passage for the reader. Thrown on his own he must continue following as best he can, without counting on any of the traditional guideposts. In mixing his techniques without warning Joyce presented the literary world with a new manifesto—the right of the artist to disregard the comfort of the reader. Such a mixture allowed the author to present direct and striking insights into characters' minds without risking the boredom of being trapped in that mind by literary convention. This was one answer to the inherent problems of inner monologue.

The second solution was the way in which Joyce amplified, varied, and extended the inner monologue as
used by Dujardin. On the technical level he showed an
awareness of certain psychological facts which had
been ignored in the past. Primary among these was the
recognition of the various levels of verbalization at
which actual thought goes on. In real life our thoughts
range from orderly presentations in sentences we are
almost speaking aloud to ourselves, to fleeting, almost
incoherent murmurings of the subconscious.   Our
thoughts may be crystal-clear in the afternoon, hallucinatory under the influence of stimulants, or aimlessly
drifting as we fall asleep. Joyce employed the inner
monologue to reflect as accurately as possible these
variations, sometimes giving us pages of unpunctuated
flowing night thoughts, sometimes representing hallu-
cinations dramatically, most often reproducing normal
thought by means of short elliptic sentences. Joyce was
not under the illusion that he could reproduce thought
completely accurately on the printed page, but he attempted it and succeeded in coming closer to that goal
than anyone before him. This achievement was recognized by the majority of German critics.

Among the most famous sections of *Ulysses* was the
final inner monologue of Molly Bloom, the episode most
often mentioned by German critics. Yet it was only one
formulation of the technique. By taking the formal
principal to its extreme and omitting all punctuation,
Joyce made this chapter memorable even in visual
terms. But the episode was equally notable for its frankness. Joyce wrote to Frank Budgen:

> *Penelope* is the clou of the book. The first sentence contains 2500
> words. . . . Though probably more obscene than any preceding
> episode it seems to me to be perfectly sane full amoral ferti-
> lisable untrustworthy engaging shrewd limited prudent indif-
> ferent *Weib. Ich bin das Fleisch das stets bejaht.*[14]

The right of the artist to depict any and all aspects of
life was an implicit assumption in *Ulysses*, and it be-

came the rallying cry for young writers all over the world, including Germany. This right was particularly underlined by the use of inner monologue. If people thought things they never said aloud then Joyce was going to reproduce those thoughts. In so doing he added a new element to the inner monologue. This contribution was summed up in Tucholsky's phrase "everything, but *everything*, is actually said." Such words, in various formulations, appeared again and again in the German press, and it is clear that this was seen to constitute a sharp line of demarcation between *Ulysses* and its predecessors.

Hardly a critic managed to write an article about *Ulysses* without bringing in the name of Sigmund Freud and/or the term psychoanalysis. The great majority agreed that Joyce was attempting, on one level at least, something like the literary expression of Freud's psychoanalytical views. The very freedom of the thoughts themselves, often touching directly or indirectly on matters of sex, seemed "Freudian." Directly connected with the characteristic range of the thoughts depicted was the psychoanalytic technique of free association. Both Dujardin and Schnitzler had shown thoughts which almost invariably proceeded logically and comprehensibly, with the associative element in only the most rudimentary of forms. Joyce allowed the thoughts of his characters to proceed under the strong influence of association, an association which was often subconscious. To this he added the psychological phenomenon of completely gratuitous thoughts (except that these too only seem gratuitous from the limited viewpoint of the reader). The result of this fidelity to actual thought processes and patterns resulted, in some cases, in near incomprehensibility. But obviously some thoughts were going to occur to Leopold Bloom during the day which, to the "listener-in," would at first be meaningless. If this had not been so his would have been a very unusual type of mind indeed.

This extension of the thought content of the inner

monologue, along with the amplified and varied formal qualities of that technique, made Joyce's contribution seem both original and important to many German intellectuals. It should not be difficult in this light to understand the reaction to *Ulysses* in 1927, nor to concur that the novel gave something new and vital to literature by its unique use of the inner monologue. Indeed one need only re-read those experimental examples in German literature already mentioned to be convinced of the gap that separates them from the achievement of *Ulysses*. Bridging this gap required ability of a very high order. Bertolt Brecht was well aware of the difficulty involved. It is the key to his remark about Tucholsky:

> Now the inner monologue is a very difficult technique to employ, and that is worth emphasizing. Without special measures which are themselves technical the inner monologue does not reproduce reality, that is, the totality of thought and association, in the way in which it seems to superficially. Here there is a *merely formal imitation* that must be watched; a falsification of reality. It is not merely a formal problem. . . . On the purely formal level we already had an "inner monologue" which we appreciated highly—I'm thinking of Tucholsky's works.[15]

The introduction of a new and viable technique which far outstripped all previous experiments was only one of the contributions of *Ulysses*. The point of establishing precisely why that contribution was a meaningful one in its literary context was to distinguish it from earlier efforts. But many of the innovations of *Ulysses* had no clear precedent in German literature. Most immediately apparent to German critics was the sharp variation in style among episodes. Besides the mixture of third person narrative and inner monologue already discussed, the novel utilized nine other major formalistic styles: formation of text into short newspaper "articles," with appropriate headlines (Aeolus); a *montage* of short passages of text interrelated in time (Wandering Rocks); a text arranged upon a musical analogy (Sirens); a first person narrative by one of the characters (Cyclops); a stylistic parody (Nausicaa); a stylistic *pastiche* tracing the development of the English language (Oxen of the Sun); dramatic form (Circe); arrangement of text into questions and answers (Ithaca); and a long single unpunctuated flow of thought (Penelope).

Many of these formalistic devices were in themselves new to German literature. But they were unlikely to engender simple imitation on the part of serious novelists—such a use would have been too obviously derivative and too trivial for writers whose own powers of expression did not require borrowed props. However the cumulative effect of the whole made itself felt, and in particular the right of the author to vary his style to suit his own particular needs within a single work.

Such a wide variety of styles employed in the same novel, and often mixed within individual episodes (or even within individual sentences), gave to the work a *montage* effect which was not lost upon contemporary novelists, particularly those interested in the art of the film. This effect was reinforced by other cinematic devices, and as early as 1925 German critics compared Joyce's technique, particularly in the Wandering Rocks episode, to that of the film. In addition Joyce's habit of inserting actual advertisements, popular songs, etc. into the body of the narrative gave to the whole a texture reminiscent of *montage* in the plastic arts—particularly the collages of Picasso and Braque.

Among the most profound results of these innovations was the recognition that a page of text could make a visual as well as a verbal impact upon the reader. Over one hundred and fifty years earlier Laurence Sterne had made use of this same discovery in *Tristram Shandy*, to humorous effect. But in *Ulysses* this element is at once more pervasive and more meaningful. At the same time that Joyce was breaking down traditional notions of narrative technique he was also beginning to break down traditional distinctions between prose and poetry (carried to the extreme in *Finnegans Wake*), and dramatic and narrative form, as well as distinctions between the arts—the novel becoming under his hand more like the film, more like science, more like music. So much so that the question whether *Ulysses* was a novel at all, for those who cared to keep their pigeonholes tidy, continued to be hotly contested. The concept of the visual possibilities of the text was closely connected with the breakdown of these distinctions. The arrangement of the words on the page could suggest poetry, or a newspaper article, or an exam paper, or music. A list of the episodes most often mentioned by German critics shows a direct correlation to those episodes which made an immediate visual impact on the reader. It seemed that many a reviewer, thinking back upon the strange novel he had just read, remembered it in visual terms.

We do not consider it surprising today that for some years German critics (and they were not alone) considered *Ulysses* an interesting, at times exciting, and certainly revolutionary work—but in the ultimate analysis unformed, chaotic, and nihilistic. The remarks above concerning variations in style and tone within the novel offer an explanation for this reaction. Yet *Ulysses* is, almost certainly, the most carefully constructed novel ever written. The structural devices extend from the large superstructure of the Homeric parallel down to the most involved reinforcement on the linguistic level. We have already seen several reasons why German critics and writers before 1930 were for the most part unaware of and consequently unimpressed by this aspect of *Ulysses*. In addition to the difficulty of the text, we have seen that the first German translation failed, particularly at the linguistic level, to reproduce the interlocking structure of the leitmotifs. With the appearance of the second, vastly improved, edition of the translation, and, equally important, Stuart Gilbert's study of the Homeric parallels (German translation 1932), the detailed overall design of the novel became apparent to any serious reader. From this point a new direction in Joycean scholarship became apparent towards a detailed analysis of this very structure. This same movement was reflected in the varying impact of *Ulysses* upon the German novel, as we shall see.

The need for careful construction in the case of *Ulysses*

was evident. If the novel was to be largely concerned with reproducing the psychic content of a few minds during an ordinary day in Dublin, then that subject matter would have to be closely controlled to prevent it from being banal and perhaps incomprehensible. If the events of 16 June 1904 were to become (in Hermann Broch's words) "the universal day of the epoch" ("Weltalltag der Epoche") the structure would have to reinforce these claims for added significance.

In his study of stream-of-consciousness in the modern English novel Robert Humphrey has listed, for convenience sake, seven types of patterns which may be imposed on the raw stuff of consciousness in literature:[16]

1. The unities (time, place, character, and action)
2. Leitmotifs
3. Previously established literary patterns (burlesques)
4. Symbolic structures
5. Formal scenic arrangements
6. Natural cyclical schemes (seasons, tides, etc.)
7. Theoretical cyclical schemes (musical structures, cycles of history, etc.)

These admittedly arbitrary classifications are useful in making the point that while many novels may utilize one or two of them, *Ulysses* makes use of them all. Now, of these, several were new to German literature (indeed to literature in general). We may pick out those which were most immediately striking to German critics. First and foremost was the rigorous adherence to the unities of time and place. The idea that an author could write a fifteen-hundred-page novel (in translation) which did nothing but describe the action of a single day in a modern city obviously overwhelmed the critics. Whether or not they approved of such single-mindedness, the impression it made is undeniable. After the improved second edition of the translation, attention turned to the amazing thoroughness with which the leitmotifs were carried through. The Homeric parallel, too, seized the imagination of readers, once Gilbert's study had outlined it more precisely. In both cases not a single critic was tempted to compare these techniques with anything that had appeared previously in German literature, in spite of the fact that these critics were well aware of the use of leitmotif in the work of Thomas Mann. Beside the extremely complex web of motifs and structure in *Ulysses*, all previous novels seemed relatively traditional. It was no doubt feeling this that Thomas Mann was moved to write: "I myself am a dull traditionalist in comparison with Joyce or Picasso,"[17] a statement reminiscent of Hermann Broch's declaration that the only name in the literary sphere worthy of being set beside Picasso was that of James Joyce.[18]

Other structural innovations were noted by German critics, but without any particular glow of enthusiasm. Even the value of the close Homeric parallel had been questioned, particularly when it obviously required such lengthy exegesis. It is perhaps not surprising therefore that other Joycean schemes of symbolic structure were largely ignored, including such involved devices as assigning an organ of the body to each episode, reflected in the language and word choice employed, so that the whole of the book might be said to symbolize the whole of the human body. The musical analogy of the Sirens episode had been largely overlooked. Yet the general idea of a literary analogy to music was of constant and recurring interest to German intellectuals, particularly the total "orchestration" of a novel by means of leitmotifs.

The impact of *Ulysses* in terms of structure and narrative techniques by no means exhausts its importance in literary history. Its influence was also to be felt on the linguistic level. Much of the effect of the novel for contemporary German writers seemed to rest in the extremely objective and, occasionally, scientific language employed. It had at one time been Joyce's goal to disappear behind his work, striving ultimately to attain the state that Samuel Beckett summed up in the words: "his writing is not *about* something; *it is that something itself*."[19] The "scientific" aspect of *Ulysses* had a particular attraction for those writers who saw in modern technology the possibility of real values and who earnestly desired to incorporate, rather than exclude, the modern world in their own writing.

The freedom Joyce took with language itself, his love of puns, neologisms, and words for their own sake, as well as the liberties he took with syntax, punctuation, and grammatical structure, made for an unusually plastic and flexible text. His constant attempt to make language reflect content led to experimentation which was often striking even in translation—particularly since many of these innovations concerned changing the form to fit the content, and a similar change of the German equivalent was often possible. Once again it was not difficult, although almost no contemporary critic bothered, to find forerunners in German literature for some aspects of Joyce's language—for example the neologisms and *Riesenwörter* of Arno Holz's "Baroke Marine." But the constant reference to Joyce's linguistic innovations in contemporary German criticism makes it clear that for them Joyce was doing something on a new and grander scale with the language. The important point for writers in Germany was that the liberties Joyce took with the English language could equally well be taken with German. The translation had already shown this to a certain extent, and German novels would make it even more apparent in the future.

1. In the front of Dujardin's copy of *Ulysses* Joyce wrote: "To E. D., annonciateur de la parole intérieure, le larron impénitent. J. J." See *Letters*, I, 287.

2. The most extended theoretical treatment of the technique involved is Robert Humphrey's *Stream of Consciousness in the Modern Novel* (Berkeley, 1954). His general definition of stream of consciousness fiction is "a type of fiction in which the basic emphasis is placed on exploration of the prespeech levels of consciousness for the purpose, primarily, of revealing the psychic being of the characters" (p. 4). He distinguishes four basic types of this technique: direct and indirect interior monologue, description by omniscient author, and soliloquy. The last two are traditional techniques, and "indirect interior monologue," as defined by Humphrey, is in fact "erlebte Rede." Only "direct interior monologue" (which we refer to simply as inner monologue) is new to the German novel in 1927, at least in the form in which Joyce presented

it. Our attention will center upon the inner monologue, and we will be distinguishing it from examples of "erlebte Rede," in which the thoughts are expressed in the third person and the tense is usually changed to the past.

3. Erich Kahler's mistaken belief that Richard Beer-Hofmann introduced the inner monologue into German literature stems from his failure to distinguish between this technique and "erlebte Rede." Thus while it is true that Beer-Hofmann's *Der Tod Georgs* (Berlin, 1900) takes as its principal object the inner experience and thoughts of one man, the technique employed is, without exception, that of "erlebte Rede." See Erich Kahler, "Untergang und Übergang der epischen Kunstform," *Die neue Rundschau*, LXIV (1953), 1-44.

4. Arthur Schnitzler, *Gesammelte Werke* (Berlin, 1912), I, 216.

5. See Schnitzler's letter to Georg Brandes of June, 1901, *Georg Brandes und Arthur Schnitzler: Ein Briefwechsel*, ed. Kurt Bergel (Bern, 1956), p. 88.

6. Bertolt Brecht, *Schriften zur Literatur und Kunst* (Frankfurt/M., 1967), III, 115.

7. Kurt Tucholsky, *Gesammelte Werke 1925-1928*, ed. Mary Gerold-Tucholsky (Reinbeck bei Hamburg, 1961), p. 395; reprinted from *Die Weltbühne*, XXII (March, 1926), 510.

8. *Ibid.*, p. 446; reprinted from *Die Weltbühne*, XXII (May, 1926), 785.

9. Many critics continue to ignore the way in which such punctuation functions as author intervention. To pick one example among many, Hartmut Binder, in *Motiv und Gestaltung bei Franz Kafka* (Bonn, 1966), pp. 231-235, continually refers to such passages as inner monologue. If such a view is accepted, inner monologue would be at least two centuries old.

10. ". . . seit diesem merkwürdigen Buch hört in Frankreich die literarische Diskussion über eine Sache nicht auf, die man den 'Inneren Monolog' getauft hat. . . . Die literarische Form ist uns nicht neu. Schnitzler . . . hatte uns schon damals im 'Leutnant Gustl' etwas Ähnliches gegeben." Tucholsky, *Werke 1925-1928*, p. 791; reprinted from the *Vossische Zeitung*, 25 May 1927.

11. "Und hier setzt nun der 'innere Monolog' ein, der so viel Aufsehen gemacht hat . . . und es muss gesagt werden, dass dies der stärkste Eindruck von allem ist. . . . Mit den winzigen Versuchen Arthur Schnitzlers und Carl Spittelers hat diese Orgelsymphonie der Gedanken nichts zu tun. Hier ist tatsächlich alles, aber auch alles, gesagt." Kurt Tucholsky, "Ulysses," *Die Weltbühne*, XXIII (November, 1927), 792; reprinted in *Werke 1925-1928*, pp. 949-955.

12. Bertolt Brecht, *Schriften zur Literatur und Kunst* (Frankfurt/M., 1967), II, 188.

13. Those critics who complained of boredom did not attribute their reaction to the use of this technique, but rather to other factors, such as extreme length, difficulty of material, etc.

14. Letter of 16 August 1921; *Letters*, I, 170. Note Joyce's play upon Goethe's *Faust*: "Ich bin der Geist der stets verneint" (Part I, vs. 1138).

15. "Nun ist der *innere Monolog* ein sehr schwierig zu verwendendes technisches Mittel, und das zu betonen ist ganz nützlich. Ohne ganz bestimmte Massnahmen wieder technischer Art gibt innerer Monolog die Wirklichkeit, das heisst die Totalität des Denkens oder Assoziierens, keineswegs so wieder, wie er das äusserlich zu tun scheint. Hier gibt es ein *Nur der Form nach*, das beachtet werden muss, eine Verfälschung der Wirklichkeit. Es handelt sich nicht nur um ein formales Problem. . . . Rein formal hatten wir einen *inneren Monolog*, den gerade wir sehr schätzten, ich denke an Tucholskys Stücke." Brecht, *op.cit.*, II, 114-115.

16. See note 2 of this chapter. Humphrey, p. 86.

17. "Ich selbst bin im Vergleich mit Joyce oder Picasso ein flauer Traditionalist." *Thomas Mann: Briefe 1937-1947*, ed. Erika Mann (Berlin, 1963), p. 390; letter of 7 October 1944.

18. Hermann Broch, *James Joyce und die Gegenwart* (Vienna, 1936), p. 23; reprinted in Broch's *Gesammelte Werke*, ed. Hannah Arendt (Zurich, 1955), VI, 183-210.

19. Samuel Beckett, "Dante . . . Bruno. Vico . . Joyce," *Our Exagmination Round His Factification for Incamination of Work in Progress* (Paris, 1929), p. 14.

6

JOYCE AND HANS HENNY JAHNN:
AN ELECTIVE AFFINITY

The creative achievement of Hans Henny Jahnn has yet to be fully assessed. As early as 1920 he was awarded the prestigious *Kleistpreis* for his drama *Pastor Ephraim Magnus*, and he continued to lead an active and often troubled literary life, much of it in exile, until his death in 1959. Yet he remains virtually unknown outside of Germany. The seven-volume edition of his works which was published in 1974 by Hoffmann und Campe Verlag of Hamburg should aid in bringing his special talents to the attention of a wider audience. Jahnn is the first of three important German novelists whose works will be examined in relationship to James Joyce's *Ulysses*.

Jahnn was born in 1894, in Hamburg-Stellingen, to an established and active family of ship-builders and makers of fine instruments. The generation to which he belonged was particularly susceptible to the widespread malaise which preceded the first world war, and as a young man Jahnn reacted strongly against the accepted order and values of the society around him. While many of his compatriots, including most intellectuals and writers, welcomed the war as a sort of catharsis, Jahnn was one of the very few who consistently opposed it. He went into exile in Norway from 1915 until 1918, an event which

marked him as an outsider early in life, and placed him
in a situation which bore obvious analogies to the re-
bellion and exile of the young artist James Joyce from
his native Ireland. Upon returning to Hamburg in 1918,
Jahnn came under the influence of the late phase of
German Expressionism. His first published work, *Pastor
Ephraim Magnus*, set the tone for much of his subsequent
production. The plays he published during the twenties
were marked by a powerful, almost baroque, handling of
language, while the subject matter was carefully calculated to shock middle-class audiences (see for example
Die Krönung Richards III, 1921, and *Medea*, 1926). Jahnn's
interest in psychological situations bordering on the
pathological was by no means unique in Germany at the
time, but his attitudes toward religion, sex, and morality
were highly individual. Throughout his life, and at a period of history in which it was by no means a popular
stand, he fought against racism, militarism, and narrow
views of human sexuality.

His subjective and idealistic *Weltanschauung* led to the
formation, in 1921, of a utopian community called the
"Glaubensgemeinde Ugrino," through which he hoped
to further both his intellectual ideals and his passion for
music. The latter aim resulted in the foundation of the
Ugrino Music Publishing House in the same year, and together with a close friend he edited seventeenth-century
organ music. Beginning in the following year, he became
active in building and restoring organs, a talent for which
he was to gain an international reputation. Throughout
the twenties his creativity in both literature and music
never flagged, yet he was still largely unknown as a literary figure when, in 1933, his works were banned by
the Nazis. This was due in large part to the unpopular-
ity of his views in general and the uncensored language
in which he expressed them. The only novel he had then
published was *Perrudja* (1929), which had appeared in a
limited edition and had sold very few copies. Under
political pressure, Jahnn once again left Germany, spend-
ing some time in Switzerland before settling permanent-

ly on the Danish island of Bornholm in the North Sea. The quiet farm life he led there allowed him to devote himself to the land, to raising horses, and to scientific research on the nature of hormones. When, at the end of the war, he returned to West Germany, he was elected president of the Academy of Arts in Hamburg, where he lived until his death in 1959.

In the fifties Jahnn had once more begun to publish: plays, stories, and a short novel *Die Nacht aus Blei* (1956). But the bulk of his creative energy during this period was devoted to his great unfinished novel, a trilogy entitled *Fluss ohne Ufer*. It consisted of *Das Holzschiff* (1949), *Die Niederschrift des Gustav Anias Horn* (1949/50), and *Epilog* (published posthumously in 1961, edited by Walter Muschg). The trilogy is an extremely long and rich portrayal of the complicated development of an artist attempting to come to terms with the world; it is a worldview steeped in the unique sensibility of the author, and Jahnn's stature as a major figure in modern German literature undoubtedly rests upon it.

It is easy to understand why Joyce appealed to Hans Henny Jahnn. The bold experimental quality of *Ulysses*, together with its extreme frankness, made it a perfect primer of artistic freedom for Jahnn during the years in which he was writing his first novel *Perrudja*. The opening pages of *Perrudja* were written in December of 1922, and it was completed only shortly before its publication in 1929. Indeed, as we shall see, Jahnn was still writing sections of the novel while other parts of it were already in press. Jahnn spoke but little of this period in later life, but we may gain some idea of his feelings then from later essays.

Jahnn saw Joyce as a literary revolutionary whose contributions could no more be denied than Galileo's critics could stop the earth from turning:

This period [the twenties] should not be forgotten . ... for it brought an expansion of sight and feeling. James Joyce may be attacked, but he cannot be refuted. Galileo too was attacked.[1]

Those who battled against Joyce were likewise battling against Jahnn (although they might not have realized it), and in defending Joyce, Jahnn was defending himself:

> It surely was not without reason that Joyce, in his *Ulysses*, led a normal man on an odyssey through several layers of consciousness. The method and goal of the description met with the objection that it could not be the purpose of existence to select out the lower and less externally obvious thoughts and sensations for special attention. . . . Such an objection is thoroughly foolish.[2]

Jahnn's own work was a constant struggle to express the complicated and many-leveled reality of the human psyche. He seems to have seen in *Ulysses* a literary expression of some of his own most personal beliefs about the world, and the expression of these beliefs had an importance that extended beyond the realms of the novel:

> In truth the philosophical objections are not at all attacks upon the method or the selection of material. It is much more a protest against the result. One sees that a revolutionary stage of art has blossomed which suggests conclusions reaching beyond art itself.[3]

After such remarks it will not be surprising to learn that the manuscript of *Perrudja* offers clear proof of a direct and profound impact of Joyce's *Ulysses* on Jahnn's first novel. In fact, as we shall see below, a connection may be established between the two novels without going beyond the published text of *Perrudja* itself.

I

Perrudja may be considered as a *Bildungsroman*; it traces the growth and emotional development of a young man towards maturity, and towards an acceptance of his place in society. Perrudja is the name of the young man, and he fits the traditional role of the naive and innocent youth, isolated from the great world outside. He has been living alone in the woods of Norway, provided for, since the death of his aunt, by a mysterious gentleman who appears periodically to furnish him with the funds he needs to live. As the novel progresses we watch the development of Perrudja's intellectual interests (science, music, literature, architecture) and sexual awareness. His love, amounting to an almost unnatural passion, is directed toward various objects: his horse, a young friend, and Signe. Signe demands from Perrudja something he seems incapable of providing—an active and vital approach to human relationships. She rejects him because he initially denies having killed a competitor for her hand; the act itself she welcomes. A major part of the subsequent narrative is devoted to Perrudja's transition from the life of a hermit to a man of the great world outside.

The mysterious visitor at last reveals that Perrudja is heir to an unlimited fortune, and hence has become the most powerful man in existence. He is forced to take up the burden and the duties of his position, and to come to terms with social and industrial evils for which he is financially responsible. Hoping to found a new utopian world colony, Perrudja must first face the decision of the timing of an inevitable war. From two coded texts he chooses the one which sets the stage for an immediate war, although he does so without realizing which message he has chosen. The novel closes with a return to Signe, and in a long final monologue we gain a last glimpse into her complicated mind. Jahnn intended to write a sequel entitled *Perrudja II*, in which he would depict "the later months" of the life of his "Nicht-Held." But this hope was dashed by Jahnn's subsequent exile, and he never finished the epic story.[4]

Without going beyond the published text of *Perrudja* it is possible to establish a connection between the novel and James Joyce's *Ulysses*. To begin with, Jahnn utilized the inner monologue extensively in his novel in a manner strikingly similar to its most common use in *Ulysses*. Such a use was completely new to the German novel in the twenties. A typical passage is the following:

> Der Hengst wurde unruhig. Die Gangart wieder ohne Beherr-
> schung. Perrudja nagte an seiner Lippe, nahm sich krampfhaft
> zusammen.
> Ich bin dem Koloss aus Fleisch und Samen nicht gewachsen.
> Kann ein Mensch so unruhig nach Frauen sein?
> Er blickte sich um, erschaute nichts. Sah vor sich und zur Seite.
> Erschaute nichts. Sein Pferd ging quer tänzelnd, nicht gradaus.
> Riecht. Wir können nicht Frauen erriechen. (p. 45)[5]

The narrative technique oscillates here between third
person narrative and inner monologue, without warning.
The reader moves in and out of Perrudja's mind at the
will of the author. This method, so characteristic of
Ulysses, is not the only technical innovation that links the
two novels. The sudden interruption of the text by poetry
or even music also appears and spurs the curiosity. Our
natural tendency is to ask whether Jahnn had read
Ulysses before the publication of his own novel. And the
answer is yes. Jahnn must have read *Ulysses* while working on *Perrudja*, for he quotes from Joyce's novel in chapter 22 of his own.

Perrudja is at home reading, and thinking to himself
(note the use of inner monologue):

> . . . 'Rotzgrünes Meer.' Ein Edelstein.[6] Erhabenes mit alten ge-
> ringen Worten sagen. Die Frommen, die uns nicht für so niedrig
> achten, dass sie nicht nachgingen unseren Verirrungen. . . .
> Er hörte deutlich, dass gegen die Tür gepocht wurde. Er sprang
> auf, warf das Buch zuboden. (pp. 296-298)

The book that Perrudja is reading is *Ulysses*, and the quotation is among the most famous lines of the opening
episode:

> —. . . A new art colour for our Irish poets: snotgreen. . . .
> —God he said quietly. Isn't the sea what Algy calls it: a grey
> sweet mother? The snotgreen sea. (5:01/05)

But Perrudja (and Hans Henny Jahnn) would be reading
the book in the German translation which had just appeared: " 'Lieber Gott,' sagte er ruhig. 'Das Meer ist
wirklich was Algy sagt: eine graue, liebe Mutter. Das
rotzgrüne Meer.' " (Vol. I, 7).

These are not the only words taken from *Ulysses*. In a long list of visitors received by Perrudja (chapter 37) near the end of the novel, we find the following name: "Almidano Artifoni" (p. 568). This is an unusual name, but set among almost seventy others of all nationalities, as it is, it is likely to go unnoticed by the reader. Yet a student of Joyce would recognize it immediately. For Almidano Artifoni was the head of the Berlitz school of languages in Trieste when Joyce taught English there.

Leaving aside the possibility that Jahnn knew Artifoni personally it is most likely that he took the name from the Wandering Rocks episode of *Ulysses*, where it becomes the name of an Italian music teacher. Jahnn no doubt lifted the name from the text of *Ulysses* for the same reasons Joyce took it from life, for its sonority and foreignness.

Thus from the printed text alone there are several reasons to believe that *Ulysses* may have had an important impact upon Jahnn's first novel. We have enough circumstantial evidence to assert that Jahnn read *Ulysses* while working on *Perrudja*. Further investigation must be based on other sources. Fortunately the original manuscript of the novel, as well as many important unpublished letters to and from Jahnn, have been preserved in the permanent collection of the Staats- und Universitätsbibliothek Hamburg. With their help it is possible to precisely define the formative influence of *Ulysses* upon the novel.[7]

II

Evidence based on his unpublished letters shows that after a brief false start in 1922, Jahnn began working on *Perrudja* in 1926 and had finished the whole of the first draft by around July of 1927.[8] Sometime in that year he began to rework the text, adding new material and substantially altering the style. *Ulysses* appeared in October, 1927, in German translation. The revision of *Perrudja* continued during the next two years, up until the publication of the novel at the end of 1929. The period from 1926 to 1929 thus represents the years in which Jahnn was actively working on the novel, and he later referred more than once to the fact that he had worked on *Perrudja* for four years.[9]

Jahnn first became aware of *Ulysses* sometime during 1926. He was almost certainly familiar with the main outline of the book and its style, through the publicity surrounding the forthcoming translation. It is also probable that he took part in the coffeehouse discussions over the form of the novel. Enough could be conveyed by these means to convince him that *Ulysses* might well be worth having—even at the extremely high price (considering his financial state) of 100 marks. He put his name on the list of subscribers and waited impatiently for his copy. In June, 1927, he wrote to the Rhein-Verlag:

> Through the publishing division of Ugrino a subscription copy of James Joyce's *Ulysses* was promised to me at the pre-publication price. Please be so kind as to send the work directly to me, or Ugrino, Publications Department, immediately upon its appearance.
>
> P.S. I see in the most recent issue of the *Literarische Welt* that the German edition probably won't appear until Autumn. Therefore please send me any English edition. Of course this doesn't mean that I cancel my copy of the German edition.[10]

This letter proves both that Jahnn was aware of *Ulysses* well before its publication in German, and that he was unusually eager to receive a copy. Considering the urgency with which he requested the novel we may assume that he read it soon after its appearance in October of 1927.[11] For Jahnn, as for so many of his contemporaries, the effect of first reading *Ulysses* must have been profound.[12] Not only was the novel the expression of a literary idea with which he himself was deeply involved, but it was also related in terms of style to a more general philosophical concept which was central to Jahnn's thought, and which he termed the creative principle of "*Form und Variantenbedürfnis.*" Thus in 1930, reviewing *Ulysses* enthusiastically, he stressed:

What is truly important in this work is only that the drive toward form and variation [*Form und Variantenbedüfnis*], the unadorned creative principle, is seen, smelled, and touched fully. The reader receives for the first time a measuring stick for judging how classical literary feelings betray contemporary man.[13]

He also noted in passing that "the phonetic basis of the language is expanded in a manner unknown up till now." At the same time, and in the same issue of *Der Kreis*, he published a general article on the novel, and it was not an accident that he stressed the same phrases:

In the beginning was the will toward form and the drive toward variation. . . . The purpose of the poet in our time is to express things and transformations which he sees, the disagreeable no matter what the cost, sometimes openly crude, offering clear blows at established morality. He must not pretend to be blind.[14]

He underlined this point in the concluding statement of the *Ulysses* review: "Buy the book, read it again and again. And whoever is shocked by it had better ask himself if his own existence is not founded upon deafness, blindness, and lies."[15] Such was the reaction of Hans Henny Jahnn to *Ulysses*, and for two years after first reading it he was hard at work on *Perrudja*; it was to appear at last in the Autumn of 1929.[16]

The first draft of *Perrudja* is contained in two bound notebooks of ruled paper, 6 3/4 X 8 1/4 inches, each comprising around two hundred pages.[17] In addition there are separate manuscripts of eight further chapters (not contained in the first draft) on large foolscap. Evidence indicates that the first draft may be roughly dated as 1926 to the Spring of 1927, while the additional chapters were most likely written in the period between the Spring of 1927 and the publication of the novel in 1929.

Three chapters of the printed version are not present at all in the manuscript, in spite of the fact that the corresponding surrounding chapters are. There is no indication in any of the manuscript material that these chapters were even being considered. They are: chapter 13, "Die

Edelmütigen oder die Geschichte des Sklaven"; chapter 17, "Der Zirkel"; and chapter 22, untitled. At least one of these may be accurately dated. Speaking of 1929 and monthly payments Jahnn received from the Enoch Brothers, he wrote:

> . . . in return I had to send them the manuscript. Under this pressure the second volume was completed. For example I wrote the chapter "Der Zirkel" in one day on which I sat down after noon and remained sitting until deep into the night.[18]

We may assume that all three of these chapters were written under this pressure during the year 1929. The contents of the first draft, as well as the separate manuscripts, and those chapters present only in the printed version are schematized in Table 4.

TABLE 4

PERRUDJA

ORIGINAL 1922-27 MANUSCRIPT	ADDED 1927-29 MANUSCRIPT CHAPTERS	PRINTED 1929 TEXT
I *Das Pferd*		
II		
III		
IV		
V		
VI		
VII	VIII *Sassanidischer König*	(story of the five boys)
	IX	(slaves story)
	X	(music added)
	XI *Ein Knabe weint*	
XII *Die anderen Tiere*		(slave's story)
		XIII *Die Edelmütigen oder die Geschichte des Sklaven*
XIV *Der Knecht und die Magd*		
XV		
XVI		
		XVII *Der Zirkel*
XVIII		
	XIX *Alexander*	
XX *Werbung und Vorhölle*		
XXI		(Ragna and Nils)
		XXII (*chapter in which Perrudja reads Ulysses*)

We may now turn to a close examination of the manuscript. The first draft contains the basic narrative substance of *Perrudja*. None of the subsequent chapters was
to add substantially to the actual "plot" of the novel.
The story is that of Perrudja, his love for Signe, and his
involvement in the international affairs of which he at
last realizes he is the primary motivating force. Keeping
in mind that this first draft had been completed by sometime in 1927, we may begin to search in its pages for
those technical and stylistic characteristics which re-
semble *Ulysses* in the published version, beginning with
the examples of inner monologue.

The first unequivocal use of inner monologue in *Perrudja* (its presence signaled by the use of the first person
singular and the present tense) occurs at the end of
chapter 2:

> Er legte sich die Handflächen auf die dunklen Brustwarzen und
> sagte bestimmt und männlich: 'Perrudja wird ein Pferd bekom-
> men.' Und über die Worte hinaus glitten Gedanken. Ein Königs-
> sohn jagte über die Hochebene.
>   *Ich streife auf schwarzem Pferd durch Wälder. Unermesslich. Eine Quelle*
> *geht auf auf grünem Moos. Meine Brustwarzen sind rund. Wozu braucht ein*
> *Mann Brustwarzen?* (pp. 32-33)

The passage I have set in italics above takes the follow-
ing form in the manuscript: "Er sah den jungen stolzen
Perrudja auf schwarzem Ross durch die unermesslichen
Wälder streifen" (ms. p. 31). Originally third person

narrative, it has been transformed and expanded in the printed version, becoming distinct inner monologue. But the manuscript gives no hint of this subsequent transformation.

The inner monologue in *Perrudja* sometimes takes the form of Perrudja speaking to himself (second person familiar). Here is an example from chapter 3:

> Seinem Atem, der träge, gegoren nach Bier roch und weisslichem Käse, den Angstschweiss in langbehaarten Achselhöhlen, seiner Mannbarkeit Regungen.
> *Du wirst einst gerichtet sein, schuldig und schuldlos zugleich, weil du faul und stinkig.*
> Das Gefühl seiner Einsamkeit kam über ihn, das Gefühl eines Durstes kam über ihn, die Sehnsucht nach Macht kam über ihn, die Pein seines Geschlechts kam über ihn. (p. 36)

Compare the italicized passage with the same passage in the first draft:

> . . . seinen Atem, der träge, gegoren nach Bier roch und weisslichem Käse. Der Angstschweiss der leicht behaarten Achselhöhel [sic], seiner Mannbarkeit Regungen. *Und ohne Adel dünkte er sich, ein Gottverlassener, der in Sünde verstrickt, und gerichtet wird, schuldlos und schuldig zugleich.* Das Gefühl seiner Einsamkeit kam über ihn, das Gefühl eines Durstes kam über ihn, die Sehnsucht nach Macht kam über ihn, die Pein seines Geschlechts kam über ihn. (ms. p. 38)

Once again it is plain that the passage in question was later rewritten as inner monologue. The surrounding text is quoted to demonstrate that only those lines we have indicated were altered significantly in rewriting. This was not a case of rewriting an entire passage; rather it represents a specific decision to introduce inner monologue into an otherwise finished text. The only other instance of inner monologue in chapter 3 (p. 38) is likewise a later alteration. In both cases in chapter 3 we may note Jahnn's tendency to set off inner monologue by placing it in separate paragraphs.

By the fourth chapter of *Perrudja*, Jahnn makes full-scale use of inner monologue in the printed version. The first instance in this chapter is typical:

Hoch auf bäumte er sich.
Du musst dich zusammennehmen, Perrudja. Lass dich nicht erkennen,
dein Herz schlägt hörbar. Es drängt dir Kot zum Darmauslass.
Misslungener Versuch. (p. 43)

In the manuscript the italicized passage is present in only
a rudimentary form (and is third person narrative):
"Hoch auf bäumte er sich, *der Reiter nahm sich zusammen.*
Ein misslungener Versuch" (ms. p. 58). The inner monologue of the following paragraphs is also written in the
third person narrative in the first draft, with no indication it was to be changed. Pages 44-45 of the printed
version contain a great deal of inner monologue completely absent in the manuscript (in any form).

It is unnecessary to multiply these typical examples;
rather we may sum up the results of a line by line comparison of the first draft with the printed version of *Per-*
rudja: with the exception of four short, separate lines in the
final chapter (39) of the first draft, there is absolutely
no use of inner monologue in the manuscript. Lines of
inner monologue in the printed version are either simply
missing in the first draft (most commonly), or present in
some other form, with no indication that the line is to
be altered, or (in a few cases) actually added or altered
at a later date in a different color ink or in pencil.
Scattered throughout the novel there are a very few examples of the traditional form "er dachte" or "er sagte
vor sich" followed by a line or two of thoughts (and
usually avoiding the first person pronoun).

The conclusion is inescapable. Jahnn first wrote the
draft of a full-length novel in more or less traditional
narrative style. This draft he completed in 1927. He then
rewrote large portions of the book utilizing inner monologue. The resulting change in effect for the whole of the
novel was striking. Such a radical change would seem to
demand an explanation. We suggest the answer lies in
Jahnn's reading of *Ulysses* in 1927.

The separate manuscript chapters on foolscap corresponding to "Sassanidischer König" (8-10) and "Ein Knabe
Weint" (11) likewise do not contain the lines of inner

monologue present in the final versions. It is thus evident that Jahnn's decision to make use of this technique was made at a later date than even the composition of these chapters. But there is an indication in the manuscripts of the point at which Jahnn first began to make extensive use of inner monologue.

The separate manuscript entitled "Das Hohelied des Gesetzes" is a very complete version of the final three chapters of *Perrudja*, written on foolscap. It is written in a form close to that of the printed text, and it contains long passages of inner monologue. We have seen that the first draft originally ended with chapter 39 ("Abraham und Isaak"). But Jahnn changed his mind and added a final section devoted to the main female character of his book, giving for the first time an intimate glimpse into her mind through the use of inner monologue. The similarity of this closing section to Molly Bloom's final soliloquy strikes the reader immediately. This similarity extends to many points of detail. The subject matter of the three chapters centers upon the erotic, and as Molly Bloom recalls her act of adultery that day, Signe is actually enacting (at least spiritual) adultery. Perhaps most striking is the comparison of the "night-thoughts" of the two women. Both are in bed, both attempting to sleep:

> MOLLY: . . . let me see if I can doze off 1 2 3 4 5 what kind of flowers are those they invented like the stars the wall paper in Lombard street was much nicer the apron he gave me was like that something only I only wore it twice better lower this lamp and try again so as I can get up early . . . (781:21)

> SIGNE: . . . Ich werde traumlos schlafen. Augen schliessen. Grünes Quadrat im roten Hof. Die Lider bewegen, es fällt, es steigt. Rotierende Kugel, rotierender Zylinder. Zehntausend Punkte. Augen öffnen. . . . Das Herz schlägt hörbar. Die grüne Kugel flammt golden, verfinstert sich wieder zu rot. Ein Haar fällt durch den Raum. Sehr gekrümmtes Haar. Ein zweites. Viele. Sehr viele, doch zählbar. Man müsste zählen. Im Verfolgen fliessen sie. . . . (p. 642)

The differences between the two flows of thought are immediately apparent, and yet the similarity of technique is evident. Signe's inner thoughts are more clearly shaped and defined, underlining the fact that Jahnn's use of the technique, here and elsewhere in the novel, remains much closer to the inner monologue of Stephen or Leopold Bloom (also the form most often employed by Joyce in his novel). Molly's thoughts are unpunctuated, drifting apparently formlessly. Nevertheless the content, basic technique, and length (one paragraph of Signe's thoughts lasts three pages) relate the two passages clearly. For both women the desire for sleep is interrupted by the needs of nature:

> MOLLY: I want to get up a minute if Im let . . . wheres the chamber gone easy Ive a holy horror of its breaking under me after that old commode . . . (769:02)

> SIGNE: Ich habe vergessen, die Blase zu entleeren, ich werde, ohne getan zu haben, nicht einschlafen. Licht. Wieder erheben. Die Notdurft verrichten. Zurück ins Bett. Licht löschen. Kaltwarme Schauer das Behagens unter der leichtwarmen Decke. Ich werde gut schlafen. Ich bin sehr müde . . . (p. 642)

For Jahnn, such scenes were part of daily life and as such deserving of artistic attention. Much of the inner monologue which was later added to the text of *Perrudja* concerns subject matter which was generally considered taboo in the twenties. In such instances the language is also noticeably franker (see for example the passages already quoted in this chapter); there can be little doubt that Jahnn was emboldened in this respect by his reading of *Ulysses*.

The addition of this last section tended to change the entire emphasis in *Perrudja* from the international affairs depicted to the relationship between Perrudja and Signe. It seems reasonable to suggest that "Das Hohelied des Gesetzes" is the first visible profound effect of Jahnn's confrontation with *Ulysses*. This would place its composition as post-October, 1927, and in the only cases in which definite dating of the addition of inner monologue is possible, both fall within this period.[19]

That the extensive use of inner monologue was post-

October, 1927, seems evident from the fact that it appears for the most part only in the printed version. And although it was often only a matter of inserting a line or two, there are also several instances of whole pages of inner monologue being added. It is perhaps significant that such additions were, for the most part, placed at the beginning or end of a chapter.[20] One of these passages in particular is strikingly similar to the Proteus episode of *Ulysses*. This is the opening of chapter 8, "Sassanidischer König," and the relevant pages are neither in the first draft nor in the separate manuscript. In the Proteus episode we find Stephen meditating on philosophical matters and writing poetry. In "Sassanidischer König" we find Perrudja doing exactly the same thing. Not only are the two young men's thoughts similar, but at times they are expressed in almost the same words:

STEPHEN	PERRUDJA
My soul walks with me, form of forms. (44:26)	Jemand hatte geschrieben: Seele, Form der Formen. Er katechisierte: Was ist das? (p. 59)
[of Aristotle] But he adds: in bodies. Then he was aware of them bodies before of them coloured. How? By knocking his sconce against them sure. . . . A very short space of time through very short times of space. (37:05)	Auch die Begriffe erhärten sich am Existenten. Auch die Seele erweist sich erst am Geschaffenen. Ohne Betätigung am Stofflichen ist sie Hypothese wie der Raum, wie der Ablauf der Zeit. (p. 59)
Ineluctable modality of the visible:[21] at least that if no more, thought through my eyes. (37:01)	Wir entrinnen (unsere Seele entrinnt) unserem Leibe nicht. Wie es geschrieben steht, wenn man es richtig erfasst. (pp. 59-60)
He comes, pale vampire, through storm his eyes, his bat sails bloodying the sea, mouth to her mouth's kiss.[22] Here. Put a pin in that chap, will you? My tablets. Mouth to her kiss. No. Must be two of 'em. Glue 'em well. Mouth to her mouth's kiss. (48:01) . . .	Rossmäulige Schenkel. Meine Seele. Rehäugige Knospen der Brüste. Saphirnes Dunkel des Nabelgrübchens. Dichtung. Man könnte Verse daraus. Rossmäulige Schenkel warten mein. In Knospen der Brüste, rehäugig, bett ich, saphirhaft umdunkelt, mich ein. . . . .

She, she, she. What she? . . . Where are your wits? (48:35)	Wen meine ich? Unbekannt. O Tollheit! (pp. 60-61)
Allbright he falls, proud lightning of the intellect, *Lucifer, dico, qui nescit occasum.* (50:24)	Luzifers Sturz, der uns nur erspart bleibt, wenn wir lügen. (p. 60)

The first of these comparisons reveals what seems to be a further actual quotation from *Ulysses*. Jahnn's phrase "Jemand hatte geschrieben . . ." alerts the reader that what follows is something Perrudja had read. Stephen first formulates this definition on page 26 of *Ulysses*: "The soul is in a manner all that is: the soul is the form of forms." Stephen has Aristotle in mind, and a passage from *De Anima*, III, 432a, where he says ". . . as the hand is the instrument of instruments, so the mind [nous] is the form of forms and sensation the form of sensibles."[23] Joyce reformulated this as "soul," and it seems likely that Jahnn was struck by the phrase.

The evidence thusfar presented indicates that Hans Henny Jahnn consciously rewrote passages of *Perrudja* inserting inner monologue, a technique essentially absent from the whole of the first draft. Several pages, and at least one entire chapter (22), seem to have been written with *Ulysses* in mind.[24] But the use of inner monologue is not the only aspect of *Perrudja* that reminds one of *Ulysses*. Jahnn also utilizes leitmotifs, plays with the language, and creates a *montage* effect by the means of insertion of snatches of poetry and musical quotations into the text. Once again we may turn to the manuscripts to determine if such effects were an integral part of the novel from its inception or whether they were added much later.

To begin with the musical quotations, we may state immediately that nowhere in any of the manuscripts is there the slightest hint that Jahnn planned to insert music.[25] Where the published text included musical quotations the original manuscript contains continuous unbroken text. It is clear that *Perrudja* was first written as a self-sufficient narrative, and that the music was added much later. This later insertion may be considered effective, but it was definitely an afterthought, and most likely was among the last additions to the novel.

If we trace a few of the primary leitmotifs in the novel we find that the situation exactly parallels that of the use of inner monologue. For those motifs we may follow through several repetitions in the printed text,[26] not one is continuously present functioning as a leitmotif in the manuscript. Rather, as we saw in the case of inner monologue, they either occur in a long passage the whole of which is missing, or they have been simply inserted for the printed text in the middle of passages that, except for these leitmotifs, already existed in the first draft. For example the motif of "gelb" and "die gelbe Blume" (to select out a few of the salient occurrences) is not present in the manuscript on the pages corresponding to pages 51, 208, 212, 220, 233, 234, and 271. Likewise the "24 Stunden" motif is undoubtedly a late addition to the novel, since the main occurrences (pp. 133, 143, 146, 173, 207, and 210) are not in the first draft. In addition the last three occurrences (on 173, 207, and 210) are from the chapter "Der Zirkel" which Jahnn himself says he did not write until late in 1929.

As for the poetry which is inserted here and there in the printed text, it too was inserted in every case as an afterthought[27] (the one exception is, as we might expect, in the final added chapters "Das Hohelied des Gesetzes," where inner monologue also occurs for the first time). The conclusion is again inescapable. The whole first draft of *Perrudja* was written without such use of poetry. Then in the added final section on foolscap lines of poetry were included. Thereafter, at a later date, he proceeded to include poetry for a *montage* effect, differentiating it from earlier traditional uses in the German novel. In *Wilhelm Meisters Lehrjahre* for example, Goethe certainly did not hesitate to insert poetry into his prose narrative. Yet these instances are always closely connected with the story at hand, and generally represent a character either singing or reciting the poem in question. Jahnn on the other hand, like Joyce, inserts lines of poetry which are not connected in a literal sense with the "story" but serve rather to convey a general mood. An example from chapter 8 is typical:

> Es erdämmerte für ihn nur eine Rettung: Müdigkeit, Feigheit, Lüge, dazu sein Herz, das zwar keine Worte erfand, keine Definitionen, keine Formulierungen, das dennoch nach schön und hässlich entschied.
>> Safrangelber Wein,
>> amethystenes Glas;
>> schwarze sterbende Lippen,
>> mondsteinfettig und nass.
>
> Hatte er sich über seinen Büchern abgefunden mit dem Ablauf der Existenzäusserungen in ihren Mannigfaltigkeiten, Widersprüchen, sprunghaften Glute . . . (p. 66)

The effect here is that of *collage* in which we might almost imagine that the lines of poetry were cut out of a magazine and pasted on the page in the middle of the text (as Alfred Döblin was actually to do in *Berlin Alexanderplatz!*) This process does not imply that the author is less in control of his effects, but only that he tends to utilize them in order to make a new kind of impact upon his readers.

Before summing up these findings, one further aspect of *Perrudja* should be examined in the light of the manuscripts—that of experimentation and play with language. Once more a simple formulation is possible: such instances are not present in their extreme forms in any of the manuscripts, and must be regarded as late additions. In the one case in which we have a few words of such a passage, in manuscript (on the back of a letter from Jahnn's parents), that passage cannot have been written before December, 1927. Effects such as letter permutation, sound-play, play with word order of a given sentence occur only in the printed version. The following passages are typical of later additions to Jahnn's novel, not present in any of the manuscripts:

> Schmetterlinge, Raupen. Wurmraupen. Wollewurmraupen. Wollewurmkriechraupen. Wollewurmkriechfressraupen. Wollewurmkriechfresskotvöllerraupen. Sind hässlich. (p. 51)

Tisch, Stuhl, Bett und Haus, Mond und Sonne, Saus und Braus,
Wind, Regen, Mühle, Trog und Stall, all überall, Knall und Fall,
Rauch und Asche, Schall und Flasche, Stock und Tasche, Buhl
und Blasche, Kemp und Tremp und Blemp und Kotz und Kater,
Mutter, Ammer, Kind und Vater, Suppenlöffel, Reichsberater—.
(p. 61).

We have now examined the major stylistic features of
Perrudja which link it with *Ulysses*. In the light of the information gleaned from the manuscripts we may assert
that such techniques as the use of inner monologue,
montage effects of music and poetry, and linguistic experimentation were late additions to the manuscript under the
direct influence of *Ulysses*. Such an influence extends occasionally to both subject matter and vocabulary, as
well as the direct (though veiled) references to *Ulysses*
already cited.

It is important to realize that the composition of *Perrudja* fell into two stages—a very complete and lengthy
manuscript of the basic narrative substance of the novel,
and then a reworking of the manner in which that subject
matter was presented. Thus the method of composition
was one of accretion, in which those characteristics of
the novel which link it with *Ulysses* were often simply
added on to a text which had already existed in its own
right. Such a method is in danger of the accusation of
superficiality. It is a mark of the literary powers of Hans
Henny Jahnn that he was able to borrow ideas and
techniques and integrate them meaningfully into his own
text. He bore an elective affinity for the work of James
Joyce, and he might well have developed in a similar
direction even without reading *Ulysses*. But it is doubtful
that *Perrudja* could have come to us in its present form
without that influence. Jahnn was able to draw direct and
profitable benefits from the pages of Joyce's major work.

By the late thirties Jahnn was writing in a style far removed from the exuberance of *Perrudja*, without using
inner monologue. His work became more reminiscent of
Kafka than of Joyce, and when he received a letter asking
him if *Das Holzschiff* (first published 1949) really portrayed

his own view of human existence, he replied that he had attempted "to view the reality of human existence in a manner as unprejudiced as Kafka's in *The Trial*."[28] Nevertheless the Joycean experience left an indelible mark upon the work of Hans Henny Jahnn. *Die Niederschrift des Gustav Anias Horn* (the second section of the *Fluss ohne Ufer* trilogy), revolving slowly through the months which form its structural skeleton, expands the hour-by-hour progress of the sections of the single day of *Ulysses*. On the textual level the insertion of musical quotations (at times identical to those in *Perrudja*) is still visually striking.

Throughout his life Hans Henny Jahnn never altered his high opinion of Joyce or *Ulysses*. Within his own work *Perrudja* stands as the most imposing witness of this literary relationship. And within German literature *Perrudja* stands among the first of a group of novels which have enriched the genre as a whole.

1. "Mann sollte diese Zeit [the twenties] nicht vergessen . . . denn sie brachte eine Erweiterung des Sehens und Empfindens. Man kann James Joyce bekämpfen: aber man kann ihn nicht widerlegen. Auch Galilei wurde bekämpft." Jahnn, *Uber den Anlass und andere Essays* (Frankfurt/M., 1964), p. 38; lecture of 25 October 1952. Hereafter cited as *Essays*.

2. "Nicht grundlos sicherlich hat Joyce in seinem *Ullysses* [sic] einen gewöhnlichen Menschen eine Irrfahrt durch viele Schichten des Bewusstseins geführt. Man hat gegen die Methode und gegen das Ziel der Beschreibung eingewendet, es könne nicht der Zweck des Daseins sein, das Untere und nach aussen hin weniger Auffällige der Gedanken und Empfindungen bevorzugt hinauszustellen. . . . Ein solcher Vorwurf ist an der Wurzel schon töricht." Jahnn, *Essays*, p. 100.

3. "In Wahrheit handelt es sich bei den philosophischen Einwänden gar nicht um Angriffe gegen die Richtung oder das Ausmass der Auswahl. Es ist vielmehr ein Protest gegen das Ergebnis. Man begreift, dass hier ein revolutionärer Abschnitt der Kunst sich aufgetan hat, der auch jenseits der Kunst Folgerungen nach sich zieht." Jahnn, *Essays*, p. 101.

4. The unfinished sequel has been published as *Perrudja II: Fragment aus dem Nachlass*, ed. Rolf Burmeister (Frankfurt/M., 1968), and in Vol. I of the 1974 Hamburg edition of Jahnn's works.

5. All page references are to the 1958 Frankfurt edition of *Perrudja*.

6. Compare with *Pastor Ephraim Magnus*, Jahnn, *Dramen I* (Frankfurt/M., 1963), p. 14: "Warum lassen sich die einfachen Dinge so schwer sagen und noch schwerer glauben?—Wer kennt sie denn noch? Oder wer hat sie wiedergefunden wie einen verlorenen Edelstein?" Paul Fechter seems to have been the first German critic to note the "snotgreen sea" quotation in *Perrudja*. See

"Peinlichkeiten," *Die neue Literatur*, I (January, 1931), p. 23. Two other critics who pointed to Joyce's influence were Lutz Weltmann (who, like Fechter, had reviewed *Ulysses* in 1928) and Klaus Mann, both of whom are quoted in Smith, pp. 105, 108 (see note 7 below).

7. Three dissertations have thusfar been devoted to *Perrudja*: Rüdiger Wagner, *Hans Henny Jahnns Roman Perrudja: Sprache und Stil* (Diss. Munich, 1965); Henry Adelmon Smith, "Sassanidischer König: Hans Henny Jahnn's *Perrudja* in Microcosm" (Diss. University of Southern California, 1969); and Thomas Freeman, "Structure and Symbolism in Hans Henry Jahnn's *Perrudja*: a Study of the Unity of the Novel" (Stanford, 1970). None of these studies investigates Jahnn's relationship to Joyce in detail, although Smith's sensitive and perceptive analysis of a single chapter of *Perrudja* includes a discussion of Joyce's possible influence on Jahnn (pp. 103-109). He suggests that an impact on the "style and technique" of *Perrudja* is probable, but maintains that "in a novel so essentially different from *Ulysses* it is obvious that only a superficial kind of influence is possible" (p. 108).

8. These conclusions are based on the following unpublished letters in the Hamburg Staats- und Universitätsbibliothek: 26 June 1926 (to Ullstein Verlag); 13 December 1926 (to Fischer Verlag); 7 July 1927 (from Fischer Verlag); 9 December 1927 (to Horen Verlag); and 8 January 1928 (to Oskar Loerke); as well as statements quoted in Walter Muschg, *Gespräche mit Hans Henny Jahnn* (Frankfurt/M., 1967), p. 165 f. (hereafter cited as *Gespräche*). Smith reaches much the same conclusions in his chapter II, "Chronology and Construction," pp. 18-35. His findings also agree with those presented in note 17 below, although he seems to have been unaware that part of the original manuscript of *Perrudja* is missing (cf. pp. 21-22 of his study).

9. "Der Perrudja hat mich vier Jahre Arbeitszeit gekostet . . ." Unpublished letter from Jahnn to Walter Herrmann, 3 October 1930.

10. "Ueber Ugrino, Abteilung Verlag wurde mir zu Subskriptionszwecken ein Exemplar des *Ulysses* von James Joyce, zum Vorzugspreise zugesagt. Ich bitte Sie doch, mir dieses Werk direkt an mich oder Ugrino, Abteilung Verlag, sofort nach Erscheinen zu senden. NS. Aus den letzten Nummer der *Literarischen Welt* ersehe ich, dass die deutsche Ausgabe wahrscheinlich erst zum Herbst erscheinen wird. Ich bitte Sie deshalb, mir irgend eine englische Ausgabe zu schicken. Damit möchte ich natürlich nicht auf ein Exemplar der Deutschen [*sic*] Ausgabe verzichten." Unpublished letter of 18 June 1927. The issue of *Die Literarische Welt* to which Jahnn refers, 17 June 1927, carried a front-page article on Joyce by Ivan Goll, as well as the pre-publication of a chapter from the German translation of *Ulysses*. Thus a specific textural example of Joyce's style had undoubtedly been seen by Jahnn as early as June 1927, during the period in which he was just finishing the first draft of *Perrudja*.

11. There is no evidence that the Rhein-Verlag was forthcoming with one of the scarce English copies, but the three-volume edition remains today in Jahnn's personal library. His daughter has informed me that both this edition and the second, two-volume, version, which was the occasion of his review of 1930, are still on the shelves: "Ich habe beide Ausgaben des *Ulysses* . . . wegen Randbemerkungen von Seiten meines Vaters durchgesehen. In beiden befinden sich keine. Übrigens befinden sich auch in literarischen Werken anderer Schriftsteller, die mein Vater sehr schätzte, niemals Randbemerkungen. Nur in Werken über Orgelbau sind hie und da Eintragungen gemacht worden." Unpublished letter of 2 November 1967.

12. It is not difficult to imagine with what mixed feelings Jahnn must have first read *Ulysses* when one considers such passages as the following, from *Pastor Ephraim Magnus*:

PETER: . . . Wenn nun ein Dichter aber die Geschichte eines Menschen schreiben will, wenn er es nun will und nichts weglassen will, nicht das Kleinste! Ja er könnte sich einen Einsideler wählen; aber er muss dann doch beschreiben, was der tut, alles—selbst, wie er seine Geschäfte erledigt—und was er dabei denkt—was man überhaupt denken kann! —(*Dramen I*, p. 170).

13. "Wichtig ist nur dass in diesem Werk Form und Variantenbedürfnis, das ungeschminkte Schöpfungsprinzip ersehen, errochen, ertastet wird. Der Leser bekommt zum erstenmal einen Massstab, um zu ermessen, dass die klassischen Literaturgefühle uns heutige Menschen verraten." Jahnn, "*Ulysses*," *Der Kreis*, VII (July-August, 1930), 472-473.

14. "Im Anfang waren Formwille und Variantenbedürfnis. . . . Der Dichter unserer Zeit nun ist dazu da, Dinge und Wandlungen auszusprechen, die er wahrnimmt, die nicht gefällig um jeden Preis, manchmal offenbar roh, offenbar Verstösse gegen die bestehende Sitte. Er darf nicht tun als ob er blind sei." Jahnn, "Der Dichter und die religiöse Lage der Gegenwart," *ibid.*, p. 407.

15. See note 9, chapter 4.

16. *Perrudja* appeared at approximately the same time as Alfred Döblin's *Berlin Alexanderplatz*, two years after the German *Ulysses*. It was published in a two-volume limited edition of 1,020 copies. The first thousand copies were bound in half-leather or linen, and twenty copies were bound in full leather and signed by the author. *Perrudja* was published by the Lichtwarkstiftung of Hamburg.

17. The first draft of *Perrudja* contains the whole of the basic narrative of the printed text, with the exception of chapters 25-34, for which the manuscript is completely missing. It is clear that there were originally *three* such notebooks—of which the two in the possession of the archive are One and Three. The extant manuscript begins with chapter 1 and ends in Notebook Three with the present penultimate section (39, "Abraham und Isaak"), which Jahnn seemingly intended to be the final chapter at that time. At this point the fragment published as *Perrudja II* begins immediately. The manuscript of *Perrudja* flows from first to last with every page covered, including the end-leaves. The uniformity of the notebooks, and the manuscript itself, strongly suggest that the first draft was composed during a period of relatively constant work, from the first chapter to the last. The added sections on foolscap were clearly written at a later date, and all during approximately the same time period.

18. "dafür hatte ich ihnen das Manuskript zu liefern. Unter diesem Druck wurde der zweite Band fertig gemacht. Ich habe z.B. das Kapitel 'Der Zirkel' in einem Tag geschrieben, indem ich mich nach Mittag hinsetzte und bis tief in die Nacht sitzen blieb." *Gespräche*, p. 166.

19. The first case occurs on p. 51 of chapter 5. Since Jahnn wrote up a long list of words to be used in this passage on the back of a letter dated 17 December 1927 it is evident that the passage was unlikely to have been written before that date. The second case concerns chapter 3, which in its final version contains two examples of inner monologue (already quoted above). It was published separately, prior to the appearance of the novel, in the 22 January 1927 issue of the *Hamburger Anzeiger*. This pre-publication follows the manuscript exactly, and does not contain inner monologue. As late as April, 1929, the chapter was reprinted (still prior to the publication of the novel) in *Der Kreis*, once more *without* the lines of inner monologue. Therefore it is evident that Jahnn altered the lines involved between the Spring and Autumn of 1929.

20. For example the opening pages of chapters 5 and 8, and the final page of chapter 23.

21. Goyert translates this "unentrinnbare Modalität des Sichtbaren."

22. The final form of this poem is: "On swift sail flaming/ from storm and south/ He comes, pale vampire,/ Mouth to my mouth" (132:12).

23. See Weldon Thornton, *Allusions in Ulysses: An Annotated List* (Chapel Hill, 1968), p. 30. Smith suggests that Jahnn's reading of Joyce may have reminded him of Aristotle, but that in this passage we simply see "a unique example of coincidental selection by two great novelists" (pp. 113-114).

24. Jahnn's use of the inner monologue is similar to its most common use in *Ulysses*, that is, in conjunction and alternating with, more traditional styles of narration. Jahnn's short elliptic sentences are also typical of much of Joyce's prose when depicting thoughts, particularly in the case of Leopold Bloom. Jahnn was unlikely to have used the extreme unpunctuated form of Molly Bloom's monologue, which having once been done, admits only of imitation. But he could utilize the more general technique that Joyce had developed, and even extend it to fit his own narrative requirements, as, for example, when he wished to enter the mind of a horse (see p. 56 of *Perrudja*).

25. Wagner, p. 26, sees special significance in these musical quotations, which he feels go beyond the limits of that which may be expressed through language alone. He states: "Fast mutet es so an, als sei der Text um die 'wortlose Kompositionen' herumgeschrieben worden." In fact exactly the opposite was the case.

26. For a discussion of these leitmotifs and the way in which they function in the novel see Wagner, p. 38 ff.

27. There are twelve such occasions in *Perrudja*: pp. 46, 60-61, 66, 135, 239-240, 297, 327, 617-618.

28. ". . . die Wirklichkeit des menschlichen Daseins so vorurteilsfrei zu sehen, wie etwa Kafka in seinem Prozess." Unpublished letter to Dr. Bermann-Fischer, 3 December 1938.

7

JOYCE AND ALFRED DÖBLIN:
CREATIVE CATALYSIS

Unlike Hans Henny Jahnn, Alfred Döblin (1878-1957) was already a leading figure in German literary circles when *Ulysses* appeared. In 1910 he had been a co-founder of the highly important Expressionist periodical *Der Sturm*; he was recognized and respected by his intellectual contemporaries both as a writer and as a literary theoretician. From the end of the first World War (in which he served as a medic) until his exile in 1933, Döblin practiced medicine in a poor section of Berlin. His early literary reputation rested primarily upon his essays, and three long novels of imaginative richness and originality: *Die drei Sprünge des Wang-lun* (1915), *Wallenstein* (1920), and *Berge, Meere und Giganten* (1924).

As the Expressionist movement died out in Germany around 1924, Döblin was among those seeking for a new direction in prose fiction. His own answer to the "crisis" of the novel was his first great popular success, *Berlin Alexanderplatz* (1929). But his new fame was cut short by the political events of 1933, and he was forced into exile in Switzerland, France, and finally the United States. During this period he continued writing novels, including *Pardon wird nicht gegeben* (1935) and the *Amazonas* trilogy (1937/1948), and began a monumental prose work entitled *November 1918: eine deutsche Revolution* (published 1938/1950).

At the end of the war Döblin attempted to find a home again in West Germany, but the result was an unhappy one. Dissatisfied with the social developments of the new Germany, and feeling lonely and ignored within the post-war literary circles, he departed for Paris in 1953. By 1956, and the publication of his final novel, *Hamlet, oder die lange Nacht nimmt ein Ende*, his health had so deteriorated that he required constant medical attention. He died in the United States on 28 June 1957.

Döblin was almost fifty years old when the German version of *Ulysses* appeared, and he was well versed in the art of the novel. His opinion of Joyce's work was therefore of special interest to his contemporaries—so much so that Bertolt Brecht, for example, selected *Ulysses* as the book of the year in 1928 primarily upon Döblin's recommendation.[1] When Döblin's own eagerly-awaited new novel appeared in October of 1929 it was a major literary event.

Berlin Alexanderplatz was an immediate best-seller and gave its author the popular recognition which a small circle of admirers had never denied him. Within five years almost 50,000 copies had been sold,[2] translations had been made into several languages, and the hero of the novel, Franz Biberkopf, had been portrayed in a film version. Thus the story of the novel's reception offers a striking contrast to that of Jahnn's *Perrudja*, which had reached very few readers, and which was selling so poorly by the early thirties that the publishers were forced to lower the price substantially in an attempt to dispense with the remaining copies.[3] Döblin's success was aided by the fact that he was already an established novelist with an enthusiastic, if limited following and a well-known publisher. But the solid basis of his success was the novel itself.

Berlin Alexanderplatz takes its title from one of the main intersections of what is now East Berlin. In many ways the city itself is the true subject of the novel, which is often regarded as the first in German literature to depict a great metropolitan center in all its fullness and complexity. The story begins as Franz Biberkopf, recently released from prison, vows to start a new life, honestly and independently. Three hammer-blows of fate are required to teach him the didactic message of the book: that it is a mistake to pit the strength of the individual against the forces of life. Before he learns this lesson he suffers betrayal by a friend, the loss of an arm, and the murder of his sweetheart. Reduced to a hospital bed in a mental institution, like a modern variant of Job, he arises only when he ceases to revile his fate. The novel ends with his spiritual resurrection. Once more he begins life in Berlin, but now with a new insight and a new hope.

Berlin Alexanderplatz was a radical departure from Döblin's previous novels (nor was he ever again to write anything quite like it). Even on first review it seemed to introduce several technical innovations to the genre and thus to serve as a dynamic response to what many novelists felt was a crisis of literary expression. The search for an explanation of its particular characteristics began, not unreasonably, with its obvious surface resemblances to *Ulysses*.

Döblin himself had not hesitated to reveal his admiration for *Ulysses*. As early as the Spring of 1928 he reviewed Joyce's novel enthusiastically and emphasized in particular its stylistic innovations. Since he was a mature writer with his own ideas about what a novel should be, it was unthinkable, however, that Döblin would simply copy *Ulysses*. His unhappiness with those critics who immediately pointed to Joyce in reviewing *Berlin Alexanderplatz*[4] was both reasonable and understandable, insofar as many of them had failed to grasp the essential meaning of Döblin's novel in their rush to categorize it. In fact, as simple-minded summations of his work continued, he became more and more insistent in pointing out that this was not his only novel and that its most significant aspects (from his own point of view) had nothing to do with Joyce.

Nonetheless, Döblin's outspoken disappointment

with the reaction to *Berlin Alexanderplatz* has long been a stumbling block to those attempting to place that novel in its literary context[5]—for Joyce's work really is of great significance as a source for Döblin's volume. Just how much *Berlin Alexanderplatz* owes to *Ulysses* will become clear, I think, from the following close comparison of the original manuscript of the novel with the printed text.[6] Such a comparison answers many questions which otherwise would be left to the realm of speculation.

It is evident from Döblin's review of *Ulysses* early in 1928[7] that he read *Ulysses* while working on his own novel. But exactly how much of *Berlin Alexanderplatz* had he actually written at that time? In 1932 he remembered having read Joyce at a time when he had written "the first fourth" of his own book.[8] His novel consists of nine books written over a period of approximately one year, and the first *two* books (written in approximately four months, from October to January) represent over one-fifth of the printed text. If *Ulysses* had any real impact upon *Berlin Alexanderplatz*, we might expect to find a noticeable change within the manuscript itself, somewhere toward the end of the second book. As we shall see, this is in fact the case.

Although Döblin stated clearly in his review that authors must not imitate Joyce,[9] he did seem to feel that *Ulysses* offered a handy reference book of styles which no author could afford to ignore.[10] He specifically pointed out, for example, those technical innovations of the novel which seemed to him particularly effective. He placed special emphasis on the work's "scientific" objectivity and could not recall a more radical formal experiment in the novel in the last twenty years.[11] Strikingly, we find a similarly radical use of narrative techniques in *Berlin Alexanderplatz*. From the facts already presented, a strong case could be made for the impact of *Ulysses* on Döblin's novel. But the case is even stronger, and a careful scrutiny of the manuscript suggests these similarities are a direct result of his reading the "reference book" Joyce had produced.

I

Döblin wrote the first draft of *Berlin Alexanderplatz* leaving ample space between the lines of the manuscript, presumably for later corrections and additions. This spacing remains constant throughout the whole. By taking a relatively clear page of the manuscript and aligning it with a page which has been heavily reworked, it is possible to separate the first draft from the later additions with little difficulty. Among the most heavily reworked pages are those which open the novel, pages which include, in the printed version, an unusually lively mixture of such narrative techniques as inner monologue, "erlebte. Rede", third- and first-person narrative. Those who were familiar with Döblin's earlier work were not surprised that he was attempting to represent thought, conscious and subconscious, by means of standard narration and "erlebte Rede". What did surprise them was the extended use of inner monologue to represent thoughts, in conjunction with the other, more standard techniques, and the radicalness with which they were mixed. Such a mixture, characteristic of *Ulysses*, was not to be found in any of Döblin's prior novels.[12] An examination of these opening pages reveals some interesting facts about the composition of the novel, and helps us understand this radical development in Döblin's career.

Inner monologue is used extensively from the first page of the published text of *Berlin Alexanderplatz*. On the surface this would indicate that Döblin, who read Joyce only after writing a fourth of his own novel, was not here acting under the impact of *Ulysses*. But such an assumption[13] ignores the obvious question: were such instances of inner monologue always present, or do they first appear in subsequent revision of the manuscript? The answer is that in every instance for the opening pages of the novel, the lines of inner monologue are later additions to the first version. The original manuscript version of the first paragraph containing such phrases, for example, was as follows:[14]

Lebhafte Strassen tauchten auf, die Seestrasse, Leute stiegen ein und aus. Mittagzeitungen, Funkzeitschriften, Illustrierte wurden ausgerufen. Er hatte sich nicht gemeldet, als der Schaffner rief. Sie gingen unbeachtet wieder aus dem Wagen. Er war unter Gewimmel, welch Gewimmel, grauenhaftes Gewimmel. Wie sich das bewegte. Was war das alles. Schuhgeschäfte, Hutgeschäfte, Restaurants. Hundert blanke Scheiben. Man riss das Pflaster am Rosenthaler Platz auf, er ging zwischen den anderen auf Holzbohlen.

This passage is written in third-person narrative with two instances of "erlebte Rede" ("Wie sich das bewegte. Was war das alles"). It is not particularly revolutionary in style,[15] nor would it strike the reader as such. But Döblin reworked it in the manuscript stage, and what emerged was a striking use of the inner monologue in conjunction with third-person narrative, in a manner similar to *Ulysses* and new to the German novel. The following is the passage as expanded in the manuscript,[16] with the later insertions italicized:

Lebhafte Strassen tauchten auf, die Seestrasse, Leute stiegen ein und aus. *In ihm schrie es entsetzt: Achtung, Achtung, es geht los . . . Seine Nasenspitze vereiste, über seine Backe schwirrte es.* Mittagzeitungen, Funkzeitschriften, Illustrierte, *noch jemand zugestiegen . . . was die Schupos jetzt für Uniformen haben.* Er hatte sich nicht gemeldet, als der Schaffner rief. Er stieg unbeachtet wieder aus dem Wagen, war unter *Menschen . . . Was war denn? Nichts. Haltung, ausgehungertes Schwein, kriegt meine Faust zu riechen.* Gewimmel, welch Gewimmel. Wie sich das bewegte. *Mein Brägen hat kein Schmalz mehr, der . . . ist ausgetrocknet . . .* Was war das alles. Schuhgeschäfte, Hutgeschäfte, Destillen. *Die Menschen müssen doch Schuhe haben, wenn sie so viel rumlaufen, wir hatten ja auch eine Schusterei, wollen das mal festhalten.* Hundert blanke Scheiben *. . . die werden dich doch nicht bange machen . . . sind eben blankgeputzt.* Man riss das Pflaster am Rosenthaler Platz auf, er ging zwischen den andern auf Holzbohlen.

It is important to note here that these additions are not simply corrections of style and subject matter such as any author might normally make in rewriting a passage. They represent a clear decision to add inner monologue to the whole chapter as a new stylistic device.

Since Döblin made a conscious decision to rewrite the

opening pages of his novel using inner monologue, we might expect that at some point in the manuscript he would begin using it in the first draft. And this is the case. Slightly more than halfway through Book Two he begins to mix inner monologue with third-person narrative (pp. 68, 81 f.) in the original draft rather than by means of additions. No instances of inner monologue before this point are to be found in the first draft (although both "erlebte Rede" and the traditional "he thought" formula are occasionally mixed with the narrative in a way characteristic of some of Döblin's earlier experiments in prose). The inner monologue on p. 18 of the printed text was added in pencil in the manuscript, while two other long passages (pp. 33-36, 37-40) using this technique were so heavily reworked that the first draft has been replaced by a fair copy (with inner monologue).[17] The final instance of inner monologue in the first book (p. 44) is not present in the manuscript.

The use of the inner monologue was not the only literary device Döblin first employed in this novel while working on Book Two. In his review of *Ulysses* he had noted that the newspaper had forced its way into literature. It had become "the most important, most widely-spread written product, the daily bread of all men."[18] The insertion of paragraphs seemingly straight out of the newspaper into the text of *Berlin Alexanderplatz* is one of the standard devices of that novel. They give to the text the flavor of city life and the effect of *montage*. In investigating the manuscript we learn that Döblin was not parodying newspaper language but reproducing it—almost without exception from actual clippings. Moreover, it was his habit to paste the clipping directly upon the page of the manuscript. It is a simple matter, then, to determine at what point he had this idea. Almost halfway through Book Two (on p. 61 of the printed text, a few pages before the point at which inner monologue is first used in the original draft), the first newspaper clipping is pasted in. Thereafter, this technique is standard procedure. Döblin also returned to the earlier pages of the

novel and inserted newspaper items, verbatim, at a later
date. These may be found on pp. 39 and 51 of the printed
text, but they are not indicated in any way in the manuscript. The clippings themselves are lying loose in a collection of separate material in the archive. Only one of
the loose clippings is dated: 16 January 1928. Thus it
could not have been added before that date. *Ulysses* had
appeared in October 1927.

In reviewing *Ulysses*, Döblin had also referred to the
visual experience of the city, "the continuously changing
scenes on the street, the business signs, the automobile
traffic."[19] Each of these elements is present in *Berlin Alexanderplatz*, as we might expect; indeed they are to be found
in some of Döblin's earlier works. But never did he make
the extended and striking use of a montage of city impressions comparable to the beginning of Book Two:
"Franz Biberkopf betritt Berlin."[20] Here the reader is even
treated to pictorial symbols of the main facets of com-
merce in the city. This is followed in the printed text by
three newspaper clippings (including the one of 16 January 1928). The passage continues with a weather report,
a description of the stops of tram number 68 and its fare
schedule, and several business signs which are quoted
verbatim. The section closes with a description of each
street which leads onto the square, along with its major
houses of business, and the portrayal of several individuals
standing at the tram stop.

Taken as a whole, the section just outlined is a perfect demonstration of what Döblin meant by the experience of the city streets. It is therefore particularly interesting that the entire section was added at a later
date. The first draft of the manuscript continues directly
from the end of Book One (skipping the pages just described) to the bottom of p. 54 in Book Two. The first
instance of a similar full-scale attempt in the manuscript
at representing the streets, shops, and people around a
square is the opening section of Book Four ("Eine Hand-
voll Menschen um den Alex"). The later addition of the
opening section of Book Two changes the entire tone of

that chapter, shifting the emphasis from Franz's story
(the constant center point of the first draft) to the entity
of the city itself. This tends to increase both the scope
and the objectivity of the presentation.

Many of the stylistic details of this opening section
are strikingly reminiscent of *Ulysses*, and in particular of
the Wandering Rocks episode, which is precisely a depiction of the "continuously changing scenes on the street"
to which Döblin refers. In his manuscript Döblin wrote:
"Ein junges Mädchen steigt aus der 41. Es ist 8 Uhr
abends, sie hat eine Notenmappe unter dem Arm. . . ."
On the opening page of the Aeolus episode of *Ulysses*,
arranged by Joyce into "newspaper articles" with headlines, Döblin could read:

IN THE HEART OF THE HIBERNIAN METROPOLIS

BEFORE NELSON'S PILLAR TRAMS SLOWED, SHUNTED,
CHANGED trolley, started for Blackrock, Kingstown and Dalkey,
Clonskea, Rathgar and Terenure, Palmerston park and upper
Rathmines, Sandymount Green, Rathmines, Ringsend and Sandy-
mount Tower, Harold's Cross. The hoarse Dublin United Tramway
Company's timekeeper bawled them off:
   —Rathgar and Terenure!
   —Come on, Sandymount Green! (116:01)

And Döblin's final version in the printed text was to become (additions italicized):

Ein junges Mädchen steigt aus der 99, *Mariendorf, Lichtenrader
Chaussee, Tempelhof, Hallesches Tor, Hedwigskirche, Rosenthaler Platz,
Badstrasse, Seestrasse Ecke Togostrasse, in den Nächten von Sonnabend
zu Sonntag ununterbrochener Betrieb zwischen Uferstrasse und Tempelhof,
Friedrich-Karl-Strasse, in Abständen von 15 Minuten.* Es ist 8 Uhr abends,
sie hat eine Notenmappe unter dem Arm . . . (p. 58)

In *Ulysses* not only the film and the newspaper force
their way into language but the world of commercial advertisement as well. Döblin uses the language of advertisement in *Berlin Alexanderplatz* in much the same way as
Joyce does. But once more the manuscript reveals an
interesting fact: it was only well over halfway through
Book Two (p. 79) that Döblin began to insert advertise-

ments into his text. All earlier instances are subsequent additions not present in the first draft. Döblin had been particularly struck by the Ithaca episode of *Ulysses* with its exact question and answer style. One such passage reads:

> Quote the textual terms in which the prospectus claimed advantages for this thaumaturgic remedy.
> It heals and soothes while you sleep, in case of trouble in breaking wind, assists nature in the most formidable way, insuring instant relief in discharge of gases, keeping parts clean and free natural action, an initial outlay of 7/6 making a new man of you and life worth living. (722:01)

The first advertisement inserted into the text of *Berlin Alexanderplatz*, in Book One, intimated it could make a new man of Franz:

> Testifortan, geschütztes Warenzeichen Nr. 365695, Sexualtherapeutikum nach Sanitätsrat Dr. Magnus Hirschfeld und Dr. Bernhard Schapiro, Institut für Sexualwissenschaft, Berlin. Die Hauptursachen der Impotenz sind: A. ungenügende Ladung . . . B. . . . Erschöpfung des Erektionszentrums. Wann der Impotente die Versuche wieder aufnehmen soll, kann nur individuell aus dem Verlauf des Falls bestimmt werden. Eine Pause ist oft wertvoll. (p. 37)

This passage is not present in the manuscript.

Another method of introducing the commercial world into the novel is through the mind of the main character. Bloom's thoughts constantly return to this sphere:

> His ideas for ads . . . You can't lick 'em. What? Our envelopes. Hello! Jones, where are you going? Can't stop, Robinson, I am hastening to purchase the only reliable ink-eraser *Kansell*, sold by Hely's Ltd, Dame Street. Well out of that ruck I am. (154:39)

Franz is likewise unable to escape the advertisements that surround him:

> Nach zwei Tagen ist es wärmer, Franz hat seinen Mantel verkauft, trägt dicke Unterwäsche . . . steht am Rosenthaler Platz vor Fabischs Konfektion, Fabisch und Co., *feine Herrenschneiderei nach Mass, gediegene Verarbeitung und niedrige Preise sind die Merkmale unserer Erzeugnisse.* Franze schreit Schlipshalter aus . . . (p. 69)

The italicized portion was added between the lines of the first draft.

A final link between the two novels may be seen in those sections of *Berlin Alexanderplatz* which parody the scientific style. The scientific "objectivity" Döblin praised in *Ulysses* may well have influenced those pages entitled "Ausmasse dieses Franz Biberkopf. Er kann es mit alten Helden aufnehmen." By its title alone this passage reminds the reader of Leopold Bloom, that other match for an old hero, Ulysses. The style of these pages is exactly that of the Ithaca episode of *Ulysses*, in which the humor comes from the unexpectedly precise scientific language employed to describe human actions. Bloom, who has forgotten the key to his house, lowers himself over the area railing and drops to the pavement. The result is described in language typical of the whole episode:

> Regaining new stable equilibrium he rose uninjured though concussed by the impact, raised the latch of the area door by the exertion of force at its freely moving flange and by leverage of the first kind applied at its fulcrum gained retarded access to the kitchen through the subadjacent scullery . . . (669:03)

Franz's attack upon Ida is described by Döblin with even greater scientific precision. The effect of the blows upon Ida "hängt zusammen mit den Gesetzen von Starre und Elastizität, und Stoss und Widerstand." In order to express exactly what happened Newton's first and second laws of motion are quoted literally. In addition the magnitude and acceleration of the force involved are expressed by means of two complicated mathematical formulas. (p. 105). He then compares Ida's death with the murder of the returning Agamemnon and notes that the signal fires of antiquity have been replaced by Hertz's wireless telegraph. ("Begeistern daran kann man sich schwer; es funktioniert, und damit fertig.")

This entire section, with its extended parody of the scientific style, is not present in the first draft. Instead it appears as "Beiblatt R," and the point at which Döblin later decided to insert it is clearly indicated in pencil in the manuscript. The length of this section, as well as its memorable visual impact through the use of formulas, results in the general impression that Döblin relies a great deal upon "scientific" presentation in the novel. But in fact, with the possible exception of the weather report on p. 51 (also a "Beiblatt" addition), the only other prior passage in this style in the novel is to be found on p. 34 (Book One) of the printed text: Franz has just failed in his purpose in visiting a prostitute. He asks himself what the problem is, and the answer follows in a long scientific description of the physiological processes of sexual potency and performance, including a listing of those psychological factors which can disturb the normal functioning of the system. Several pages of manuscript in this section have been rewritten and inserted in place of the first draft. Yet even in this rewritten section of the manuscript the "scientific" passage is not present (nor is there even any indication that a later addition is intended). The conclusion must be that the "scientific" passage represents an addition even later than the period of rewriting which introduced inner monologue into the text.

These findings may be summed up briefly. In 1928 Alfred Döblin had suggested that *Ulysses* should be studied by all serious writers since it was a valuable reference book of stylistic devices. While working on his own novel Döblin praised many aspects of *Ulysses* which were to be found in a similar form in the published version of his own novel two years later. The manuscript shows that the first book and half of the second were originally written without inner monologue, without the *montage* effects of inserted newspaper articles and advertisements, and without parodies of the scientific style. These elements were later additions to the manuscript, and reflected a conscious decision to employ new techniques in the novel, and not random rephrasing. As might be expected, other formal elements of the novel were even later additions. The introductory passages to each book, as well as the titles for the various sections (sometimes obviously intended to remind the reader of newspaper headlines), are not present in any stage of the manuscript, with the exception of the introduction to Book Nine, which is on a separate loose leaf. The voice which, beginning with the first paragraph of the novel, intermittently interrupts the text to speak to Franz between brackets is present only in the later books of the manuscript.[21]

On the basis of this evidence we may assert that Döblin, having read *Ulysses* sometime in the winter of 1927-28, made use of those elements in it which particularly appealed to his own sense of what a novel should be. These elements were to him only a means to an end very different from that of *Ulysses*. That the critics chose to concentrate upon those characteristics of the work which were reminiscent of *Ulysses* and to ignore what Döblin himself considered to be the actual substance of the work, the language of his city, Berlin, and the spiritual odyssey of Franz Biberkopf, came to anger him more and more in the coming years. Until disillusion set in he continued to praise *Ulysses*, and even to identify himself with Joyce. Max Tau, whose critical essay on Joyce had been published by *Die neueren Sprachen*, tells of a telephone call he received immediately after he had attacked Joyce on a radio program in the early thirties:

> I had hardly left the studio when I was called to the phone. 'Max Tau,' said a very likeable voice, 'this is Alfred Döblin. I understood you. You spoke against James Joyce and had me in mind. We must talk soon.'[22]

This is a telling comment upon the extent to which Döblin identified with Joyce in a literary sense.

II

Previously undiscovered evidence suggests that Döblin may have received a further, indirect, impetus from Joyce's work through Hans Henny Jahnn. In an unpublished letter of 24 February 1929, Jahnn wrote to Döblin asking him to read two chapters of the manuscript of *Perrudja*, and requesting him, "wenn Sie sie für passabel halten, einige Worte darüber zu schreiben." There is no indication which two chapters were involved. But they arrived in Döblin's hands eight months before either *Perrudja* or *Berlin Alexanderplatz* was published.[23] It is conceivable, although unlikely, that Döblin never looked at these chapters until his own novel was published. But the use of a mixture of inner monologue and third person narrative would undoubtedly have appealed to him, as well as Jahnn's own type of montage effects. Döblin would certainly have recognized stylistic similarities with his own work. The first definite proof that Döblin read *Perrudja* is in an unpublished letter of 21 January 1930. But by that time he was reading the printed version. There is no indication why he waited so long to answer Jahnn. He writes: "I'm reading *Perrudja* daily. There are splendid things in it, it's giving me great pleasure—when I'm finished I'll publish a few notes on it."[24] Around this time Döblin was asked by a periodical to recommend twelve books to readers. His reply is revealing:

> This puts me in a very bad position. I can't think of twelve books—not even twelve books from world literature before the war. If I have time, and peace and quiet, and think it over, I have an author with me who fills this time with quiet pleasure. My first choice for the time being—the daily newspapers. After that I might occasionally look into James Joyce's *Ulysses*, and Hans H. Jahnn's recently published private edition of *Perrudja*; I'd sleep a lot, and leave the reading to others.[25]

Among those interested in *Berlin Alexanderplatz* was Eugene Jolas, editor of *transition* and Joyce's personal friend. By 1931 he had translated the novel into "American," and, predictably, the advertisements termed it "the first novel in modern German literature to adopt the influential Joyce technique."[26] By 1932, Döblin was beginning to tire of his first great popular success's being called an imitation. He stressed the fact that he had not read Joyce until he had written the first fourth of his own novel, and continued:

> Later his work delighted me, as I've said and written many times, and it was a good wind in my sails. Similar, even identical, effects may be produced at the same time in different places, independently of each other.[27]

Döblin was never to become precise about in which sense Joyce was a good wind in his sails—or whether this might be taken to refer specifically to the last three-quarters of his novel. During his lecture in 1932 he stressed his own inability to analyze Joyce's influence on his work:

> Joyce is a magnificent writer, a pioneer of style, and thus also of narrative technique. I myself am not able to analyze whether and which Joycean influences are demonstrable in my last book. I do know, however, that Joyce has nothing to do with the essential parts of my work; only peripheral similarities are concerned.[28]

It is not difficult to understand what Döblin means here. He does not deny an influence from Joyce, but only maintains that such an influence would touch only the surface qualities of the book, and not its essential nature. For Döblin both the special use of the German language and the basic message and intent of the novel were aspects having nothing to do with *Ulysses*. As he was to write in 1955:

> What they didn't construe later as a model or influence! I'm said to have imitated the Irishman Joyce. I don't find it necessary to imitate anyone. All I need is the living language surrounding me, and my past provides me with all imaginable material.[29]

Döblin's later distaste for crude references to imitation is particularly understandable in the light of his own unhappy position. When he left Germany for the second time, in 1953, his bitterness towards a public he felt had forgotten him was common knowledge among his fellow writers. Jahnn wrote to him sympathetically: "I well understand that you feel betrayed and sold, at any rate isolated, sick and tired. But it is *not* the case that all of us have forgotten you."[30] Whereas before the war Döblin was willing to admit some influence from Joyce upon at least the surface qualities of the work, by 1955 he was obviously profoundly tired of the whole question.

Paradoxically enough, it was the tremendous success of *Berlin Alexanderplatz* which was at the root of much of Döblin's anger. Had his novel been spared the critical spotlight for a few years, as was Jahnn's *Perrudja*, he too might have continued unabated in his praise for *Ulysses*, recommending that serious young writers should study it. But in fact the public in general was impressed by what he considered the surface qualities, and demonstrated a total lack of concern for what he felt was the real substance of the novel. In later years he tended to turn away from many of those stylistic features which related his work to that of Joyce. Just as Hans Henny Jahnn felt unable to return to the "expressionistic" forms of *Perrudja* in later life, so Alfred Döblin was never to repeat the stylistic innovations of *Berlin Alexanderplatz* on such a scale. If one, for example, glances at his *Pardon wird nicht gegeben* (1935), another novel set in Berlin, the complete change in approach is immediately obvious. Yet the extensive use of inner monologue is retained. *Berlin Alexanderplatz* was the turning point in Döblin's use of this technique.

Joyce's importance in Döblin's development is not lessened by the fact that *Ulysses'* influence may have been largely catalytic. It is true that much may be found in Döblin's early work to indicate the direction he later took. And certainly Döblin was able to work creatively with whatever impulses he received. But without Joyce the evidence suggests that *Berlin Alexanderplatz* might never have achieved its final form. In the final analysis the novel stands both as a witness to the impact of *Ulysses* upon Döblin's development as a writer, and as a testimony to his own power, skill and originality. Much more widely read than *Perrudja*, *Berlin Alexanderplatz* was the first German novel to introduce to a wide circle of readers a number of new literary techniques which were to become, in the course of time, the common property of all writers.

1. ". . . weil er [*Ulysses*] nach Ansicht Döblins die Situation des Romans verändert hat und als Sammlung verschiedener Methoden der Betrachtung (Einführung des inneren Monologs und so weiter) ein unentbehrliches Nachschlagewerk für Schriftsteller darstellt." Bertolt Brecht, *Schriften zur Literatur und Kunst* (Frankfurt/M., 1967), I, 82.

2. See Walter Muschg, "Nachwort," *Berlin Alexanderplatz* (Olten, 1961), p. 509. By way of comparison, *Ulysses*, in German translation, had sold a total of around sixty thousand copies by 1956, according to the Rhein-Verlag edition of that year.

3. Unpublished letter of 26 February 1933 to Jahnn from J. Meyer.

4. Including Walter Muschg, who later denied the influence he attributed to Joyce in his review of *Berlin Alexanderplatz* in 1930: "Es ist mit Händen zu greifen, dass [der Roman] unter dem Eindruck des Joyce'schen *Ulysses* entstanden ist." "Ein Stoss Bücher," *Schweizerische Monatshefte für Politik und Kultur* (April, 1930), p. 48. Reprinted in *Alfred Döblin im Spiegel der zeitgenössischen Kritik*, ed. Ingrid Schuster and Ingrid Bode (Bern, 1973), pp. 246-247; hereafter cited as *Döblin Kritik*. This collection of contemporary essays includes reprints of twenty-six reviews of *Berlin Alexanderplatz*. Among those critics referring specifically to Joyce in connection with Döblin's novel were Julius Bab (p. 210), Efraim Frisch (p. 218), Herbert Ihering (p. 226), H. A. Wyss (p. 241), Axel Eggebrecht (p. 244), Walter Benjamin (p. 251), Felix Bertaux (p. 254), and Albin Stübs (p. 266), as well as Muschg and Hans Henny Jahnn. Although Joyce's name was often invoked, there was, from the start, sharp disagreement about the extent and importance of his influence on Döblin. I have suggested below that Döblin may have received an indirect impetus from *Ulysses* through his reading of two manuscript chapters of Jahnn's *Perrudja*. Jahnn's own review of *Berlin Alexanderplatz* is particularly interesting in this connection: "Vor einem Jahr oder vor zweien rief Alfred Döblin seinen Mitdichtern und Mitmenschen zu: lest den *Ulysses* des James Joyce! Wie viele sich mit ihm im Lob dieses katholischsten, unerschrockensten, vielleicht besten neueren Romanes vereinigt haben, der ein Wendepunkt des Schreibstils, eine Steigerung der Ausdrucksmöglichkeit jetziger Sprachen bedeutete, weiss ich nicht. Doch in dem neuen Buch Döblins ist zu erkennen, er selbst hat sich viele Übungen des irischen Dichters zum Vorbild genommen." *Der Kreis*, VI (1929), 735; reprinted in *Döblin Kritik*, pp. 227-228.

5. The primary studies which have dealt with Joyce and Döblin in some detail are: H. Szulanski, "Eine Parallele zwischen James Joyce und Alfred Döblin" (Diss. Brussels, 1949); Helmut Becker, *Untersuchung zum epischen Werk Alfred Döblins am Beispiel seines Romans Berlin Alexanderplatz* (Diss. Marburg, 1962), pp. 202-213; Francis Lide, "*Berlin Alexanderplatz* in Context: Alfred Döblin's literary Practice" (Diss. Illinois, 1966); C. Zalubska, "Parallelen der Erzähltechnik in den Werken von Alfred Döblin und James Joyce," *Studia Germanica Posaniensia* I (1971), 59-67; and Andrew McLean, "Joyce's *Ulysses* and Döblin's *Alexanderplatz Berlin*," *Comparative Literature*, XXV (1973), 97-113. All of these studies are based solely on the printed version. More recently Joris Duytschaever has reiterated the suggestion that Joyce functioned simply as a catalyst for Döblin, and points to such works as *Der schwarze Vorhang* to support his point. See Duytschaever, "Joyce—Dos Passos—Döblin: Einfluss oder Analogie?" *Materialien zu Alfred Döblin: Berlin Alexanderplatz*, ed. Matthias Prangel, Frankfurt/M., 1975, pp. 136-149.

6. The original manuscript of *Berlin Alexanderplatz* is now in the possession of the Deutsches-Literaturarchiv, Schiller-Nationalmuseum, Marbach/Neckar. It consists of scores of individual "Hefte," which are often numbered in Döblin's hand and are arranged according to the printed text. The individual sections of the manuscript are loose-leaf and the pages are unnumbered. The whole of the first draft is written on pages 6 1/2 by 8 1/4 inches. In addition there are a great number of "Beiblätter" (as Döblin labelled them) on

various-sized paper which contain text to be inserted at certain indicated points in the manuscript.

7.   Döblin, "*Ulysses* von Joyce," *Das deutsche Buch*, VIII (1928), 84-85; reprinted in *Alfred Döblin: Aufsätze zur Literatur*, ed. Walter Muschg (Olten, 1963), pp. 287 ff. In his review Döblin refers to having read Alexander West's "careful analysis" of *Ulysses*, which had been published in 1927. West's article may have been seminal. He speaks of Bloom as "der Sohn der grossen Mutter, welche Stadt heisst," and continues: "Die genaue Schilderung des städtischen Menschentyps . . . ist ja die Entweihung des einstigen hochpersönlichen Ziels: eine sublime, parodierende Rache an der Übermacht der Städte." John Alexander West, "Über den *Ulysses*," *Annalen*, I (1927), 510-516. Döblin may well have been strengthened in his own ideas with regard to Franz Biberkopf and Berlin by this early article on Joyce's work.

8.   "Mein Buch *Berlin Alexanderplatz* 1932," reprinted in Walter-Verlag edition of the novel, p. 506.

9.   ". . . man muss es nicht so machen, wie es Joyce gemacht hat. Die Bahn ist nicht eingleisig. Dies ist ja auch ein Experimentierwerk, weder ein Roman noch eine Dichtung, sondern ein Beklopfen ihrer Grundelemente." *Aufsätze zur Literatur*, p. 288 (see note 7 of this chapter).

10.   *Ibid.*, p. 290. "Es ist ein literarischer Vorstoss aus dem Gewissen des heutigen geistigen Menschen heraus. Es sucht auf seine Weise die Frage zu beantworten: wie kann man heute dichten? Zunächst hat jeder ernste Schriftsteller sich mit diesem Buch zu befassen . . ."

11.   *Ibid.*, p. 287.

12.   There is no instance of inner monologue, for example, in *Die drei Sprünge des Wang-lun*, which is at all like the extended use of that technique in *Berlin Alexanderplatz*. In all of *Wallenstein* there is only one line written in inner monologue and using the first person (p. 464). In none of the longer novels can one speak of an extended use of the inner monologue, although "erlebte Rede" is fairly common. In his shorter prose works Döblin's tendency is in the direction of the techniques of *Berlin Alexanderplatz* is clearly evident, although still in a very unrefined stage. What he seemed unable to do was to develop and utilize these techniques effectively in the novel (see note 20 below).

13.   See Lide, p. 187. A similar assumption is made by Klaus Müller-Salget, in *Alfred Döblin: Werk und Entwicklung* (Bonn, 1972) pp. 286-293.

14.   This transcription of the first draft does not take into account the manuscript additions and revisions. Becker, p. 172, quotes the opening page of the manuscript without distinguishing between the phases of its composition.

15.   The first draft is very typical of Döblin's earlier attempts at depicting human consciousness in interaction with the real world. The mixture of "erlebte Rede" and third-person narrative, at times even within a sentence, the rush of sensory impressions obscuring the distinction between narration and thought, a sort of incipient *montage*—all are present. But in the past Döblin had been able to go no further.

16.   Compare with p. 13 of the printed text. This passage still exhibits some variations from the final version. Words which Döblin inserted between the lines and then crossed out have not been transcribed. Words which were not taken over into the printed text have been omitted (indicated by ellipses). All page references to the printed text are to the 1961 Walter Verlag edition of *Berlin Alexanderplatz*.

17.   This is particularly clear in the manuscript on those pages corresponding to p. 33 of the printed text. Lines of inner monologue are either absent or additions between the lines up to "Er mit den Augen immer hinter ihr her." At this point the first draft is completely crossed out and on the following (loose) pages the passage (including the new form of the half-page scratched

out) is rewritten very clearly and with very few additions or corrections. This rewritten passage continues to p. 36 of the printed text.

The manuscript of *Berlin Alexanderplatz* is notoriously difficult to decipher and Klaus Müller-Salget has recently suggested that one previous example of inner monologue (ten words in length) is in fact present in the manuscript corresponding to page 31 of the printed text. To my mind this does not materially affect the basic strength of the argument presented here. See Müller-Salget, "Zur Entstehung von Döblins *Berlin Alexanderplatz*," *Materialien zu Alfred Döblin: Berlin Alexanderplatz*, ed. Matthias Prangel, Frankfurt/M., 1975, pp. 117-135.

18. Döblin, *Aufsätze zur Literatur*, p. 288. ". . . die Zeitungen sind gross geworden, sind das wichtigste, verbreitetste Schrifterzeugnis, sind das tägliche Brot aller Menschen."

19. *Ibid.*, p. 288. "Zum Erlebenisbild der heutigen Menschen gehören ferner die Strassen, die sekündlich wechselnden Szenen auf der Strasse, die Firmenschilder, der Wagenverkehr."

20. Compare for example with Döblin's early novel set in Berlin, *Wadzeks Kampf mit der Dampfturbine* (Berlin, 1918) which he himself considered a failure. The novel also makes an interesting comparison from the point of view of the use of inner monologue, and illustrates clearly the gap between the very infrequent and tentative attempts at this technique in Döblin's early work, including *Der schwarze Vorhang*, and its full and effective use in *Berlin Alexanderplatz*.

21. The prepublication of the opening pages of the novel in *Die neue Rundschau*, XXXIX (1928), pp. 124 ff., does not include these phrases, although the inserted lines of inner monologue are present.

22. "Ich hatte kaum das Studio verlassen, da wurde ich ans Telephon gerufen. "Max Tau," sagte eine sehr sympathische Stimme, "hier ist Alfred Döblin. Ich habe Sie verstanden. Sie haben gegen James Joyce gesprochen und mich gemeint. Wir müssen uns bald sprechen." Max Tau, *Das Land das ich verlassen musste* (Hamburg, 1961), p. 203.

23. In an unpublished letter of 21 March 1929, Jahnn wrote to Oskar Loerke (whom he had asked to deliver the chapters) that he had no word yet from Döblin. Loerke replied that he had given them to Döblin (unpublished postcard of 22 March 1929).

24. "Ich lese täglich *Perrudja*. Es hat herrliche Sachen, ich habe grosse Freude daran—wenn ich durch bin werde ich ein paar Notizen darüber veröffentlichen."

25. "Ich bin da in einer sehr schlechten Lage. Zwölf Bücher finde ich nicht zusammen—nicht einmal zwölf Bücher aus der Weltliteratur der Vorkriegszeit! Wenn ich Zeit und Ruhe habe, denke ich selbst nach, habe einen Autor bei mir, der diese Zeit mit Ruhe und Freude an sich reisst. Mein nächster Autor für die Dauer—die Tageszeitungen. Dann würde ich gelegentlich in den *Ulysses* von James Joyce sehen, in Hans H. Jahnns eben erschienenen Privatdruck: *Perrudja*, ich würde viel schlafen und das Lesen anderen überlassen." Undated clipping in the miscellaneous Döblin file, Deutsches-Literaturarchiv, Schiller-Nationalmuseum.

26. Quoted from the dust jacket.

27. "Später hat mich ja sein Werk, wie ich auch öfter gesagt und geschrieben habe, entzückt, und es war ein guter Wind in meinen Segeln. Dieselbe Zeit kann unabhängig voneinander Ähnliches, ja Gleiches an verschiedenen Stellen erzeugen." Döblin, p. 506 (see note 2 of this chapter).

28. "Joyce ist ein grossartiger Schriftsteller, ein Pionier im Stilistischen und darum auch in der Darstellungsweise. Ich vermag selbst nicht zu analysieren, ob und welche Einflüsse von Joyce bei meinem letzten Buch nachweisbar sind. Ich weiss aber dass mit wesentlichen Bestandteilen meiner

Arbeit Joyce nichts zu tun hat, es kann sich nur um periphere Ähnlichkeiten handeln." Döblin, unpublished typescript for his lecture before the "Lesezirkel Hottingen" in Zurich, February, 1932. The typescript gives Döblin's answers to several questions sent to him in advance.

29. "Was hat man später als Vorbild oder Anregung konstruiert! Ich soll den irischen Joyce imitiert haben. Ich habe is nicht nötig, irgend jemanden zu imitieren. Die lebende Sprache, die mich umgibt, ist mir genug, und meine Vergangenheit liefert mir alles erdenkliche Material." Döblin, p. 508 (see note 2 of this chapter).

30. "Ich verstehe wohl, dass Sie sich verraten ud verkauft, jedenfalls vereinsamt, krank und müde fühlen. Aber es ist doch nicht so, dass wir alle Sie vergessen hätten." Unpublished letter of 15 May 1953.

8

JOYCE AND HERMANN BROCH:
THE READER DIGESTS

Joyce's name was linked to that of Hermann Broch from the very start of the publicity campaign which surrounded the appearance of *Die Schlafwandler*. What few people then realized was that the comparison was suggested, indeed insisted upon, by Broch himself. When later critics referred to him as an "Austrian Joyce, and an almost Biedermeier-Joyce,"[1] Broch simply witnessed the fruits of the seeds he himself had sown.[2]

Broch (1886-1951) turned to writing relatively late in life. As a student his dream had been to become a professor of mathematics, but his family background led him towards the industrial world and his father's factories. He was by no means forced to take this course, but he desired to unite all of these possibilities into one life. As he expressed it:

> . . . suddenly I was in charge of my father's factories, there was the war, post-war and crises, and I rose in rank in the industrial world. I became what is called a captain of industry, and seemed trapped for life, all the more so because I had slowly taken over responsibility for my whole family, including my aged parents.[3]

In 1927 he succeeded in selling his factories (which proved, in the light of later events, to have been a fortu-

nate financial move) and devoted himself once more to
the study of mathematics and philosophy. He was interested in writing, and in particular in creating a literary
synthesis of science, mathematics, and literature.

His first novel-trilogy, *Die Schlafwandler* (1931/1932),
placed him immediately among a handful of writers
whose literary creativity was accompanied by intellectual
ability of the highest order. His quiet life as a writer was
interrupted in 1938 when he was arrested by the Gestapo
during the occupation of Austria. With the help of some
influential friends he was allowed to leave for France and
subsequently the United States. A second major work,
Der Tod des Vergil, appeared in 1945. In it Broch approached the problem of the artist and his relationship to
the state, in a parallel with obvious overtones for his own
questions about the justification of art removed from the
world. In 1950 he became professor of German literature at Yale University, and was nominated in that same
year for the Nobel Prize. He died in New Haven in 1951.

Die Schlafwandler consists of three sections set at fifteen-
year intervals: *Pasenow oder die Romantik 1888*, *Esch oder
die Anarchie 1903*, and *Huguenau oder die Sachlichkeit 1918*.
In them Broch traces the dissolution of German middle-
class society, the disintegration of values, and the rise of
the new, spiritually impoverished man. The three volumes are linked with each other by both theme and character. In the first novel, set in Berlin, the military officer
Joachim von Pasenow still lives in a society marked by
empty notions of honor and a rigid conventionality.
Forced to enter civilian life as the manager of his father's
estate, he finds the desire to make a "proper" marriage
stronger than his natural inclinations for a girl he truly
loves. He marries another woman, with the approval of
society, and gives himself up to a life of form without
content. In the second volume Esch, a bookkeeper whose
goal in life is to rise socially at all costs, represents the
development of the age around 1903 toward the typical
city-dweller of the German Rhineland. The third and final
volume shows the triumph of Huguenau, a completely

amoral deserter from the army (thus representing the final breakdown of that military order which was Pasenow's security in 1888). In the disturbed world of 1918, Huguenau alone seems truly at home.

This carefully constructed trilogy occupies an important place in German literature not only for its perceptive and sensitive depiction of German society over a thirty-year period but also for its formal innovations. The structure of each book in part reflects the social stage depicted, and the general fragmentation of man is reflected in an increasingly fragmented narrative style. By the third book, philosophical essays alternate with short narrative sections in a way unknown in previous German literature. The whole structure of the trilogy makes it one of the most carefully built works of art in the twentieth century. The full import of the carefully interwoven symbols and leitmotifs is granted to the reader only through close study.

The coincidence of the publication of the German Ulysses and Broch's return to the active intellectual life in 1927 was of course pure chance. Although he could scarcely have escaped hearing about Ulysses in Vienna, he did not actually read the novel until he had completed the first version of his own work in 1930.[4] As a result the impact of Ulysses upon Die Schlafwandler differed in several essential respects from the literary relationship of Joyce, Döblin, and Jahnn. Only by taking into account both the development of critical appreciation and the improvement of the German translation, can Broch's attitude toward Joyce's work be properly set in its literary and historical context.

I

Hermann Broch's high opinion of Joyce can be gathered from his letters and essays, as well as from the thirty-two-page pamphlet he devoted to Joyce, entitled James Joyce und die Gegenwart (published in 1936, based primarily upon a lecture delivered in 1932). Broch's in-

terest amounted at times to an obsession, and his admiration for the Irish writer was repeatedly evident in his
letters. In 1931 he wrote to Willa Muir:

> Concerning my relationship to Joyce I can only say one thing: if I
> had known *Ulysses* before I had written *Die Schlafwandler* it would
> have remained unwritten—for I see in *Ulysses* a perfect realization
> of everything which it is possible to express in a novel. That goal
> which I had in mind in my work, "to get beneath the skin" in my
> writing, I find completely fulfilled in Joyce, and I am convinced
> that literature, insofar as it remains an expression of modern life,
> will come more and more under the Joycean influence.[5]

It is difficult to imagine how a literary work could have any
greater impact than the one implied here—but only implied, for Broch after all is talking about what might
have happened. The actual story of the literary relationship involved is a complex one. As with Döblin, the
sweeping generalizations of those who dismissed Broch
as simply an Austrian disciple of James Joyce were misleading in the extreme, and Broch felt called upon,
many years later, to defend himself against this charge:

> Superficial observers believe that I am seeking to emulate Joyce,
> because I have occupied myself with him in regard to matters of
> theory. After what has been said I need not even protest that that
> is far from my intention. In order to follow his path I would have to
> bring my own methods and technique to an intensity to match his.
> Leaving aside the fact that my strength is probably not equal to
> the task, it is also not my ambition.[6]

Broch's continuing high regard for Joyce is obvious, but
for those who think he is still striving to emulate Joyce in
1951 he continues: "In the time I have remaining in life
I wish to complete my theory of perception and my other
scholarly work, simply because I consider them more
important than literature."[7]

Of course Broch's attitude to Joyce and *Ulysses* developed and changed during the course of the years, just
as did his attitude toward his own work over the same
period. What we are concerned with, however, is his attitude in the early thirties, when he was rewriting the
third section of his own novel; for in spite of Broch's

statement that he would never have written *Die Schlaf-wandler* had he known Joyce's work, manuscript evidence shows conclusively that he did in fact revise and greatly expand the third section of his novel, after reading *Ulysses*.[8]

II

Broch began writing *Die Schlafwandler* in 1928, and by early 1930 the novel was in what he then thought to be its final form.[9] It consisted of the two sections "Pasenow" and "Esch" (of approximately equal length) and a short "Epilog"; he intended to publish them together as a one-volume novel. It is clear that at this point he considered *Die Schlafwandler* finished, and had no intention of altering it significantly. He began to look for a publisher and turned first to the Fischer Verlag. Fischer, who had had phenomenal success twenty-five years earlier with Thomas Mann's first novel *Buddenbrooks*, advised Broch to suppress parts II and III of the novel and simply continue "Pasenow" as a "type of family novel."[10]

It was at this point that Broch first read *Ulysses*,[11] and its effect was immediate and profound:

> . . . since reading *Ulysses* I have stopped work on a second novel which I had already begun, because I see a parallel direction in our efforts and too great a gap in our abilities. . . first I must digest the Joyce phenomenon.[12]

Broch's use of the term "digest" (verdauen) pointed to the core of the problem: Joyce and *Ulysses* had to be converted in some manner, assimilated into Broch's own creative life. His notion of the ideal novel, as expressed in this same letter to Frank Thiess, reads like a description of *Ulysses* itself, and Broch continued:

> What I admire in Joyce is his close approximation to the ideal state I demand, and indeed in a fullness, breadth, and depth of the irrational such as I have not previously experienced. Naturally I know that the path that I seek to the work of art, and that Joyce has taken so decisively, is not the only one which leads to the goal, and that there are also other possibilities to seize unity and the irrational . . . but for me, probably because of my mathematical-constructivist talent, another path seems hardly practicable.[13]

Broch's decision to reject Fischer's suggestion, and insist upon the publication of all three sections of *Die Schlaf-wandler*, may have been the first positive result of his reading of *Ulysses*. He considered Fischer's idea "a maximum concession to the publisher and public with which I will have nothing to do."[14] Broch realized the danger of an overly difficult text. Yet he felt compelled to express himself freely in his own way, and let the average reader fend for himself. Joyce's example was a decisive one:

> Joyce seems to me important with regard to the problem of the "reader" . . . *Ulysses* is a thoroughly unlikeable book which takes no account of the reader and if possible slaps him in the face on every page. . . . I am convinced that one gets nowhere with "concessions to the reader." I find it a terribly difficult problem, for expressing myself as a writer and scholar is a vital necessity to me.[15]

This same letter contains the first indication of Broch's interest in the firm which was finally to publish *Die Schlaf-wandler*: "I would have a certain tendency toward the Rhein-Verlag simply because my literary super-ego Joyce was published there."[16] One week after these lines were written the manuscript of Broch's novel arrived at the Rhein-Verlag offices.[17]

An agreement was soon reached, and in June, Broch was making a few minor alterations in the text of the first section, at the suggestion of the director Daniel Brody. But Brody's wife played an even more important role at this point by helping to free Broch from his initial paralysis in the face of Joyce's achievement. Broch wrote to her:

> . . . there doesn't seem to be anything else to do but to write further novels, in spite of Joyce. I even believe—this became clear to me on the way home after our conversation of Sunday afternoon; thus I owe it to you!—that it will be possible.[18]

Broch had concluded that what he was seeking was a "novel of perceptual theory" rather than a psychological novel, and in this sense "something that does not lie in the direction of Joyce (and that was lost to me in fright over

Joyce)."[19] The possibility of a new literary form lay in this direction, and Broch promised to send Frau Brody a few chapters of this "future book."

Freed at least in part from Joyce's inhibiting effect, Broch tactfully suggested to his publishers that his name be coupled with Joyce's in promoting *Die Schlafwandler*. Fischer had already warned him against such a proposal:

> . . . since all the bookdealers were said to be having unpleasant difficulties with their customers because of Joyce: if *Ulysses* hadn't been sold through subscription 9/10ths of the readers would have given the book back to the bookhandlers as unreadable. Now he maintains that making a parallel between *Ulysses* and *Die Schlafwandler* would give it the stigma of unreadability from the beginning. . . . I think that neither objection holds water, particularly because the parallel with Joyce is such an honor to me that I would even sacrifice for it.[20]

This parallel indeed became part of the standard advertisements for *Die Schlafwandler*, and Broch was obviously pleased. For in spite of his denial in later years that he wished to emulate Joyce, that was certainly his ambition in the early thirties:

> . . . *Die Schlafwandler*, as I well know, is a very important book. . . . The reputation of the Rhein-Verlag is founded upon the absolute work of art, *Ulysses*; *Die Schlafwandler* must maintain this level: I would never have come to you if this had not been my ambition.[21]

In August of 1930 Broch reached two important decisions which were to affect the text of *Die Schlafwandler*. This first was to delete almost the entire first chapter of the original version of "Huguenau":

> Now I am on Huguenau, and I would like to ask you a few things: you remember that Huguenau opens with a (certainly light) parallel to Odysseus, and that the analogy to the Odyssey is mentioned a few more times in the course of events. Do you consider it necessary to remove this, because of *Ulysses*?[22]

In spite of Brody's feeling that this was unnecessary,[23] Broch followed through on his own suggestion, the only case of a substantial deletion of material from the original form of the novel. As Broch had indicated, the parallel to the *Odyssey* was only lightly touched upon, and he did not bother to delete those brief references which reoccurred later in that section. But it is clear that, after *Ulysses*, he found it impossible to start Huguenau with a sentence which began "Wurde Odysseus in vorgerückten Jahren, da er täglich nur noch vor den Palast sich bringen liess, um sein erkaltendes Blut auf der besonnten Stein-bank neben dem Tore zu wärmen . . . ."

This "negative" impact upon the text of *Die Schlafwand-ler* was balanced by Broch's other decision, to expand the "Huguenau" section:

> Now I am facing the problem of whether or not to enlarge Hugue-nau by about 20 pages, particularly since Esch has grown some-what in size and the disproportion is rather great.[24]

Broch mentioned his intention to introduce a new figure, Marguerite, into the narrative, and asked for three weeks in which to complete this work. But once having started to expand "Huguenau" he found it difficult to stop. A month later he wrote: "Now I have involved myself with Huguenau to the extent that I could make a 300-page novel out of it. I have to keep applying the brakes constantly to keep it from growing too large."[25] By Jan-uary of 1931 he had added four new chapters to the novel.[26]

By early 1932 Broch had completed the new version of "Huguenau."[27] He had added the amazing total of al-most fifty new chapters to this section, and what had originally been planned as an "epilogue" had increased in length until it was only slightly shorter than the first two sections put together. Moreover the basic structure of the section had been radically altered. This startling transformation took place at a time when Broch was deeply involved with studying *Ulysses*, including the preparation of an introductory essay to Joyce's collected works. In order to assess the complex relationship in-volved, it is necessary to examine both the scope and quality of the changes Broch introduced into *Die Schlaf-wandler* between 1930 and 1932.

III

The 1930 version of "Huguenau"[28] consists of a straightforward narrative told in a traditional style; it concerns the story of Huguenau, Esch and his wife, and the Major. There are only two departures from standard narrative techniques: the dialogue of chapter 59 (Das Symposium) and the final sonnet of chapter 87. Neither of these departures could be considered revolutionary, although they do indicate tentative attempts to break out of the conventional story-teller's mold.

The 1932 version, five hundred pages in the final type-script, was expanded both quantitatively and qualita-tively. The additions include: 1) new narrative material; 2) utilization of new narrative techniques, and 3) de-velopment of a new overall structure. Broch himself re-ferred to his "additive method" in rewriting "Huguenau"[29] and, with the exception of the Odysseus parallel already mentioned, there was no substantial deletion of material from the first version. For the sake of clarity the new nar-rative elements, as well as new narrative techniques, in-troduced after Broch read *Ulysses*, are schematized below:

Die Schlafwandler ("Huguenau")

1930 version	*added for printed version 1932*
story of:	*story of*:
Esch	
Frau Esch	
Huguenau	
Major Pasenow	
	Marguerite
	Gödicke (and the doctors)
	Jaretzke
	Hanna Wendling
	Salvation Army Girl
	Bertrand ("Zerfall der Werte")

techniques:	*techniques:*
third person narrative	
Platonic dialogue (59)	dialogue expanded
newspaper article (33)	article "edited" to highlights
sonnet (87)	poetic form (16, 17, 53, 67, 83)
	philosophical essay ("Zerfall der Werte": 12, 20, 24, 31, 34, 44, 55, 62, 73, 88)
	formal abstraction (57, pp. 524-525)
	"labyrinth" (60, "Siegesfeier")
	epigrammatic (65)

The numbers in parentheses in both columns refer to the chapters in the final printed version.

Had Hermann Broch simply added the strands of several new stories to his original version, without basically altering the manner in which those stories were told, the result would not have been so striking. But Broch was interested in a totally new approach to narration:

> . . . in Huguenau a new technique is attempted. . . . The book consists of a series of stories which turn about the same theme. . . . These separate stories, interwoven like a tapestry, each represent a different layer of consciousness: they rise out of the wholly irrational (story of the Salvation Army girl) to the complete rationality of the theoretical sections (Zerfall der Werte). . . . I am somewhat conscious of the fact that the book is, in this respect, something new in literary expression, certainly too, something risky.[30]

The drastic renovation of Huguenau strongly suggests that Broch's preoccupation with *Ulysses* played a direct and important role in his development as a writer.

Broch's interest in Joyce's novel was never greater than during the period in which he was rewriting "Huguenau." In January of 1931 (at which point he had written four of the fifty chapters he was to add to his novel) he wrote to Brody: "Thanks for the letter, Joyce commentary, Goll's letter. . . . I have announced a lecture on Joyce for radio."[31] In that same year he prepared an introduction for a proposed German edition of the collected works of Joyce (to be published by Rhein-Verlag). By 1932 he had written a long essay on Joyce, which was published in 1936 as part of *James Joyce und die Gegenwart*. His theoretical speculations on the nature of the novel were continually measured against Joyce's achievements. He saw a similarity of goals, even when he was expressing those goals in his own particular terms: ". . . the essential thing in Joyce is that which I (at a suitable distance) have also strived for, and to a certain extent achieved, namely *architectonic polyphony*."[32] His declaration that the time was ripe for the "polyhistorical novel" was accompanied by the statement that no author had managed to unite science and literature except Joyce. And in specific reference to the philosophical chapters entitled "Zerfall der Werte" he wrote:

> . . . the breadth of perception of the total work has undergone an expansion, by means of these chapters, of a type unknown (Joyce always excepted!) to creative literature.[33]

It is clear that the general literary and intellectual affinities which so often found expression in Broch's utterances on Joyce should also have left traces on the text of *Die Schlafwandler* itself. The first and most obvious characteristic of the "new" "Huguenau" which links it with Joycean precedent is the imposition of a totally intellectual superstructure. *Ulysses* utilized the skeleton of the Homeric myth, "Huguenau" an abstractly schematized representation of human consciousness from the lowest (irrational) level to the highest (rational-philosophical). The intellectual pattern determined, in each case, both the general subject matter and the way in which that matter was presented—that is, the pattern was reflected both in content and in form. Thus Joyce's modern parallel to Circe consisted of fittingly chosen subject matter (men in a brothel) and narrative technique (dramatized hallucinatory images). Broch, in a similar fashion, presents the highest level of human consciousness by matching form (the philosophical essay) and content (philosophical ideas) without regard for traditional fictional conventions. In each case scant attention was paid to the reader's comfort.

The relationship of the episodes to one another are also dependent upon broader structural considerations in both Joyce and Broch. Broch described his goal as follows:

> . . . in the contrapuntal structure I attempted to bring the flow of events in a continuous relationship to the islands of rationality and exactly the same for the lyrical sections—in other words to do what the mason Goedicke does within his soul; through continuous propping to achieve complimentary supports to the whole edifice . . .[34]

Such an arrangement determined the rhythm of the book, involving the reader in the forward movement of the whole narrative line while at the same time providing both lyrical and philosophical points of rest. This careful control of tempo was one of the things Broch most admired about *Ulysses*:

> . . . the unheard of concentration with which all these stylistic means and forms of expression are united in an artistic whole, the truly symphonic mastery with which they are used for architectonic acceleration and retardation of events . . . refutes the charge of eclecticism . . . for in just such new unity and constraint do the alloyed styles prove their productivity and their right to exist.[35]

In this attention to structural relationships lies the first evidence of a qualitative difference between the impact of *Ulysses* on Hermann Broch, and its impact on Alfred Döblin or Hans Henny Jahnn. The simple fact of the matter was that neither Döblin nor Jahnn were aware of the structural details of Joyce's novel. Their appreciation of the novel had been limited to its narrative and stylistic innovations (such as the inner monologue) as well as its frank and open expression of life. Hermann Broch, on the other hand, owed his sharper eye for detail in *Ulysses* largely to an improved German version and Stuart Gilbert's commentary. Broch himself was well aware of his privileged position:

> . . . *Ulysses* became famous after the change of generations around 1930. The new generation was the first to break through

the "organic mystery" which, until then, surrounded it; the new generation was the first for whom the banal day of the Ulysses-hero Mr. Bloom became the "universal day of the era" . . . that generation alone could feel all the anonymous epochal strengths summed up in, and streaming forth from, this work.[36]

In the same essay Broch stressed *Ulysses'* complexity: "it requires a lengthy commentary the likes of Stuart Gilbert's to comprehend it."[37] Gilbert's work was in his hands by January of 1931, the year in which he both prepared his own lecture on Joyce and extensively re-worked "Huguenau."

Ulysses provided Broch with a striking example of how a novel could be structured and controlled, but it also served as a stimulus to stylistic variation from episode to episode. The new "Huguenau" was not only expanded in length but also contained completely new fictional techniques (Joyce always excepted!). Both the philosophi-cal essays of "Zerfall der Werte" and the extensive new use of poetry in the Salvation Army episodes point directly toward Broch's admiration for such narrative mixtures in *Ulysses*, where, he noted: "the old traditional narrative forms, the epic, the lyric, and the dramatic have been fused into unity."[38]

A further example of such departures from more tra-ditional styles is found in chapter 33 of "Huguenau," where Major Pasenow's newspaper article is reproduced (446). Ziolkowski has pointed out[39] that although this arti-cle is in the earlier version of the novel it is not given its present "impressionistic" form, in which only phrases of the article are reproduced, with the omitted passages indicated by dotted lines. He makes no suggestion as to what may have induced Broch to make this formal al-teration. The resulting visual effect, in which the high-points of the article are isolated on that page in a man-ner analogous to the manner in which they might be picked out by a reader only skimming the newspaper, calls to mind a very similar effect in *Ulysses* which may have served as a stimulus to Broch. Stephen is quickly skimming a letter Mr. Deasy has handed him for inser-tion in a local newspaper:

—I have put the matter into a nutshell, Mr Deasy said. It's about the foot and mouth disease. Just look through it. There can be no two opinions on the matter.

May I trespass on your valuable space. That doctrine of *laissez faire* which so often in our history. Our cattle trade. The way of all our old industries. Liverpool ring which jockeyed the Galway harbour scheme. European conflagration. Grain supplies through the narrow waters of the channel. The pluterperfect imperturbability of the department of agriculture. Pardoned a classical allusion. Cassandra. By a woman who was no better than she should be. To come to the point at issue. (32:40)

Such attempts to suit style to psychological situation were still strikingly unusual in 1922, and Broch's decision to utilize abnormally long ellipses to create an analogous impression in Major Pasenow's article was, if anything, even more daring in its disregard for the normal reader's expectations.

Two other stylistic innovations appear in the new version of "Huguenau." The first is a highly stylized dialogue (chapter 57, p. 524) which runs (in part):

Das Kind sagte: 'Niemand hört's, wenn man lügt.'
Der Major sagte: 'Gott hört es.'
Huguenau sagte: 'Niemand hört einen Deserteur, niemand kennt ihn, auch wenn er mit allem, was er spricht, recht behält.'
Esch sagte: 'Keiner sieht den andern im Dunkeln.'
Der Major sagte: 'Sichtbar, und doch einer vor dem andern versteckt.'
Das Kind sagte: 'Der liebe Gott hört es nicht.'

This abstract and formalized conversation, in which each person seems to be speaking past, rather than to, the others creates a visual impact on the page as well. Such an effect is also noticeable in the newly added chapter 65, p. 571. The entire episode consists of epigrams, and functions as an intellectual counterpart to the "Siegesfeier" of chapter 60—that is, it serves as a meeting place for the various strands of which "Huguenau" is composed, united here on a purely rational level, in contrast to the distinctly lower level of discourse in the "Siegesfeier." As with Broch's other additions to the new version of "Huguenau," such an episode is a clear departure from conventional narrative effects within a novel.

The various innovations introduced into the new "Huguenau" were clearly motivated by Broch's desire to unite form and content in a way similar to that which he praised in Joyce. The result, as we could expect from a writer of Broch's stature, is a novel which is both original and powerful. It would never occur to a contemporary reader to term it an "imitation" of Joyce, as critics did with Döblin and Jahnn. This is not because contemporary critics had any special understanding of Broch's work; rather it was due to the fact that *Ulysses* had very little impact on the linguistic level of the novel, and it was only on this level that critics were prepared to react to it. In the case of both Döblin and Jahnn, critics could point immediately to the use of inner monologue, and they all "knew" that Joyce had introduced this technique into the novel. It was particularly on the level of stylistic parody, wordplay, *montage* effects, and leitmotifs that critics thought they could recognize a relationship to Joyce. But Hermann Broch made very little use of inner monologue in *Die Schlafwandler*, nor did he indulge in parody or playful linguistic effects. Thus on the linguistic level there was little to link the novel to *Ulysses*. In fact one is tempted to speculate that had not Hermann Broch himself so insistently called the attention of others to the parallels between Joyce's work and his own, most critics at the time would have overlooked it completely.

Having said this much, it should be added that Joyce's use of inner monologue and leitmotifs did undoubtedly affect the text of the *Schlafwandler*, albeit in a quantitatively minor way which passed unnoticed at the time. Leslie Miller has shown[40] that in chapter 5 of "Huguenau," the rewritten version includes a form of inner monologue rather than the indirect narrative typical of the 1930 version. The "relative brevity and scarcity" of such passages in the whole of "Huguenau" prevents the assumption of any major influence, but it is unlikely that Joyce would not have been in the back of Broch's mind as he added such passages, particularly considering his continuing involvement with Joyce's work at this period.

The increased use of leitmotifs in the final section of the novel provides a second instance of Broch's interest in Joyce. Broch's conscious effort to reinforce these motifs while working on the final version of his novel was accompanied by his own speculations on the exact nature of Joyce's technique. Broch pointed out the way in which the Joycean leitmotifs function as interlocking supports for the whole structure of the novel. In rewriting "Huguenau" he gave increasing emphasis to precisely this aspect of the work, introducing several new leitmotifs, and attempting to make sure that some of the themes developed for the first time in the third section of *Die Schlafwandler* were worked into the first two sections as well, so as to provide points of reference in the reader's mind for later developments. Even after the German text of the novel was set, Broch wrote to Willa Muir, who was working on the English translation, to ask "whether it might not be necessary to work certain motifs from the Epilogue into the preceding books. That the Epilogue consists mostly of such leitmotifs hardly needs mentioning."[41] Because he felt that the English text should not diverge too greatly from the published German version, he finally settled upon the inclusion of just one further motif: "I've at last become very modest. That is, I would like simply to introduce the term 'verlorenes Geschlecht' into the first two volumes."[42] His suggestion was followed, and as a consequence the English version has remained, in this respect, more true to his intentions than any German edition. Of the new motifs introduced into the rewritten "Huguenau," several were relatively extended,[43] while others tended to be restricted to brief verbal links between two episodes.[44] The total effect, however, was to give a special texture to the final version which might never have existed had Broch not been deeply impressed by what he himself termed this "complicated and subtle technique" which formed "the true center of the Joycean narrative art."[45]

The surprising and radical revision of the third section

of *Die Schlafwandler* is a testament to the originality and creativity of its author. Broch was seeking to give expression to a world-view that was particularly his own. The whole philosophical structure of *Die Schlafwandler* distinguishes it sharply from *Ulysses*; as Broch suggested, the final version of "Huguenau" represents a direction new to literature in many respects. The "erkenntnistheoretischer Roman" was Broch's own contribution to the development of the genre. Yet the very decision to rework the novel, at a point in time when Broch considered it finished, indicates an event in his intellectual and spiritual life great enough to disrupt the course of his literary development. It is abundantly clear that the impact of *Ulysses* was such a force, and that it colored not only his theoretical approach to the novel, but also the way in which he revised *Die Schlafwandler*. Obviously Broch's cultural background was rich and varied, but *Ulysses* remained the primary literary experience in his life.

Broch's own theory about the history of literature[46] was based on the belief that advances in literary expression, just as advances in science, were simply a "function of the times," and that it was Joyce's misfortune to be twenty years in advance of everyone else, so that he ran the risk of being viewed simply as a forerunner of a subsequent literary development. Seen in this light, Joyce might be regarded simply as a catalyst, who crystalized certain tendencies in Broch's development (much as Döblin claimed in later years that Joyce had merely been a "good wind in his sails"). If the impact of *Ulysses* were limited to this basic catalytic action, it would still have to be viewed as the most important event in Broch's literary life. But the chemical analogy is only partially helpful, for chemicals only react—they do not learn. Hermann Broch reacted to *Ulysses*, but he also learned from it.

In 1936 Broch sent a copy of *James Joyce und die Gegenwart* to Joyce himself, with a warm dedication. Joyce on

his part, did not forget Broch, and was even able to aid
him in leaving Austria in 1938. Joyce wrote to Brody in
that year:

> Glad also to be able to tell in an anniversary message that last
> evening my friend in the French F.O. rang up to say that permis-
> sion for H. Broch to enter France had been telegraphed to the
> French C.G. in Vienna. I am trying to get two other people into
> America and hope I shall succeed.[47]

Joyce was even able to make use of Broch, as well as
Döblin, in *Finnegans Wake*. Familiar with the fact that both
authors were said to be influenced by him (although
there is no evidence he ever looked into their works)
he wove their names into passages of text where the notion
of *Doppelgänger* seemed appropriate. In both cases he suggested that the German writers had "borrowed" his literary discoveries, and no doubt he felt it was a case of
true poetic justice that he could use their names in turn.[48]

In the late thirties Broch's attitude toward the position
of the novelist in society began to change, under the direct pressure of the events of the time. The question was
whether or not the writer had the moral right to withdraw
into the ivory tower of art in times of political and social
upheaval. The beginning of such unrest was to be seen as
early as 1932, immediately upon completion of *Die Schlafwandler*. Broch wrote to Frau Brody:

> Again and again the frightening thought surfaces, that everything
> literary and poetical has become completely uninteresting, that
> it has lost its right to existence. Even Joyce and so on. Please
> tell me that it isn't so!!!, for I must keep working.[49]

It was the pain of this dilemma which ultimately forced
Broch to reassess his own work, and to see in *Finnegans
Wake* the symptoms of the unacceptable withdrawal he
feared. By the end of his life, as we have seen, he wished
to devote himself solely to his philosophical work, simply
because he considered it "more important than literature." But in the thirties his major work *Der Tod des Vergil*
(1945) still lay before him. In it he confronted directly

the very artistic dilemma which had troubled him. The novel makes extended use of inner monologue, and is structured around four books: water, fire, earth, and air. It depicts the last eighteen hours of Vergil's life. In spite of the fact, as Broch insisted, that the novel bore as little resemblance to a work like *Finnegans Wake* as a "dachshund to a crocodile" *Der Tod des Vergil* stills bears ample witness, both stylistically and structurally, to the continuing fructifying power of the Joycean experience.

1. Heinz Politzer, "Zur Feier meines Ablebens," *Der Monat*, III (September, 1951), 631.

2. A detailed picture of Broch's personal insistence upon the parallel between Joyce's work and his own in the advertisements of the Rhein-Verlag is provided in *Hermann Broch / Daniel Brody: Briefwechsel 1930-1951*, ed. Bertold Hack und Marietta Kleiss (Frankfurt/M., 1971). See, for example, letters 12, 14, 17, 20, 39, and 42. Cited hereafter as *Briefwechsel*.

3. ". . . ehe ich mich versah, hatte ich die Leitung der väterlichen Fabriken inne, und es war Krieg und Nachkrieg und Krisen, und ich stieg zu industriellen Würden auf, würde das, was man einen Industriekapitän nennt, und schien für mein ganzes Leben lang gefangen, umsomehr, als ich die Verantwortung für meine ganze Familie, inklusive meiner alten Eltern nunmehr langsam übernommen hatte." Hermann Broch, *Gesammelte Werke*. [various eds.] (Zurich, 1952-1961), X, 330. *GW* = *Gesammelte Werke* in all later references. All page references to *Die Schlafwandler* are to the edition which is Volume II of the *GW*.

4. *GW*, X, 316.

5. "Über mein Verhältnis zu Joyce kann ich bloss eines sagen: hätte ich den Ulysses gekannt, ehe ich die Schlafwandler geschrieben hatte, so wären diese ungeschrieben geblieben, da ich im Ulysses ein vollkommenes Realisat dessen sehe, was im Roman überhaupt ausdrückbar ist. Dasjenige, was mir bei meinen Büchern vorgeschwebt ist: 'unter der Haut zu schreiben,' das finde ich bei Joyce restlos erfüllt, und ich bin überzeugt, dass die Literatur, so weit sie überhaupt Ausdruck des modernen Lebens bleiben wird, sich immer mehr und mehr unter der Joyceschen Einfluss begeben wird." *GW*, X, 316.

6. "Oberflächliche Beobachter glauben, dass ich Joyce nachstrebe, weil ich mich theoretisch mit ihm befasst habe. Nach dem Gesagten brauche ich nicht eigens zu beteuern, dass mir derlei fern liegt. Ich müsste, sofern ich seinen Wegen folgte, meine eigene Methode, meine eigene Technik zu einer Intensität bringen, die sich an der seinen messen liesse, doch abgesehen davon, dass meine Kräfte wahrscheinlich hiefür nicht ausreichen, es ist auch nicht mein Ehrgeiz . . ." Letter to Karl Horst of 11 April 1951; *4gw*, VIII, 415.

7. ". . . ich will in der mir noch verbleibenden Lebensspanne meine Erkenntnistheorie und meine sonstigen wissenschaftlichen Arbeiten fertigbringen, einfach weil ich sie für wichtiger als Literatur halte." *GW*, VIII, 415.

8. The first critic to draw attention to this fact was Theodore Ziolkowski, who considered it beyond the scope of his study to pursue the question of Joyce's influence (Ziolkowski, "Zur Entstehung und Struktur von Hermann

Brochs *Schlafwandlern," Deutsche Vierteljahresschrift*, XXXVIII [1964], 40-69). The one study devoted solely to the question of Joyce's relationship to Broch was Manfred Durzak's "Hermann Broch und James Joyce: zur Aesthetik des modernen Romans," *Deutsche Vierteljahresschrift*, XL (1966), 391-433. This material appears, with a few points of detail corrected, in his book *Hermann Broch: der Dichter und seine Zeit* (Stuttgart, 1968), pp. 76-113; the specific relationship of Joyce to *Die Schlafwandler* is treated on pp. 99-105. As a result of the attempted scope of his whole investigation, he makes no attempt to actually compare the texts of *Ulysses* and *Die Schlafwandler*, nor does he refer, except briefly, to the specific changes in the typescripts. The burden of this section of his essay, in which he admits "eine gewisse Anlehnung an Joyce in der Technik des Leitmotifs" is to show Joyce's influence as "sehr bedingt" in *Die Schlafwandler*. His conclusion is based almost solely upon selected quotations from Broch's letters. A later formulation of Joyce's total impact on Broch is expressed more positively: "Die grosse Bedeutung von Joyce für Broch liegt darin, dass seine Dichtung wie ein Katalysator auf Broch's Kunstwollen gewirkt hat. Die Konfrontation mit Joyce hat Brochs eigene Intentionen freigesetzt und geklärt. In dieser Hinsicht ist Joyces Einfluss gross. Es ist jedoch ein Einfluss dialektischer Art. Paradox formuliert, könnte man sagen, dass Brochs Romane grösstenteils gegen Joyce geschrieben worden sind" (p. 113).

Among studies which assert Joyce's influence, without being aware of the manuscript evidence, are: Karl Robert Mandelkow, *Hermann Brochs Die Schlafwandler* (Heidelberg, 1962), p. 94; George C. Schoolfield, "Broch's Sleepwalkers: Aeneas and the Apostels," *The James Joyce Review*, No. 1-2 (1958), pp. 21 ff.; Egon Vietta, "Hermann Broch in memoriam," *Der Monat*, III (September, 1951), 616-629; and Jack Hirschman, "The Orchestrated Novel: a study of Poetic Devices in Novels of Djuna Barnes and Hermann Broch, and the Influences of the Work of James Joyce upon Them" (Diss. Indiana, 1961).

Hartmut Steinecke, in *Hermann Broch und der Polyhistorische Roman* (Bonn, 1968) denies that Broch was strongly dependent upon Joyce, citing Durzak's study. Hartmut Reinhardt, on the other hand, leaves the question open in *Erweiterter Naturalismus: Untersuchungen zum Konstruktionsverfahren in Hermann Brochs Romantrilogie "Die Schlafwandler"* (Cologne, 1972), while suggesting that Durzak's study is inconclusive because it does not analyze the narrative structure of the novel (p. 33, note 62).

9. See his letter to Frank Thiess of 6 April 1930; *GW*, VIII, 14.

10. "eine Art Familienroman" *GW*, VIII, 16.

11. This conclusion is based on Broch's statement that he had written *Die Schlafwandler* before reading Joyce (that is, before he had completed the first version), and the date of the first letter in which he mentions Joyce: 6 April 1930. He would have been reading the second German edition.

12. ". . . seit ich den Ulysses gelesen habe, stocke ich mit der Arbeit an einem zweiten Roman, den ich bereits angelegt hatte, weil ich eben eine Parallelität der Bestrebungen und einen zu grossen Abstand in den Ausführungsmöglichkeiten sehe. . . . Vor allem muss ich eben das Phänomen Joyce erst verdauen." *GW*, VIII, 15.

13. "Was ich an Joyce bewundere, ist seine weitgehende Annäherung an diesen von mir geforderten Idealzustand u. zw. in einer Fülle und Breite und Tiefe des Irrationalen, wie ich es bis dahin nicht erlebt habe. Natürlich weiss ich, dass der Weg, den ich zum Kunstwerk suche und den Joyce mit aller Dezision gegangen ist, nicht der einzige ist, der zum Ziel führt, und dass es auch andere Möglichkeiten gibt, um die Einheit und das Irrationale zu erfassen . . . aber für mich ist, wahrscheinlich infolge meiner mathematisch-konstruktivistischen Anlage, ein anderer Weg kaum gangbar." *GW*, VIII, 14. Note the resemblance to Döblin's remarks note 49, chapter 3.

14. ". . . eine Maximalkonzession an Verleger und Publikum, an die ich vorderhand nicht denken will." *GW*, VIII, 16.

15. "Joyce erscheint mir aber auch wichtig zum Problem des 'Lesers' . . . Der Ulysses ist ein vollkommen unliebenswürdiges Buch, das auf den Leser überhaupt keine Rücksicht nimmt und ihm womöglich auf jeder Seite ins Gesicht schlägt. . . . Dazu bin ich überzeugt, dass man mit "Konzessionen an den Leser' überhaupt nichts machen kann. Für mich ein entsetzlich schweres Problem, denn mich schriftstellerisch und wissenschaftlich auszudrücken, ist mir ja doch Lebensnotwendigkeit . . ." *GW*, VIII 15.

16. "Eine gewisse Neigung hätte ich zum Rhein-Verlag, einfach deswegen, weil mein schriftstellerisches Über-Ich Joyce dort erschienen ist." *GW*, VIII, 16.

17. Letter to G. H. Meyer, Rhein-Verlag, 10 April 1930: "Das Manuskript ist vorgestern abgegangen." *GW*, VIII, 17.

18. ". . . wird wohl nichts anderes übrig bleiben, als weiter Romane zu schreiben, trotz Joyce. Ich glaube sogar—mir ist dies auf der Heimreise klar geworden, in Anschluss an unser Gespräch am Sonntag Nachmittag; ich verdanke es also Ihnen!—, dass es gehen wird." Letter to Frau Brody, 16 July 1930; *GW*, VIII, 23.

19. "erkenntnistheoretischer Roman"; "etwas, das nicht in der Richtung Joyce liegt (etwas, das mir im Schrecken über Joyce abhanden gekommen war)." *GW*, VIII, 23.

20. ". . . da alle Buchhändler unangenehme Differenzen mit ihren Kunden wegen Joyce hätten: wäre der Ulysses nicht unter Subskription abgegeben worden, so wäre den Buchhändlern das Buch von 9/10 der Käufer als unlesbar zurückgegeben worden. Er behauptet nun, dass die Parallelstellung der Schlafwandler mit dem Ulysses ihnen im vorhinein das Odium der Unlesbarkeit anheften würde. . . . Ich halte beide Einwürfe *nicht* für stichhaltig, besonders da mir persönlich die Parallelstellung mit Joyce so ehrend ist, dass ich sogar dafür Opfer bringen würde." Letter to Rhein-Verlag, 19 July 1930; *GW*, VIII, 25.

21. ". . . die Schlafwandler sind, dessen bin ich mir vollkommen bewusst, ein durchaus bedeutsames Buch . . . Die Reputation des Rhein-Verlags ist auf dem absoluten Kunstwerk Ulysses begründet; die Schlafwandler müssen dieses Niveau halten: sonst wäre ich nie zu Ihnen gekommen, wenn ich nicht diesen Ehrgeiz gehabt hätte." Letter to Daniel Brody, 21 December 1930; *GW*, VIII 41.

22. "Jetzt bin ich beim Huguenau, und da möchte ich Sie einiges fragen: Sie werden sich erinnern, dass der Huguenau mit einer allerdings leichten Parallele zum Odysseus eingeleitet wird und dass die Odyssee-Analogie auch einigemale im Laufe der Begebenheit wieder angedeutet wird. Halten Sie es für notwendig, dies mit Rücksicht auf den Ulysses zu entfernen?" Letter to Daniel Brody, 31 August 1930; *GW*, VIII, 28.

23. "Bezüglich Ihre Frage: 'Odysseus' soll ruhig stehen bleiben. Niemand wird eine Analogie zum 'Ulysses' herausfinden. Und wenn ja, umso besser." Letter from Daniel Brody to Broch, 2 September 1930; *Briefwechsel*, letter 30.

24. "Weiter stehe ich vor dem Problem, ob der Huguenau nicht etwa doch um 20 Seiten bereichert werden soll, besonders da der Esch nun auch etwas stärker geworden ist und die Disproportion doch ziemlich gross ist." *GW*, VIII, 28.

25. "Jetzt habe ich mich derart in den Huguenau hineingelebt, dass ich einen Roman von 300 Seiten daraus machen könnte. Ich muss unaufhörlich bremsen, dass es nicht zuviel wird." Letter to Frau Brody, 27 September 1930; *GW*, VIII, 31.

26. See his letter to the Rhein-Verlag, 14 January 1931; *GW*, VIII, 43.

27. "Huguenau" was published early in 1932, and Broch mentioned his own copy in a letter of 14 April 1932; *GW*, VIII, 70.

28. The typescript of the 1930 version of *Die Schlafwandler* consists of 27 chapters, and is one hundred and fifty-one pages in length. As Leslie Miller has pointed out ". . . only two complete versions of *Die Schlafwandler* exist: the novel as it was accepted for publication by Rhein-Verlag early in 1930, and the final published version which appeared in 1931 and 1932" (Leslie Miller, "Hermann Broch's *Die Schlafwandler*: a Critical Study in the light of his letters, exposés and an unpublished manuscript version of the novel"; Diss. Berkeley, 1964, p. 36).

29. "additives Verfahren" Letter to Frank Thiess, 6 April 1932; *GW*, VIII, 67.

30. ". . . im Huguenau ist eine neue Technik versucht . . . Das Buch besteht aus einer Reihe von Geschichten, die alle das gleiche Thema abwandeln. . . . Diese einzelnen Geschichten, untereinander teppichartig verwoben, geben jede für sich eine andere Bewusstseinslage wieder: sie steigen aus dem völlig Irrationalen (Geschichte des Heilsarmeemädchens) bis zur vollständigen Rationalität des Theoretischen (Zerfall der Werte). . . . Ich bin mir ziemlich bewusst, dass das Buch damit ein Novum für den literarischen Ausdruck ist, sicherlich auch ein Wagnis." Letter to Frau Brody, 23 July 1931; *GW*, VIII, 56.

The roots of this new technique, it has been suggested, may lie in part within the work of John Dos Passos. Manfred Durzak has stated flatly "Die Wurzel dieser neuen Technik liegt jedoch nicht in Joyces, sondern Dos Passos' Romanen" (Durzak, *Hermann Broch*, p. 102). But Broch's interest in Dos Passos was of an entirely different nature and intensity. In the 547 letters printed in the *Broch/Brody Briefwechsel*, the name Dos Passos does not occur a single time. That of Joyce is found on approximately 150 different occasions. In the letters published in the *Gesammelte Werke*, Dos Passos is mentioned only twice, and on both occasions he is immediately compared less than favorably with Joyce. Durzak quotes Broch's positive formulation of Dos Passos' technique (p. 102), but neglects to point out that his final word on the subject in the same letter runs as follows: "Was aber die Zersprengung der Form anlangt: ich hoffe sehr, dass Sie jetzt in Steinhude Zeit für Joyce finden werden." Letter to Frank Thiess, *GW*, VIII, 54.

We know that Dos Passos himself was impressed with *Ulysses*, and that it "disposed of the current theory that the English novel was dead" (Dos Passos, *The Best of Times*, London, 1968, p. 131). The "Querschnitt" technique employed by Dos Passos is an expansion of what Joyce had already done in microcosm in the Wandering Rocks episode of *Ulysses*, where the individual sections are precisely "untereinander teppichartig verwoben." Broch's passing interest in Dos Passos and *Manhattan Transfer*, although obviously far from profound, no doubt reinforced the impact of this one facet of *Ulysses* as well.

31. "Dank für Brief, Joycekommentar, Gollbrief. . . . Ich habe einen Joyce-Vortrag im Radio angekündigt." *GW*, VIII, 44.

32. ". . . was das Wesentlich bei Joyce ist, was ich (im gebührenden Abstand) gleichfalls angestrebt und zum Teil immerhin verwirklicht habe, nämlich die *architektonische Vielstimmigkeit*." *GW*, VIII, 33.

33. ". . . die Erkenntnisbreite des Gesamtwerkes [hat] durch diese Kapitel eine Ausdehnung erfahren, wie sie in der Belletristik (Joyce immer ausgenommen!) nicht vorhanden gewesen ist . . ." Letter to Daniel Brody, 23 September 1931; *GW*, VIII, 61.

34. ". . . in [der Kontrapunktik] kam es mir darauf an, den Fluss des Geschehens in eine fortgesetzte Verbindung mit den rationalen Inseln zu bringen, genau so wie mit den lyrischen, m.a.W. das zu tun, was der Maurer Goedicke innerhalb seiner Seele tut; durch fortgesetzte Verstrebungen gegenseitige Stützungen des Gesamtgerüsts zu erreichen . . ." *GW*, VIII, 68.

35. "Indes die unerhörte Konzentration, mit der alle diese Stilmittel und

Ausdrucksformen zur künstlerischen Einheit gebunden, die wahrhaft symphonische Meisterschaft, mit der sie zur architektonischen Akzeleration und Stagnation des Geschehens verwendet werden . . . entkräftet den Vorwurf des Eklektizismus . . . denn erst in solch neuer Einheit und Gebundenheit erweisen die legierten Stile ihre Tragkraft und ihre Existenzberechtigung." *GW*, VI, 191.

36. ". . . der Ulysses ist nach dem Generationswechsel um 1930 berühmt geworden, erst die neue Generation hat die 'Organische Unbekanntheit' durchbrochen, die das Werk bis dahin umgeben hat, für die neue Generation erst wurde der banale Alltag des 'Ulysses-Helden' Mr. Bloom zum 'Welt-Alltag der Epoche' . . . und ihr war es vorbehalten gewesen, all die anonymen Epochekräfte zu erfühlen, deren Totalität . . . in diesem aufstrahlt und vereinigt ist. . . ." *GW*, VI, 186.

37. ". . . sie [benötigt] aber auch zu ihrem Verständnis eines ausgedehnten Kommentars wie etwa den Stuart Gilberts." *GW*, VI, 193. Interestingly enough, Brody maintained that Gilbert's book had hurt the sales of *Ulysses*, and did not sell well itself. See letter 190 in the Broch/Brody *Briefwechsel* (with reference to the German edition of Gilbert's study). Gilbert's work was available as early as 1930 in English, and in the same year was made available in its general outlines in Bernhard Fehr's article, in German. Already in October of 1930 Broch was waiting eagerly to read it: "Was aber die architektonische Vielstimmigkeit angelangt, so warte ich schon sehr auf den Joyce-Kommentar . . ." *GW*, VIII, 33.

38. ". . . die althergebrachten Darstellungsformen, also die epische, die lyrische, die dramatische [sind] zur Einheit verschmolzen . . ." *GW*, VI, 190.

39. Ziolkowski, p. 44.

40. Miller, p. 224. (See note 28 of this chapter).

41. ". . . ob man gewisse Motive aus dem Epilog nicht schon in die vorhergehenden Bücher hineinarbeiten müsste. Dass der Epilog zum grossen Teil aus solchen Leitmotiven besteht, brauche ich ja nicht weiter zu erwähnen. . . . Für die deutsche Ausgabe ist natürlich nichts mehr zu machen . . ." Letter of 10 February 1932; *GW*, X, 332.

42. "Ich . . . bin schliesslich sehr bescheiden geworden. D.h., ich möchte . . . bloss die Vokabel vom 'Vorlorenen Geschlecht' in den beiden ersten Bänden anbringen." *GW*, X, 333.

43. Typical of the more extended leitmotifs which Broch worked into "Huguenau" after 1930 is that connected with Hanna Wendling, "der Einbruch von unten." This is the title of a newspaper article she has read recently. It comes to symbolize both sexual assault and political upheaval, as well as the invasion of the irrational into a supposedly sane world. It appears on page 613 (chapter 78), 639 (chapter 85), 651 (chapter 85), and is finally linked into the whole of the novel in the final chapter, on page 661.

44. A typical example of such verbal links may be seen in chapters 43 and 44 (both later additions to the 1930 version). Jaretski speaks: ". . . sozusagen bloss aus Gerechtigkeitssinn habt Ihr es getan, weil ich dem Franzosen damals die Handgranate zwischen die Beine geschmissen hab' . . . (p. 474). And the following chapter (Zerfall der Werte 6) begins immediately with the declaration: "Zur Logik des Soldaten gehört es, dem Feind eine Handgranate zwischen die Beine zu schmeissen . . ." (p. 474). This is one of the first hints that the author of the philosophical essay is also the author of the novel, and it links the two chapters in an immediately striking way in the mind of the reader.

45. "höchst komplizierte und subtile Technik"; "eigentliches Zentrum der Joyceschen Darstellungskunst" *GW*, VI, 192.

46. See his letter to Willa Muir, 19 July 1931; *GW*, X, 317.

47. Letter to Daniel Brody, 16 June 1938; *Letters*, III, 424.

48.   See Breon Mitchell, "Swobbing broguen eerisch myth brockendootch: two German Novelists in the *Wake*," *A Wake Newslitter*, VI (1968), 10-11, for a discussion of the passages in question.

49.   "Und immer wieder taucht es beängstigend auf, dass alles Literarische, alles Dichterische völlig interesselos geworden ist, dass es keine Daseins-berechtigung mehr hat. Selbst Joyce nicht u.s.f. Bitte sagen Sie mir, dass es nicht so ist!!!, denn ich muss doch weiter arbeiten." *GW*, VIII, 71.

CONCLUSION:
THE WIDENING CIRCLE

Ulysses is not merely an English novel; it has taken its place within that realm of literature which ignores national boundaries. It is one of the great paradoxes of literary creation that a work of art strictly localized in time and place can speak with so many tongues. In Germany, too, *Ulysses* struck a chord of sympathy with the age, and no other twentieth-century English novel has meant more to German writers. Yet few tasks are more arduous than showing just how a particular work affected the development of the whole range of its art.

Influence studies are notoriously risky. We cannot enter the poet's mind, nor can we ever be sure we understand even partially the magical chemistry that produces great works. The present study has been an attempt to say something meaningful, in a positivistic sense, about literary influence. In concentrating as far as possible upon the "facts" available to us—manuscripts, letters, reviews—some challenging questions have inevitably been avoided, or only lightly touched upon. It is hoped that the results of this investigation might be an aid in answering at least some of them. Value judgments in particular have, on the whole, been expressed rather than justified through literary analysis. It was not within the scope of this study to investigate in detail the artistic quality of the novels discussed, nor to show the success with which the authors integrated new techniques and ideas into their works. The knowledge of the various stages through which the relevant novels passed may provide some new insights into the value of the final products. And, of course, it should be obvious that we have traced but one thread in the incredibly rich and complex tapestry of literary creation.

The three German novelists discussed were selected in the belief that they are representative of the most direct and profound influence which Joyce seemed capable of exerting upon his contemporaries. It is natural to seek the common factor that made all three particularly susceptible to Joyce's work. For each, Joyce was perhaps primarily a reflection of something they felt very deeply about art. They were united by their common interest in experimentation with narrative prose techniques, and in widening the possibilities of their art. Taken together, they present a revealing spectrum of the kinds of influence one novelist may exert on another.

Hans Henny Jahnn clearly felt a natural affinity for Joyce's broader view of the human mind and human nature. He thought Joyce was honest in his approach to life, and that he saw with a vision that was whole and clear. *Perrudja* presents us with perhaps a classic case of the direct impact of one novel on the style and narrative technique of another. Jahnn seems to have taken over directly, and made wide use of, literary techniques he formerly knew little or nothing about. He may have learned more from Joyce than anyone else. Alfred Döblin's case is more complex, in that he was already an established novelist with an experimental bent when he first read *Ulysses*. Joyce's influence may have been largely catalytic, prodding Döblin in directions toward which he naturally tended. But the evidence presented leaves little doubt that Döblin fundamentally changed the narrative style of *Berlin Alexanderplatz* after reading Joyce's novel. He found more in Joyce than simply the courage to try his own literary convictions. Hermann Broch's case is perhaps most interesting of all. *Die Schlafwandler* is least like *Ulysses* in style and technique. But Broch's constant concern with the work of James Joyce demonstrates a closer affinity with him, in the final analysis, than we find in either of the other two novelists. It is doubtful that *Die Schlafwandler* would have ever achieved its present form had Broch never read *Ulysses*, but his assimilation of the Joycean experience was so complete that one must reconstruct it with considerable care. Taken together the three novelists represent, in their varying relationships to Joyce, something like the varieties of literary experience.

Ulysses was a unique and concrete example of formal and stylistic innovations, and as such it was invaluable to these three novelists in the process of forming their own works. In turn they provided concrete examples of similar innovations for many of their countrymen who had never read *Ulysses*. By the mid-thirties, for example, it would not be surprising to see a German writer mix inner monologue and third-person narrative in his novel without ever having read a word of Joyce—provided he had read *Berlin Alexanderplatz* or *Perrudja*.

During the Third Reich the works of James Joyce were banned by the fascists in Germany. Yet what is perhaps less well known is that his works were also attacked by the literary officialdom of the communist party in Moscow. Joyce was, as one critic had prophetically remarked at an earlier date, an annoying writer to partymen of all political persuasions. In this period of polarization, only individual voices were heard speaking out in Joyce's defense. Bertolt Brecht, for example, had to warn his political friends against dismissing Joyce on ideological grounds, and he pointed out that he himself had attempted to make use of Joyce's inner monologue technique in *Der Dreigroschen Roman* (1935). But Joyce was to continue in disfavor until the end of the war. Within Germany, into the late thirties, theses on Joyce still occasionally appeared, and at least at some universities

there were unsuccessful attempts to have his name removed from the banned list. The outbreak of the war
stifled most literary discussion, and even outside of Germany 1939 was an unfortunate year for the appearance
of a novel like *Finnegans Wake*.

At the end of the bleak war-years there seemed to be,
once again, a time and a place for literature. Almost immediately German periodicals rediscovered Joyce, and
large printings of his works were made available to the
average German reader for the first time. A controversy
over the quality of the German translation of *Ulysses*
aroused heated discussion by the mid-fifties, and it soon
became evident that Joyce was to be a meaningful figure
for postwar German literature. It was Arno Schmidt who
began the debate over the merits of Goyert's translation,
and when the Rhein-Verlag proved unwilling to alter
the "authorized" translation, Schmidt announced his
determination to translate it himself (and publish it when
the copyright expired on the old version). Other major
writers proved equally interested in Joyce's works, and
only *Finnegans Wake* remained a closed book to them. Indeed, even this most difficult of all novels (a chapter of
which has been translated into German by Wolfgang
Hildesheimer) has not been completely without influence, as a glance at Schmidt's work will reveal. In Max
Frisch's *Mein Name sei Gantenbein*, only a hypothetically
blind character is absolved of having to pretend he's
read *Finnegans Wake*.

The widening circle of Joyce's influence becomes increasingly difficult to assess as we move away from the
center of the impact. The year 1933 was deliberately
chosen as the terminal date for this study, both because
it is a reasonable stopping place, and because the type
of positivistic investigation attempted here relies heavily
on measuring influence as close to the source as possible. After 1945 it becomes difficult to name a major
novelist who does not owe a literary debt to Joyce. He
has, quite simply, become a part of the intellectual climate of our age. An increasingly sophisticated reading

public finds Joyce's work increasingly accessible in Germany. A new, complete edition of his works is currently being published there, and the new translation of *Ulysses* by Hans Wollschläger has just been issued, almost fifty years after the first English edition was quietly smuggled into English speaking countries from Paris. During its long journey it has survived many storms of censorship and misunderstanding. Joyce, were he alive today, would be pleased at the manifold evidence of its continuing power. But his mind, we may be sure, would be upon that future novel beyond the wake.

BIBLIOGRAPHY OF WORKS CITED

Note: The following bibliography is simply that of works cited in this study, and obviously does not constitute a complete selection of the most important secondary literature on the individual authors discussed. Major studies of Joyce, Jahnn, Döblin, and Broch have been omitted unless they addressed themselves directly and significantly to the topic at hand.

Becker, Helmut. *Untersuchungen zum epischen Werk Alfred Döblins am Beispiel seines Romans Berlin Alexanderplatz.* Diss. Marburg, 1962.

Beckett, Samuel. "Dante . . . Bruno. Vico . . Joyce." *Our Exagmination Round his Factification for Incamination of Work in Progress.* Paris, 1929, pp. [3]-22.

Bericht über das grösste Prosawerk des XX. Jahrhunderts. [Basel, 1926]. Advertising pamphlet, Rhein-Verlag.

Binder, Hartmut. *Motiv und Gestaltung bei Franz Kafka.* Bonn, 1966.

Binz, Artur. "Der abstruse *Ulysses*," *Saarbrücker Zeitung*, 21 April 1928.

Blass, Ernst. "James Joyce und der Dulder Ulysses," *Vossische Zeitung*, 18 August 1932.

B[lei], F[ranz]. "James Joyce: *Ulysses*," *Neue Revue* (1930), p. 139.

Budgen, Frank. *James Joyce and the Making of Ulysses.* London, 1934.

Brecht, Bertolt. *Schriften zur Literatur und Kunst.* 3 vols. Frankfurt/M., 1967.
Broch, Hermann. *Gesammelte Werke.* 10 vols. Zurich, 1952-1961.
    Vol. 2: *Die Schlafwandler.* 1952.
    Vol. 3: *Der Tod des Vergil.* 1952.
    Vol. 6: *Dichten und Erkennen: Essays,* ed. Hanna Arendt. 1955.
    Vol. 8: *Briefe,* ed. Robert Pick. 1957.
    Vol. 10: *Die unbekannte Grösse, mit den Briefen an Willa Muir,* ed. Ernst Schönweise and Eric Herd. 1961.
——. *James Joyce und die Gegenwart.* Vienna, 1936; reprinted in the *Gesammelte Werke,* Vol. 6.
——. *Hermann Broch / Daniel Brody: Briefwechsel 1930-1951,* ed. Bertold Hack and Marietta Kleiss. Frankfurt/M., 1971.
Connolly, Thomas E. *The Personal Library of James Joyce: A Descriptive Bibliography.* Buffalo, 1955.
Curtius, Ernst Robert. "James Joyce," *Die Literatur,* XXXI (November, 1928), 121-128.
——. "Philologie oder Literaturkritik," *Die literarische Welt,* VII (April, 1931), 7.
——. "Technik und Thematik von James Joyce," *Neue Schweizer Rundschau,* XXII (January, 1929), 47-68; translated in *transition,* No. 16-17 (June, 1929), 310-325.
——. "Das verbote Buch: *Ulysses,*" *Die literarische Welt,* I (October, 1925), 1.
Deming, Robert H. *A Bibliography of James Joyce Studies.* Lawrence, Kansas: 1964.
Döblin, Alfred. *Ausgewählte Werke,* ed. Walter Muschg. 10 vols. Olten, 1960-1965.
    Vol. 1: *Die drei Sprünge des Wang-lun.* 1960.
    Vol. 2: *Pardon wird nicht gegeben.* 1960.
    Vol. 3: *Berlin Alexanderplatz.* 1961.
    Vol. 8: *Aufsätze zur Literatur.* 1963.
    Vol. 10: *Wallenstein.* 1965.
——. *Der schwarze Vorhang.* Berlin, 1918.
——. *Ulysses* von Joyce," *Das deutsche Buch,* VIII (1928), 84-85; reprinted in *Ausgewählte Werke,* VIII, 287-290.
——. *Wadzeks Kampf mit der Dampfturbine.* Berlin, 1918.
——. *Alfred Döblin im Spiegel der zeitgenössischen Kritik,* ed. Ingrid Schuster and Ingrid Bode. Bern, 1973.

——. *Materialien zu Alfred Döblin: Berlin Alexanderplatz*, ed. Matthias Prangel. Frankfurt/M., 1975.

Dos Passos, John. *The Best of Times*. London, 1968.

——. *The 42nd Parallel*. New York, 1930.

——. *Manhattan Transfer*. New York, 1925.

Dujardin, Edouard. *Les lauriers sont coupés*. Paris, 1887.

Durzak, Manfred. *Hermann Broch: der Dichter und seine Zeit*. Stuttgart, 1968.

——. "Hermann Broch und James Joyce: zur Aesthetik des modernen Romans," *Deutsche Vierteljahresschrift*, XL (1966), 391-433.

Duytschaever, Joris. "Joyce—Dos Passos—Döblin: Einfluss oder Analogie?" *Materialien zu Alfred Döblin: Berlin Alexanderplatz*, ed. Matthias Prangel. Frankfurt/M., 1975, pp. 136-149.

Ehrenstein, Albert. "James Joyce," *Berliner Tageblatt*, 5 April 1928; also printed in *Ostseezeitung* (Stettin), 9 May 1928; reprinted in *Albert Ehrenstein: Ausgewählte Aufsätze*, ed. M.Y. Bengavriel (Darmstadt, 1961), pp. 71-76.

Ellmann, Richard. *James Joyce*. New York, 1959.

Enkenbach, Walter. "Die Odyssee der verspäteten Schüler," *Der Scheinwerfer* (Essen), No. 14 (April, 1930), pp. 7-10.

"L.F." "James Joyce: *Ulysses*," *Das Kunstblatt* (Berlin), XII (1928), 63-64.

Fechter, Paul. "James Joyce und sein *Ulysses*," *Die schöne Literatur*, XXIX (May, 1928), 239-243.

——. "Peinlichkeiten," *Die neue Literatur*, I (January, 1931), 22-25.

——. "Der *Ulysses* des James Joyce," *Deutsche Allgemeine Zeitung*, 22 January 1928.

Fehr, Bernhard. "Bewusstseinstrom und Konstruktion: James Joyce," *Die englische Literatur der Gegenwart und die Kulturfragen unserer Zeit* (Leipzig, 1930), pp. 56-68.

——. "James Joyces *Ulysses*," *Englische Studien*, LX (1925), 180-205.

——. "Vom englischen Roman der Gegenwart," *Archiv für das Studium der neueren Sprachen und Literaturen*, LXXX (1925), 49.

——. "*Ulysses* von James Joyce," *Frankfurter Zeitung*, 18 June 1930.

——. "Der Roman *Ulysses* von James Joyce," *Basler Nachrichten*, 16 August 1925; reprinted in *Von Englands geistigen Beständen: Ausgewählte Aufsätze von Bernhard Fehr*, ed. Max Wildi (Frauenfeld, 1944), pp. 162-167.

Fischer, A. J. "James Joyce in Salzburg," *Salzburger Volksblatt*, 25 August 1928.

Franke, Rosemarie. *James Joyce und der deutsche Sprachbereich: Übersetzung, Verbreitung und Kritik in der Zeit von 1919-1967*. Diss. Berlin, 1970.

Franzen, Erich. "Zum *Ulysses* von Joyce," *Die literarische Welt*, IV (April, 1928), 5-6.

Freeman, Thomas. "Structure and Symbolism in Hans Henny Jahnn's *Perrudja*: a Study of the Unity of the Novel." Diss. Stanford, 1970.

Frisch, Efraim. "Jugendbildnis eines Dichters," *Frankfurter Zeitung*, 12 September 1926.

——. "*Ulysses*: zu dem Werk von James Joyce," *Frankfurter Zeitung*, 11 January 1928.

Die fünf Weltteile: Ein unidyllisches Verlegerjahrbuch [Zurich, 1928]. Rhein-Verlag advertising brochure.

Gaupp, Fritz. "Kritisches zum *Ulysses* von James Joyce," *Badische Presse* (Karlsruhe), 4 April 1928.

Georg, Manfred. "Der *Ulysses* des James Joyce," *Badische Presse* (Karlsruhe), 4 January 1928; also printed in *Kölner Tageblatt*, 16 January 1928.

Giedion-Welcker, Carola. "James Joyce," *Frankfurter Zeitung*, 3 February 1932; also printed in *Mannheimer Tageblatt*, 5 February 1932.

——. "Zum *Ulysses* von James Joyce," *Neue Schweizer Rundschau*, XXI (January, 1928), 18-32.

——. "Work in Progress: ein sprachliches Experiment von James Joyce," *Neue Schweizer Rundschau*, XXII (September, 1929), 660-671.

Gilbert, Stuart. James Joyce's *Ulysses*. London, 1930.

Goll, Ivan. "Der Homer unserer Zeit: über James Joyce," *Die literarische Welt*, III (June, 1927), 1-2; also printed in *Badische Presse Literarische Umschau* (Karlsruhe), No. 42, 1927; reprinted in *Zeitgemässes aus der Literarischen Welt von 1925-1932*, ed. Willy Haas (Stuttgart, 1962), pp. 98-101.

——. "James Joyce," *Die Weltbühne*, XXVIII (February, 1932), 216-218.

——. "Ein Tag in dem Leben eines Genies," *Der Quer-schnitt*, XII (July, 1932), 492.

——. "*Ulysses, sub specie aeternitatis*," *Die Weltbühne*, XXIII (December, 1927), 960-963.

Gottgetreu, Eric. "Joyce der Spiesserschreck," *Der Homer unserer Zeit: Deutschland in Erwartung des Ulysses von Joyce* [Basel, 1927], pp. 7-9. Reprinted from the *Neue Leipziger Zeitung* and the *Neue Wiener Journal*, no dates given.

Goyert, Georg. "James Joyce," *Prisma* (Munich), No. 17 (1948), pp. 17-18.

——. "Noch einmal: *Ulysses* in Deutschland: Antwort des Übersetzers Georg Goyert," *Frankfurter Allgemeine Zeitung*, 6 December 1957.

Guillemin, Bernhard. "Die Irrfahrt des James Joyce in seinem Roman *Ulysses*," *Berliner Börsen-Courier*, 7 March 1928; also printed in the *Magdeburger Zeitung*, 4 March 1928, and in the *Hamburger Fremden-blatt*, 14 April 1928.

——. "James Joyce," *Die Literatur*, XXXIV (March, 1932), 384; reprinted in part from the *Berliner Tageblatt*, 2 February 1932; also printed in the *Mannheimer Tage-blatt*, 5 February 1932.

Haas, Willy. *Die literarische Welt: Erinnerungen*. Munich, 1957.

Hennig, Artur. "Grundsätzliches zu James Joyce *Ulysses*," *Die Tat*, XX (1928), 223-224.

Hentze, Rudolf. *Die proteische Wandlung im Ulysses von James Joyce und ihre Spiegelung im Stil*. Diss. Marburg, 1933; published as Beiheft 27 of *Die neueren Sprachen* (1933).

Hirschman, Jack. "The Orchestrated Novel: a Study of Poetic Devices in Novels of Djuna Barnes and Hermann Broch, and the Influences of the work of James Joyce upon them." Diss. Indiana, 1961.

Hodgart, Matthew and Mabel Worthington. *Song in the Works of James Joyce*. New York, 1959.

Der Homer unserer Zeit: Deutschland in Erwartung des Ulysses von Joyce. [Basel, 1927]. Rhein-Verlag advertising brochure.

Humphrey, Robert. *Stream of Consciousness in the Modern Novel*. Berkeley, 1954.

Jahnn, Hans Henny. "Alfred Döblin: *Berlin Alexanderplatz*," *Der Kreis*, VI (1929), 735; reprinted in *Alfred Döblin im Spiegel der zeitgenössischen Kritik*, ed. Ingrid Schuster and Ingrid Bode. Bern, 1973.

——. "*Ulysses*," *Der Kreis*, VII (July-August, 1930), 472-473.

——. *Werke*. Frankfurt/M., 1958-1968.
Perrudja. 1958.
Fluss ohne Ufer. 1959-1962.
    1. *Das Holzschiff*.
    2. *Die Niederschrift des Gustav Anias Horn*. 2 vols.
    3. *Epilog*, ed. Walter Muschg.
Dramen I. 1963.
Über den Anlass und andere Essays. 1964.
Dramen II. 1965.
Perrudja II: Fragment aus dem Nachlass, ed. Rolf Burmeister. 1968.

——. *Werke und Tagebücher*, ed. Thomas Freeman and Thomas Scheuffelen. 7 vols. Hamburg, 1974.

Joyce, James. *Anna Livia Plurabelle*. Frankfurt/M., 1970. With German versions by Wolfgang Hildesheimer, Georg Goyert, and Hans Wollschläger.

——. *James Joyce: sa vie, son oeuvre, son rayonnement*. Paris, 1949.

——. *Letters of James Joyce*. [Vol. I], ed. Stuart Gilbert. New York, 1957. Vols. II and III, ed. Richard Ellmann. New York, 1966.

——. *Ulysses*. New York, 1961.

——. *Ulysses*, trans. Georg Goyert. 3 vols. [Basel], 1927. Second edition, 2 vols. Zurich, 1930. Reprinted, Zurich, 1956.

Jung, Carl. "*Ulysses*: ein Monolog," *Europäische Revue*, VIII (September, 1932), 547-568; reprinted in *Wirklichkeit der Seele* (Zurich, 1934), pp. 132-169.

Kahler, Erich. "Untergang und Übergang der epischen Kunstform." *Die neue Rundschau*, LXIV (1953), 1-44.

Knapp, Otto. "Das Bild des Menschen im neuen englischen Roman," *Das Hochland*, XXX (September, 1933), 539-542.

Kolb, Annette. "Randglossen zur heutigen englischen Literatur," *Die neue Rundschau*, XLII (1931), 114-123.

K[orrodi], E[duard]. "Kritizismus im europäischen Roman," *Neue Zürcher Zeitung*, 11 November 1927.

Kulemeyer, Günther. *Studien zur Psychologie im neuen englischen Roman.* Diss. Greifswald, 1933.

Lide, Francis. "*Berlin Alexanderplatz* in Context: Alfred Döblin's Literary Practice." Diss. Illinois, 1966.

Lieven, Hugo. "Das Rätsel Ulysses," *Dresdener Neueste Nachrichten*, No. 84, 1932.

Magalaner, Marvin and Richard Kain. *Joyce: the Man, the Work, the Reputation.* London, 1957.

Mahler-Werfel, Alma. *Mein Leben.* Berlin, 1960.

Mandelkow, Karl Robert. *Hermann Brochs Die Schlafwandler.* Heidelberg, 1962.

Mann, Thomas. *Thomas Mann: Briefe 1937-1947*, ed. Erika Mann. Berlin, 1963.

Marcu, Valeriu. "Des Mystikers James Joyce Weltruhm," *Berliner Börsen-Courier*, 8 September 1926; reprinted in *Hamburger Fremdenblatt*, 22 January 1927.

Marinoff, Irene. *Neue Wertungen im englischen Roman.* Leipzig, 1932.

McLean, Andrew. "Joyce's *Ulysses* and Döblin's *Alexanderplatz Berlin*," *Comparative Literature*, XXV (1973), 97-113.

Meyer, Joachim. *Verzeichnis der Schriften von und über Hans Henny Jahnn.* Berlin, 1967.

Miller, Leslie Lewis. "Hermann Broch's *Die Schlafwandler*: a critical Study in the light of his letters, exposés, and an unpublished manuscript version of the novel." Diss. Berkeley, 1964.

Mitchell, Breon. "Swobbing broguen eerisch myth brockendootch: two German Novelists in the *Wake*," *A Wake Newslitter*, VI (October, 1968), 10-11.

Moore, Frederic L. "Blickpunkt: *Ulysses* and the Changing Perspective: a Translation and Evaluation of German Criticism from Three Decades." M.A. thesis, Northern Illinois, 1966.

Müller-Salget, Klaus. *Alfred Döblin: Werk und Entwicklung.* Bonn, 1972.

――. "Zur Entstehung von Döblins *Berlin Alexanderplatz*." *Materialien zu Alfred Döblin: Berlin Alexanderplatz*, ed. Matthias Prangel. Frankfurt/M., 1975, pp. 117-135.

Muschg, Walter. "Der deutsche *Ulysses*," *Annalen*, II (January, 1928), 19-24.

——. "Ein Stoss Bücher," *Schweizerische Monatshefte*, X (April, 1930), 48-49; reprinted in *Alfred Döblin im Spiegel der zeitgenössischen Kritik* (Bern, 1973), pp. 246-247.

——. *Gespräche mit Hans Henny Jahnn*. Frankfurt/M., 1967.

Offenburg, Kurt. "Joyce: *Ulysses*," *Münchener Post*, 31 May 1928; also printed in *Deutsche Republik*, II (1928), 1137-1139.

Peitz, Wolfgang. *Alfred Döblin Bibliographie 1905-1966*. Freiburg i. Br., 1968.

Pender, R. Herman. "Die moderne englische Literatur: ein Überblick," *Deutsche Rundschau*, CCIII (June, 1925), 285-286.

Pohl, Gerhart. "*Ulysses*," *Die neue Bücherschau*, V (November, 1927), 224-228.

——. "*Ulysses* und die deutsche Literatur-Kritik," *Die neue Bücherschau*, VI (1928), 87-98.

Politzer, Heinz. "Zur Feier meines Ablebens," *Der Monat*, III (September, 1951), 630-632.

Pound, Ezra. "James Joyce's *Ulysses*," *Der Querschnitt*, IV (1924), 137-141; translated from *The Dial*, LXXII (June, 1922), 623-629.

Reinhardt, Hartmut. *Erweiterter Naturalismus: Untersuchungen zum Konstruktionsverfahren in Hermann Brochs Romantrilogie "Die Schlafwandler,"* Cologne, 1972.

Russe, Ellen. "Englische Literatur," *Das geistige Europa*, II (Paderborn, 1926), 201-205.

"H.S." "Der Rundfunk regt sich," *Das Tagebuch*, XII (April, 1931), 632-633.

Schirmer, Walter. *Der englische Roman der neuesten Zeit*. Heidelberg, 1923.

Schlawe, Fritz. *Literarische Zeitschriften: 1910-1933*. Stuttgart, 1962.

Sch[lien?], H[elmut]. "*Ulysses* von James Joyce," *Der Bund*, Beilage: *Der kleine Bund*, 7 January 1928.

Schmits, Walter. "James Joyce," *Die Kölnische Zeitung*, 3 November 1927.

Schnitzler, Arthur. *Gesammelte Werke*. 7 vols. Berlin, 1912.

——. *George Brandes und Arthur Schnitzler: ein Briefwechsel*, ed. Kurt Bergel. Bern, 1956.

Schoolfield, George C. "Broch's Sleepwalkers: Aeneas and the Apostles," *The James Joyce Review*, No. 1-2 (1958), pp. 21-38.

Slocum, John and Herbert Cahoon. *A Bibliography of James Joyce: 1882-1941*. London, 1953.

Smith, Henry Adelmon. "Sassanidischer König: Hans Henny Jahnn's *Perrudja* in Microcosm." Diss. Southern California, 1969.

Steinecke, Hartmut. *Hermann Broch und der polyhistorische Roman*. Bonn, 1968.

Szulanski, H. "Eine Parallele zwischen James Joyce and Alfred Döblin." Diss. Brussels, 1949. Not available to author.

Tau, Max. "James Joyce," *Die neueren Sprachen*, XX (August, 1932), 344-354.

———. *Das Land das ich verlassen musste*. Hamburg, 1961.

Theile, Harald. "Credo der Ausgestossenheit: zu James Joyces *Ulysses*," *Eckart*, IX (February, 1933), 70-78.

Thieme, Karl. "Der Unsägliche und die Sprache: eine Studie über Marcel Proust, James Joyce und Paula Schlier," *Christliche Welt*, XLIII (1929), 290-298.

Thornton, Weldon. *Allusions in Ulysses: an Annotated List*. Chapel Hill, 1968.

Tucholsky, Kurt. *Gesammelte Werke*, ed. Mary Gerold-Tucholsky and Fritz Raddatz. 4 vols. Reinbeck bei Hamburg, 1961.

———. ("Peter Panter"). "*Ulysses*," *Die Weltbühne*, XXIII (November, 1927), 788-793; reprinted in *Gesammelte Werke*, II, 949-955.

Venn, Artur. "Ein Übersetzer: zum Tode von Georg Goyert," *Frankfurter Allgemeine Zeitung*, 14 May 1966.

Vietta, Egon. "Hermann Broch in memoriam," *Der Monat*, III (September, 1951), 616-629.

Vowinckel, Ernst. *Der englische Roman der neuesten Zeit und Gegenwart*. Berlin, 1926.

Wagner, Rüdiger. *Hans Henny Jahnns Roman Perrudja: Sprache und Stil*. Diss. Munich, 1965.

Weiss, Ernst. "James Joyce," *Die Literatur*, XXXIV (March, 1932), 384; reprinted in part from *Berliner Börsen-Courier*, No. 71, 1932.

Weltmann, Lutz. "Momentaufnahme: James Joyce," *Bayerische Israelitische Gemeindezeitung*, VIII (February, 1932), 36-37.

W[eltmann?], L[utz]. "*Ulysses*," *Deutsche Zeitung Bohemia* (Prague), 24 February 1928.

Werner, Bruno E. "Der *Ulysses* des James Joyce," *Deutsche Rundschau*, LIV (June, 1928), 268-270.

West, John Alexander. "Über den *Ulysses*," *Annalen*, I (1927), 510-516.

Zalubska, C. "Parallelen der Erzähltechnik in den Werken von Alfred Döblin und James Joyce," *Studia Germanica Posnaniensia* I (1971), 59-67.

Zarek, Otto. "Der *Ulysses* des James Joyce," *Das Tagebuch*, VIII (December, 1927), 1963-1966.

Ziolkowski, Theodore. "Zur Entstehung und Struktur von Hermann Brochs *Schlafwandlern*," *Deutsche Vierteljahresschrift*, XXXVIII (1964), 40-69.

Zweig, Stefan. "Anmerkung zum *Ulysses*," *Die neue Rundschau*, XXXIX (October, 1928), 476-479; also printed in *Wiener Allgemeine Zeitung*, 30 October 1928.

INDEX